Islamic Renaissance
a new era has started

Kassim Ahmad

I0167672

Dedicated to my parents, who raised me up with love, care, and hope for better lives, but for whom I, obsessed with politics, failed to return enough of these three. May God forgive me.

Brainbow Press

© 2012, Kassim Ahmad

All rights reserved. No part of this book may be used, transmitted, or reproduced in any form or by any means whatsoever without the written permission of the author except in the case of brief quotations in reviews and critical articles. For permission requests or other information, contact the publisher or Kassim Ahmad electronically at:

www.kassimahmad.blogspot.com
www.brainbowpress.com
www.islamicreform.org
www.19.org

9780982586723

Cover Design: Uğur Şahin

Printed in the United States of America by Brainbow Press

10 9 8 7 6 5 4 3

Kassim Ahmad is Malaysia's foremost thinker and philosopher. Kassim was born on 9 September, 1933 in Kedah, Malaysia. He received his Bachelor of Art's degree in Malay language and literature, but also read widely in political science and Islamic philosophy.

Kassim grabbed national headlines in the 1950s with his dissertation on the characters of Hang Tuah (Perwatakan Hang Tuah), the Malay literary classic. He taught Malay language and literature for a time in the London's School of Oriental and African Studies and then in a secondary school in Penang where he has been staying with his family since 1966.

Kassim was jailed for nearly five years under the ISA for daring to express openly his political views, an experience which he recounted in his book, Universiti Kedua (Second University).

Like many modern reformists, after comparing the teachings of Hadith to the Quran, Kassim experienced a paradigm change. He shook the Malay world with his *Hadith: A Re-Examination* in which he challenges the infallibility of the purported words of Prophet Muhammad.

He is awarded an honorary doctorate in Letters by the National University of Malaysia. He has written several books on Malay literature as well as on Islamic subjects. His English and Malay articles are published at:

www.kassimahmad.blogspot.com

Table of Contents

Appendices

ACKNOWLEDGEMENT

At the outset, I would like to state that this work would not have been possible had not friends, supporters, and even critics and outright opponents, gave me the strength and the will to do so (in case of critics and opponents, to prove them wrong). When I published my *Hadis – Satu Penilaian Semula* in 1986, I was presented or sent books and research materials, by not only friends and supporters, but by some anonymous individuals. Their encouragement and support through numerous letters, e-mails, telephone calls and direct and indirect conversations, was crucial. Their number is too many that I cannot mention all their names. I can only say: "Thank you, all. May God bless you."

However, I would like to mention four names who presented me with excellent English translations of the Quran: Haji Noh Hansen of Malaysia, the five-volume English translation of the Quran and Commentary by the Ahmadiyyah Movement; my late teacher and friend, Dr. Ahmad Zaki Badawi of Egypt (at that time resident in London) with another excellent translation of the Quran and commentary by the late Muhammad Asad, the late Dr Rashad Khalifa for his equally excellent, albeit controversial, English translation of the Quran, and Edip Yuksel, for his (and two other collaborators) English reformist translation. Ahmad K of

Singapore, presented me with an Arabic Concordance of the Quran, which I find very useful, and, last but not least, our dear friend and fine teacher, journalist and author, Adibah Amin, for presenting me with a very useful *Life Application Bible*, New International Version. She also wrote a memorable review of my *Hadith* book on the editorial page of the *New Straits Times* a few days after it came out.

Even before this, I would like to mention three scholar-friends (themselves fine writers) who had given me great encouragement in my works. One was the late scholar and friend, Rustam A. Sani, who did me great honour in his eloquent oration for the *Universiti Kebangsaan Malaysia*'s honourary Doctorate of Letters to me on 17th August, 1985. Another is the scholar-friend (himself a fine poet), Dato' Baharuddin Zainal, (popularly known as Baha Zain) when delivering his fine speech at the National Association of Malaysian Writers' (*GAPENA*) award to me on 18th August, 1987. Yet another is the novelist, painter and Fine Arts lecturer Dr. Zakaria Ali, a dear friend, who wrote several pieces in the *New Straits Times* in appreciation of my works and also painted a portrait of me at the age of 40.

Four scholar-and-writer friends read some or all the final drafts of this book: Dr. M. Bakri Musa, a Malaysian from Negeri Sembilan, a surgeon who is himself a prolific writer and who now has a home and a clinic in California, U.S.A. Dr. Bakri also designed my website and wrote the most perceptive and eloquent introduction of my works to readers; Nik Abdul Aziz Hassan, a close friend, who is former *University Kebangsaan Malaysia* lecturer and an active member of the Shah Waliyullah group in Kota Baharu, Kelantan; and Edip Yuksel, a Turkish Kurdish author, a social activist, a lawyer and philosophy professor, resident in the U.S. (Edip has done a fine modern reformist translation of the Quran into English with two other collaborators; Edip belongs to what is known as a "Quran-alone" movement). Also Dr. Chandra

7

Muzaffar, a Muslim scholar and famous social activist. All four have read, commented on and criticized some or all the chapters of my final drafts. They provide the criticisms that I need, and made useful suggestions for improvement.

I have the highest respect for these scholar-friends and wish to express my deep-felt gratitude for their help. They are not responsible for errors found in the book: the errors are mine.

To my wife, my children and grand-children: "Thank you, all" They look with wonder and disbelief at my writing habits, for I awake daily to write from midnight till dawn – they provide me with wonderful solace and support. My wife, Sh. Fawziah Yusoff, is the most hard-working house-wife in the world. She looked after me to perfection single-handedly. As for my writing, she leaves me to my own devises, while before she used to help me with the typing of the manuscripts. The computer (what a marvelous creature it is!) has released her of that chore.

With all this support, in spite of the joy, yet at times I felt lonely, fearful (of making mistakes) and tired (I was not in the best of health) when writing this book. It was only my deep faith in God's Truth that propelled me to the finishing post. First and last, therefore, all praise be to God, the Lord of the Worlds!

Kassim Ahmad

Kulim, Kedah,
Malaysia
November, 2010

FOREWARD

The purpose of this book

This book, "Islamic Renaissance: A New Era Has Started", planned and written on the heels of the publication of my memoirs,[1] is precisely designed to give me the vehicle to carry my thoughts on the whole panorama of human life. Does God exist? Surely God is a Great Mystery – the Great Unknown.[2] That explains the existence of many diverse religions – some monotheistic, some polytheistic, and some even theistic. It is the proverbial the case of blind men describing an elephant: all giving different answers!

Yet the real and true elephant exists. It is the same with religion. It is to examine the phenomenon of religion, the highest of which, in my view, is God's religion of Islam[3] – the essence of which is, in the words of Abul Kalam Azad, "devotion to God and righteous living."[4] Yet Islam today, as I shall show, has become corrupted.

---

[1] Published by Zaid Publications in May, 2008. It was launched in Kuala Lumpur on 2nd Mei, 2008 by Prof. Ungku Aziz. After this book, I looked forward to a period of rest. It was not to be!

[2] "No vision comprehends Him, but He comprehends all vision." (Quran, 6:103)

[3] "The only religion approved by God is 'submission'." (Quran, 3:19). For those who object to the authority of the Quran, see Quranic epistemology in chapter 33.

[4] Abul Kalam Azad, *The Opening Chapter of the Quran*, (1962); p. 163.

This book, therefore, is not for Muslims alone. It is for those who uphold the truth.

I shall examine how the two religions, monotheism and its opposite polytheism, came into existence and lived side by side, how the original monotheism of the Divine prophet-messengers from the earliest times five thousand years ago or even earlier, developed through prophets Abraham, Moses, Jesus, and ending in the final Prophet Muhammad of 7[tbh] Century Arabia. As we know, this original monotheism of one Divine religion called "submission", in the valleys of the Nile, the Tigris and Euphrates broke up and deteriorated to become three religions, each with its own beliefs, myths and rituals. This is the Abrahamic tradition.

Then there is the non-Abrahamic tradition, called the *sabi'in* in the Quran[5] – Hinduism, Buddhism, Taoism, Confucianism, Zoroastrianism and the rest. Confucianism may not be termed a religion, as it is more of a social philosophy. Buddhism began as a personal search (by Gautama Buddha, 563 B.C. – 483 B.C.) for release from suffering in the concept of Nirvana, which is akin to the concept of Paradise in Judaism, Christianity and Islam.

Why the deterioration from the strict monotheism of original Islam? Does it mean that God has failed? That is a thought no believer would entertain. What are the methods that God employ to overcome the deterioration? Thus the dramas of the so-called "Second Coming" of Jesus Christ, the rise and fall of nations, and, the author, being from the Malay World, the fate of that world, and further, of all mankind, form the subject-matter of this book.

To say that it is an ambitious book is an understatement. I can justly be accused of foolhardiness in undertaking to write it. That is why I said at times I felt fearful when writing it. But I strongly believe in taking the bull by the horns.

---

[5] See 2:62.

Return to the religion of divine unity

Although we cannot see God, it is the assumption of this book that it is He Who creates, nourishes and guides the world to its conclusion. Since Plato is right to say that God is the Good, in spite of the evils, the world and the entire universe is headed towards betterment. Evil is the result of rebellion against God – those who disbelieve in Him, act to spread evil, and are punished by the just laws of God. It will take time for the better world to come into being, because it has to fight against the forces of deterioration. The forces of deterioration come from the earth, the lowly world from which Man, the *Homo sapiens*, emerged between 400,000 to 100,000 years ago. This event is described by one historian as momentous.[6] The Quran describes the emergence of Man, God's vicegerent on Earth (Ar. *khalifa*), as a new creation.[7]

The impulse to good, inherent in men (as equally the impulse to bad), pushes men upwards. The impulse to evil, although it had brought trails of destruction along the way of men's progress, cannot vanquish men's upward journey. Thus God's religion, *submission*, has deteriorated at every step of the way: the religion of Moses becoming Judaism, of Jesus becoming Christianity, and of Muhammad becoming Muhammadanism (the false religion of Muhammad created by the later newly-emergent priesthood), losing its pristine belief in the One God for all humanity.

Overcoming deterioration and realizing God's purpose

As the Quran says, God's purpose cannot be frustrated.[8] This is because the whole of Nature, including Man, is stamped with God's purpose.[9] The teachings of God, according to the Quran,

---

[6] J. M. Roberts, *History of the World* (1976); p. 36.

[7] Quran, 23:12-14.

[8] Quran, 24:57.

[9] Quran, 3:83 and 30:30.

11

have been sent to every human community, some it has named, others not.[10] It is, therefore, logical to expect these teachings to be reflected in all societies and to converge in the World Society that has definitely been formed as a result of the Second World War. The United Nations Organization, formed in 1945, is certainly a concretization of this convergence of the World Society. Firstly, is it a concrete embodiment of internationalism, which brings together nations regardless of creed and colour – a new era in history which actually began with Prophet Muhammad. Secondly, it is brings into practice continuous dialogues and discussions among nations to solve and resolve all conflicts and problems – a basic teaching of Islam.[11] As one historian says, "In the end the greatest importance of the United Nations was to prove to lie not in its power to act, but in the forum it provided for discussion. For the first time, a world public linked as never before by radio and film – and later by television – would have to be presented with a case made at the General Assembly for what sovereign states did. This was something quite new. The United Nations gave a new dimension to international politics rather than a new instrumentation for dealing with problems."[12]

The Universal Declaration of Human Rights, adopted on 10th December, 1948, may be seen as a major success by the United Nations at promulgating international law. To us, this Universal Declaration of human Rights reflects the true universal teachings of the Quran. This is nowhere clearer than in the absolute freedom of religion given in the Quran.[13]

---

[10] Quran, 4:164.
[11] Quran, 42:38.
[12] J. M. Roberts, *History of the World* (1976); p. 884.
[13] Quran, 2:256. Note that this verse comes directly after the "Throne Verse" that speaks about the limitless might of God, implying that even such power does not negate man's absolute freedom to choose his or her religion.

We may go to an earlier period, the formation of the League of Nations, after the First World War. Although it failed, it was the first practical step taken by the international community.

At present, the United Nations Organization is still under the undemocratic control of the five veto-baring Permanent Members, the United States, Great Britain, France, Russia and China with several rotating Non-Permanent Members, representing every continent. This undemocratic nature of its Security Council, a realistic necessity at the time of its formation, is a great defect of the organization. The so-called Nuclear Club consisting of the five Permanent Members of the U.N. Security Council plus Israel, India and Pakistan, applying non-proliferation against others, represents an unjust international law and constitutes a major bone of contention in international relations. Then there is the unsolved Arab-Israeli conflict, spanning over a period of sixty-one years and six wars, the on-going conflict between North and South Korea, and the conflict between Taiwan and China.

These are very serious weaknesses of the United Nations, some of which may, God forbid, lead to a Third World War. Yet it still represents a major hope for mankind to move towards its betterment. The fast rate of the development of science and technology as well as humankind's new-found consciousness for its own betterment augurs well for humanity's future, although science and technology have their negative destructive side. The Just New World Order that the Special Session of the U.N. General Assembly in 1974 with its resolution on New International Economic Order set in train is a practical objective that may be attained before the end of this 21st Century.

In fact, there is not a matter that this book does not touch on – the book's title sees to that. Each of the 34 chapters can constitute a book in itself. But I am not writing a fat book Fatness in a book is not automatically a good quality. My purpose is to outline the way forward, based on a new scientific understanding of God's Final Scripture, the Quran, after tracing mankind's historical steps.

The meeting point of religion, philosophy and science

One wonders at men's vast capability at every step to approve of their own misdoings. I have mentioned this in cases of the Jews, the Christians and the Muhammadans (later followers of Muhammad who have deviated; the term "Muslims" cannot be used here). Reason, therefore, is a double-edged sword. It can solve men's problems; it can also make men's misdoings appear good to them.

How are we to resolve this seeming dilemma?

The East, it is said, is rich in spiritual traditions. Look at Hinduism and its profound scripture, the Bhagavad Gita with its undifferentiated concept of Reality. Then there is the atheistic belief of Buddhism and its Noble Eightfold Path to gain release from human suffering and entrance into the blessed state of nothingness, that is, Nirvana. Then there is the social and ethical philosophy of Confucianism and the rather dry metaphysics of Taoism. What does one make of these religious-moral-philosophical traditions? How much do these shape the modern life of those living in these traditions? Or, perhaps, they are no more relevant now, except as rituals for the dying, for marriage and for worship. They have become customs into which one is born and bred.

The West (Judeo-Christian world) is, perhaps, less steeped in religion, but nevertheless is not devoid of it. The West is stronger in its science and technology. However, modern science and technology, run *amuck* without ethical restraint and self-control, have proved beyond doubt to be massively destructive, as the terrible destructions of the First and Second World Wars have shown. The greed bred among the rich nations has caused starvation, poverty and diseases in countries of the South. The modern scientific and technological world has proved to be a materialistic world without a sense of justice, not to say feelings of love and compassion. The next one decade or two must bring a change to this, if mankind is to survive certain doom.

Thus the post-World War Two world has arrived at a very critical juncture. Both the East and the West have to re-evaluate their civilizational inheritances to make the three major epistemological sources of religious, scientific and philosophical knowledge meet at a harmonious unifying point.[14] It is my belief that humanity's further development depends solely on his ability to seek and arrive at this harmonious unifying point. It is also my belief that God's religion, the Religion of Truth, as contained in the Quran, God's Final Scripture to mankind, confirming and superseding all previous scriptures, can take mankind forward on his long evolutionary journey to everlasting happiness.

Kassim Ahmad
Kulim, Kedah, Darul-Aman,
Malaysia
January, 2009

*****

---

[14] World-renown British physicist, Stephen W. Hawkins, in his book *A Brief History of Time* (1988), mentions the possibility of a unified theory that would answer the riddles of the Universe.

16

CHAPTER 1

Introduction

1. What is the purpose of religion?

The phenomenon of religion seems natural to man. No human community, whether literate or non-literate, has been known to be without its religious beliefs. This religion may be called animism, shamanism, polytheism in its various forms, and monotheism in its various forms. This is because the wonder, awe and mystery regarding the Universe and surrounding man's life: birth, death, sickness, suffering and joy – these give rise to his religious beliefs.[15]

---

[15] The Quran puts this wonder and consequent supplication thus, "In the creation of the heavens and the earth, and the alternation of night and day, these are signs for those who possess intelligence. They remember God while standing, sitting, and on their sides, and they reflect upon the creation of the heavens and the earth: 'Our Lord, You did not create all this in vain. Be You glorified. Save us from the retribution of Hell. Our Lord, whomever You commit to Hell are the ones You have forsaken. Such transgressors have no helpers. Our Lord, we have heard a caller calling to faith and proclaiming: "You shall believe in Your Lord, " and we have believed. Our Lord, forgive us our transgression, remit our sins, and let us die as righteous believers.'" (3:190-93)

There seems to be no precise definition of religion. We now know of many religious traditions, formed over many generations, in many parts of the world, especially in the Middle East and East Asia. The nature and structure of these traditions depended on many factors, including the mental and intellectual developments of the community, its existing culture, and the personalities involved in the ensuing and developing religious drama.

There is a tradition of monotheism, developed as early as the time of Adam and Eve, a million years ago, and clarified at the time of Prophet Abraham, about 5,000 years ago in the Ur or present-day Iraq, and further developed through Prophets Moses and Jesus, and ending in Prophet Muhammad in Seventh Century Arabia. Directly opposed to this tradition and existing side by side is that of polytheism.[16]

In South and East Asia, there was the religion of Hinduism, seemingly polytheism with a perceptible core of belief in a supreme being, the Brahman.[17] There was Buddhism, a seemingly atheistic religion, a belief in a life of liberation from grief to be found in Nirvana, founded by Siddarta Buddha (563-483 B.C.). However, this atheistic religion, after the death of its founder, developed into a religious worship of its founder.

There are other religions or rather philosophies that have sprouted in East Asia: Confucianism and Taoism. Confucianism is a social philosophy, a social code of conduct to be followed, without a belief in God or gods. Taoism is a philosophy about Reality, again without a belief in God or gods.

These religious traditions, outside the Abrahamic traditions, arose as the same time as Abraham, about five thousand years ago.

---

[16] Quran, *Surah* 109.
[17] See New Encyclopedia Britannica.

2. The difference between Islam and other religions.

Muslims believe that Islam – the religion of divine unity -- is the religion approved by God for mankind.[18] Its purpose is to bring mankind out of darkness into light[19] as well to guide him to attain success and felicity in his life individually and collectively.[20]

The religion of Islam began with Prophet Adam, but Prophet Adam was so early in man's history, about a million years ago, that he had no clear conception of God. Then came Prophet Noah and the Great Floods, which drowned all the disbelievers of that time, including his rebellious son.[21] When the time of Prophet Abraham, two thousand years ago, came, the picture and conception of this monotheistic religion became much clearer. The many gods that Abraham's father and his co-disbelievers of that time believed in were demolished by Prophet Abraham in both brilliant argumentation as well as by his practice.[22]

According to the Quran, it was he who began the rituals of Islam, the five daily prayers, fasting, the pilgrimage to the House of God, and the poor rate (*zakat*).[23] Again, according to the Quran, Prophet

---

[18] "The only religion approved by God is Islam. Ironically, those who received previous scripture are the ones who disputed this fact, despite the knowledge they have received, due to jealousy. For such rejecters of God's revelations, God is most strict in reckoning." (Quran, 3:19)

[19] Quran, 65:11.

[20] Quran, 5:3.

[21] Quran, 11:25-49 for the story of how God dealt with the disbelievers, including his rebellious son, of his time.

[22] See Quran for Abraham's brilliant intellectual discovery of the True God (21:51-67) and his equally brilliant refutation of the idols his father and fellow-disbelievers worship (6:74-81)

[23] Quran, 2:127-28

Abraham had his scripture,[24] which may be taken to mean his teachings about the worship of One God.

Then came Moses and his brother Aaron, teachers of the Jews, to whom God gave the Old Testament. Then came Jesus of Nazareth, also to the Jews, with the New Testament. God told him of a coming Messiah, i.e. Muhammad, who would reveal to men what he, Jesus, cannot yet reveal to them.[25] The Old Testament also foretold the coming of Muhammad.[26]

That is the Abrahamic tradition. Outside the Abrahamic tradition, to the east, we find the religions of Hinduism, Buddhism, Zoroastrianism, Taoism and Confucianism. This tradition is referred in the Quran as *Sabian*.[27] The Quran has already acknowledged the existence of believers in God among the various religious groups, implying that there were and are disbelievers among them as well.[28] Gandhi's famous statement about his being a Hindu, a Christian, a Muslim, and a Jew all at the same time refers to this situation.

We have recourse to refer to the various components of religion as a way of life in a separate chapter. They are a world-outlook (metaphysics, cosmology, epistemology and eschatology) law,

---

[24] Quran, 87:18-19.

[25] In John 16:12-14, Jesus is said to have stated, " I have much more to say to you, more than you can now bear. But when the Spirit of truth, comes, he will guide you into all truth. He will not speak on his own; he will speak only what he hears, and he will tell you what is yet to come."

[26] "The Lord God will raise up for you a prophet like me from among your own brothers. You must listen to him... The Lord said to me , 'I will raise up for them a prophet like you from among their brothers; I will put my words in his mouth, and he will them everything I commend him. If anyone does not listen to my words that the prophet speaks in my name, I myself will call him to account.' " (*Deut.*, 18:15-19)

[27] Quran, 2:62.

[28] The verse 2:62 indicates this.

politico-economic doctrine, customs, and rituals of worship. It turns out that not only the world-outlook, but also the other components are different in all religions. The difference may lie in the language. For instance, the concept of "Afterlife" does not refer to life after death; it refers to this worldly life, but at a later time. This world-outlook is wrapped up in speculations and mysticism about the nature of reality – what the Universe is, how it began, and what its purpose is.

Obviously, religion precedes science, because science is knowledge of what earlier was based on speculation. So, as science develops and its methods improve, untested beliefs give way to more reliable knowledge. The Quran informs us of the comprehensibility of the world to man in a beautiful metaphor.[29] This is an extremely important characteristic of man, against the position of many skeptical philosophers, ancient and modern. So it stands to reason that religion and science will one day meet at a point when the one coincides with the other. Since, as the Pakistani poet-philosopher Muhammad Iqbal says, Islam's advent at the time of Muhammad, its last prophet, opens the way to the Age of Modern Science and Technology.[30] It is highly significant that the first revelation that Muhammad received touched on

---

[29] Quran, 2:31-33.

[30] In his brilliant book, *The Reconstruction of Religious Thought in Islam* (1958), Iqbal said, "…the Prophet of Islam seems to stand between the ancient and the modern world. In so far as the source of his revelation is concerned, he belongs to the ancient world; in so far as the spirit of his revelation is concerned, he belongs to the modern world. In him life discovers other sources of knowledge suitable to its new direction. The birth of Islam is the birth of the inductive intellect. In Islam prophecy reaches its perfection in discovering the need of its own abolition. This involves the keen perception that life cannot forever be kept in leading strings; that in order to achieve full self-consciousness, man must finally be thrown back on his own resources." (p. 126)

21

reading and writing, thus unleashing a revolution leading to science and knowledge.[31]

It was the French philosopher, Auguste Comte (1798-1857), who divided the development of man's thought into three stages of the theological, the metaphysical and the positivistic. In the first theological stage, reference was made to supernatural beings to explain events, in the second metaphysical stage, events are explained by more abstract forces, while in the third positivistic stage, men seek causes in a scientific and practical manner not only in physics and biology, but also in the domains of morality and society, thus founding the science of society, namely sociology.

This classification by Comte has been criticized as not being precise and sound, but nonetheless, it agrees with Iqbal's statement about Prophet Muhammad's advent marking a new era between the Greek speculative pre-scientific thought and modern scientific thought. It is true that although the Arab-Muslim renaissance began this scientific age brilliantly, it fell to modern Europe and the West, after the Renaissance, that inherited and continued this scientific movement to its maturity to all the cultural areas of the world: Japan, China, back to the Arab world, and to all parts of the world by the end of the 20th Century.

As things turned out, the Islam of Moses became Judaism, and the Islam of Jesus, Christianity, for whom Paul rather than Jesus became its founder, with the belief of a risen Christ and his Second Coming at the end of time. When Prophet Muhammad, the true messiah, came to complete the Islam, the religion of divine unity, at dawn of the Era of Modern Science and Technology, the Jews and the Christians rejected him. Thus, one

---

[31] "Read in the name of your Lord, who created. He created man from an embryo. Read, and your Lord, Most Exalted. Teaches by means of the pen. He teaches man what he never knew." (Quran, 96:1-5)

religion became three. However, Islam, after a brilliant carrier of world leadership in all fields, broke into sects and deviated to become the corrupted Islam of a new religious priesthood. This spelt its downfall.

As we know, Islam is distinguished from other religions in that it represents the divine teaching of strict monotheism ("There is no god, but God, and we should worship Him Alone"). It was this creative and dynamic inspiration and impulse that took them to the pinnacle of world leadership in a very short time.

3. The deterioration of Islam

However, as we things turned out, Muhammad's followers could not maintain this pure monotheism for long. About 300 years after Prophet Muhammad's death, it broke into theological factions, set us a priesthood in imitation of Christianity and Hinduism, separated knowledge into worldly and religious knowledge, and idolized Muhammad through the so-called *Hadith/Sunnah* Their polytheistic culture of the past re-emerged in various guises. Thus, Islam also became corrupted with polytheistic beliefs, and became like the other religions.

But God's design is not to be thwarted. In His omniscience, He has preserved his Religion of Truth[32], in a perfectly protected Quran through the awesome mathematically-structured compositional methodology known as Code 19.[33]

---

[32] Islam is referred to in the Quran as God's religion, or the true religion in 9:33; 48:28; 61:9; and 110:1-3.

[33] See Rashad Khalifa, *The Computer Speaks: God's Message to the World*, Renaissance Productions International, Tucson, 1981. See also Kassim Ahmad, *Hadis—Jawapan Kepada Pengkritik*, Media Indah, Kuala Lumpur, 1992; Chapter 6. The Quran is the only scripture in the world, whose purity is divinely protected. (Quran, 15:9)

4. Polytheism and atheism

It should be noted that the modern religious strain of atheism does not seem to be recognized in the Quran. This is highly interesting. A creator-god is assumed in the Quran. Men either believed in the One True God, as the prophets and their true followers did, or they believed in many false gods.[34] Thus the disbelieving Pharaoh of Moses's time believed himself to be the chief god of the Egyptians.[35] The disbelievers are confronted with the facts of God's creation, of God's kingship of the universe, of God's sovereignty over everything, and of God being the source of all succour. They then acknowledge God, but persist in believing in many gods.[36]

Let us examine the statements of some famous scientists who profess atheism. Albert Einstein, the greatest scientist of the 20th century and one of the supreme intellects of all time, said:

> *I have never imputed to Nature a purpose of a goal, or anything that could be understood as anthropomorphic. What I see in Nature is a magnificent structure that we can comprehend only very imperfectly, and that must fill a thinking person with a feeling of humility. This is a genuinely a religious feeling that has nothing to do with mysticism.*

---

[34] Quran, 23:84-89. A Russian philosopher remarked, "It must be acknowledged that out-and-out consistent godlessness does not exist. Man is more inclined to be an idolator than an atheist. He recognizes the "divine" even when he denies God and there is in him a need of the "divine" which cannot be overcome. He deifies the most diverse objects, he deifies the cosmos, man and humanity, he deifies society, he deifies race, nationality or class, he deifies a particular social order, socialism, and he makes a god of his own godlessness." (Nicolas Beydyaev, *Truth and Revelation*, London, 1953; p. 90).

[35] Quran, 28:38.

[36] Quran, 23:84-89.

I do not believe in a personal God and I have never denied this but have expressed it clearly. If something is in me which can be called religious, then it is the unbounded admiration for the structure of the world so far as our science can reveal it.[37]

Another famous scientist, Carl Sagan, wrote:

How is it that hardly any major religion has looked at science and concluded, 'This is better than we thought! The Universe is much bigger than our prophets said, grander, more subtle, more elegant'? Instead they say, 'No, no, no! My god is a little god, and I want him to stay that way.' A religion old or new that stressed the magnificence of the Universe as revealed by modern science might be able to draw forth reserves of reverence and awe had tapped by conventional faith.[38]

I want to quote Steven Weinberg as the third testimony of this professed atheism of modern science:

Some people have views of God that are so broad and flexible that it is inevitable that they will find God wherever they look for him. One hears it said that 'God is the ultimate' or 'God is our nature' or God is the universe.' Of course, like any other word, the word 'God' can be given any meaning we like. If you want to say that 'God is energy,' then you can find God in a lump of coal.[39]

Can such statements be described as atheistic?

---

[37] Quoted in Richard Dawkins, p. 15. Compare this statement to Verse 3-4 of Chapter 67, which states: " He created seven universes in layers. You do not see any imperfection in the creation of the Most Gracious. Keep looking; do you see any flaw? Look again and again; your eyes will come back stumped and conquered."

[38] *Ibid.*, p. 12.

[39] *Ibid.*, p. 12-13.

However, look at this one by the British philosopher of Logical Positivism, the dead end of Western empiricism, Bertrand Russell. Note the pessimism is poignant and the language almost poetic.

> *Such, in outline, but even more purposeless, more void of meaning, is the world in which science presents itself for our belief. Amid such a world, if anywhere, our ideals henceforth must find a home. That Man is the product of causes which had no prevision of the need they were achieving; that his origin, his growth, his hopes and fears, his loves and his beliefs, are but the outcome of accidental collocations of atoms; that no fire, nor heroisms, no intensity of labours of the ages, all the devotion, all the aspirations, all the noonday brightness of human genius are destined to extinction in the vast death of the solar system, and that the whole temple of Man's achievement must inevitably be buried beneath the debris of a universe of ruins – all these things, if not quite beyond dispute, are yet so nearly certain, that no philosophy which rejects them can hope to stand. Only within the scaffolding of those truths, only on the firm foundation of unyielding despair, can the soul's habitation henceforth be built.[40]*

Can we say that Russell here makes a god of his own despair, his egoism for that passion?

5. What the future hold?

For us, there is no doubt that man is wonderful creation of God. The Quran informs us that he occupies an honoured place on the entire scale of creation.[41] The whole created universe is made to

---

[40] *Mysticism and Logic*, Allen and Unwin, London, 1910; p. 41.

[41] "Surely We have honoured the Children of Adam, and We carry them in the land and the sea, and We provide them with good things, and We have made them to excel highly most of those whom We have created." (Quran, 17:70)

serve him.[42] The greatest dramatist, Shakespeare, wondered in his great play, *Hamlet,* about the human being we call man. "What a piece of work is man!" his character of the name is made to reflect.[43] The Quran gives us a clue, in the simultaneous status of man as God's slave (Ar. *'abd*), completely under His control and doing His bidding, and God's vicegerent on Earth (Ar. *khalifa*) with powers to do good as well as to do evil.[44] The famed atheistic French philosopher and novelist, Jean-Paul Sartre (1905-1980), cursed man's freedom of choice.[45] God, however, took the side of man; God, the All-Knowing, knows what all others, including the angels, do not know. God knows that man will prevail, that goodness and truth will prevail. Why? Because that is what His Grand Design for creation is, and because Man is God-Manifested. Remember that God is the First and the Last, the Manifest and the Hidden.[46] He is also present in man's self when a breadth of the Divine Spirit is blown into him at his creation.[47]

The concept of the One True God is the concept of a lawful universe,[48] being held together and sustained by one truthful law

---

[42] "He committed in your service everything in the heavens and the earth, all from Himself." (Quran, 45:13)

[43] *Hamlet*, Act II, Scene ii.

[44] Come to think of it, it is really amazing that this important status and role is given to Man, regardless of whether he is a believer or non-believer. However, God's action is completely logical and reasonable. Quran, 2:30.

[45] He is reputed to have made the remark, "Man is condemned to be free."

[46] Quran, 57:3.

[47] "Your Lord said to the angels, 'I am creating a human being from aged mud, like the potter's clay. Once I perfect him, and blow into him from My spirit, you shall prostrate before him.'" (Quran, 15:28-29)

[48] "Everything We created is precisely measured." (Quran, 54:49) "Say, 'You disbelieve in the One who created the earth in two days, and you set us idols to rank with Him, though He is Lord of the universe.' He placed on it stabilizers, made it productive, and He calculated its provisions in four days, to satisfy the needs of all inhabitants. The He turned to the sky when it was still gas, and said to it and to the earth, 'Come into existence, willingly or unwillingly.' They said, 'We come willingly.' Thus, He completed the seven

hierarchically-leveled in an ascending order, peeking in the crowning glory of Man, the *Homo sapiens,* God's vicegerent on Earth. Man is the highest physical manifestation of the Pure Spirit that is God. When that point is reached, God's grand design is realized, and the universal drama of creation comes to an end. The universe collapses upon itself and dies, and God Alone, the Pure Spirit, remains.[49]

---

universes in two days, and set up the laws for every universe. We adorned the lowest universe with lamps, and placed guards around it. Such is the design of the Almighty, the Omniscient." (Quran, 41:9-12)

[49] "Everyone on earth perishes. Only the presence of your Lord lasts, Possessor of Majesty and Honour." (Quran, 55:26-27) "You shall not worship beside God any other God. There is no other god beside Him. Everything perishes except His presence. To Him belongs all sovereignty, and to Him you will be returned." (Quran, 28:88)

CHAPTER 2
Pointer from the Opening Chapter

The opening chapter summarizes the teachings of the Quran

Let us quote the Opening Chapter in full in three translations, by Abdullah Yusuf Ali and Mohammed Marmaduke Pickthall, and a a new and unorthodox translation by Dr. Rashad Khalifa[50]:

1. In the name of Allah, Most Gracious, Most Merciful.
2. Praise be to Allah the Cherisher and Sustainer of the Worlds;
3. Most Gracious, Most Merciful;
4. Master of the Day of Judgement.
5. Thee do we worship, and Thine aid we seek.
6. Show us the straight way,
7. The way of those on whom Thou hast bestowed Thy Grace, Those whose (portion) is not wrath, and who go not astray.

1. In the name of Allah, the Beneficent, the Merciful.
2. Praise be to Allah, Lord of the Worlds,
3. The Beneficent, the Merciful.
4. Owner of the Day of Judgememnt,
5. Thee (alone) we worship; Thee (alone) we ask for help.
6. Show us the straight path,
7. The path of those whom Thou hast favoured; not (the path) of those who earn Thine anger nor of those who go astray.

---

[50] See *The Computer Speaks God's Message to the World*, Islamic Productions, Tucson, Arizona, U.S.A., 1981.

1. In the name of God, Most Gracious, Most Merciful.
2. Praise be to God, Lord of the universe.
3. Most Gracious, Most Merciful.
4. Master of the Day of Judgement.
5. You alone we worship; You alone we ask for help.
6. Guide us in the right path;
7. the path of those whom You bless; not of those who have deserved wrath, nor of the strayers.

The Opening Chapter of the Quran, *Al-Fateha*, is also known variously as the *Umm'ul-Quran* (the Core of the Quran), *Al-Kafiy* (the Sufficient), *Al Kanz* (the Treasure House, and *Asasul-Quran* (the Basis of the Quran)[51] Therefore, we shall scrutinize this chapter to get at the gist of Divine teachings to believers and disbelievers alike. We shall put the whole of the teachings of the Quran under the microscope of this chapter.

We should note that it begins with the *Basmallah* ("In the name of God, Most Gracious and Most Merciful") and is the only one that is numbered in the whole Quran. It contains two of the most important names and qualities of God, Most Gracious and Most Merciful. God, the Creator, Sustainer and Cherisher of the Worlds are assumed, and not specifically stated in this verse.

We should note that in this Opening Chapter, mankind speaks to the Lord in the plural 'we'. This proves that Islam is a social doctrine to be practiced as a revolutionary way of life, as opposed to a quietist, individualistic mysticism. Also note that the two dimensions of man, man the servant of God (Ar. *abdul-Allah*), and man, the vicegerent of God (Ar. *khalifa*), are implied but not specifically mentioned.

---

[51] See Abul Kalam Azad, *The Opening Chapter of the Quran*, (1962); p. 5.

Also note that this 'we' does not refer to any exclusive grouping. It refers to the entirety of mankind, proving Islam's all-embracing, inclusive and unifying universalism.

Three-part teaching: glorification, principles of monotheism, and supplication

The whole chapter is mankind's prayer to the Lord. It is divided into three parts. The first part (verses 1-4) consists of mankind's praise to the Lord and His wonderful qualities of beneficence, mercy and justice that spell also His awesome power to exact retribution. The verses sum up Islam's two main beliefs: belief in One God and belief in man's accountability to Him. The second part (verse 5) tersely states the extremely important principles of the religion of divine unity: Man must worship God alone and none other; to God alone, and to none other, man must ask for help.

The third part (verses 6-7) puts beautifully mankind's supplication to the Lord. Compared to the Lord's Prayer in the Christian Gospel,[52] the *Fateha* is a most comprehensive prayer, covering all levels of human wants –spiritual, moral and material– beautifully avoiding the obvious materialism of the of the Lord's Prayer, which was a characteristic of the Israelites of that time. The Lord's Prayer was specific to the Israelites of a particular time, whereas the Muslim Prayer is a universal prayer of all mankind.

Note the terminology "Lord of the Universe" or "Lord of the Worlds". This means that God is the Creator, Sustainer and Cherisher of all creations. The whole vast created order is

---

[52] "Our Father which art in heaven, Hallowed be thy name. Thy kingdom come. Thy will be done in earth, as it is in heaven. Give us this day our daily bread. And forgive us our debts, as we forgive our debtors. And lead us not into temptation, but deliver us from evil; For thine is the kingdom, and the power, and the glory, forever. A'-men." *Matt*:6:9-13.

beholden to Him. There is a plurality of worlds, made up of the physical, moral and spiritual worlds – plural but unified under a hierarchy of His laws in the various worlds.[53]

We are to note also that what appears to the naked eye as a physical universe (prompting scientists to be atheists)[54] is only a partial universe, witnessed by the senses. Actually, this is a moral and spiritual universe, created by God, with its hierarchy of laws, expressing His Will. This is proved by the fact that the world's behaviour, since it came into being, has not been capricious, but orderly, harmonious and evolving towards a purposive and better future for both the world and mankind.[55]

The narrow, truncated Western empirical epistemology strangely does not recognize inspiration or revelation as a form of knowing, considering it to be unscientific. Inspiration, or knowledge that comes to you suddenly, sometimes called revelation from God, although is widely experienced by writers, musicians, artists, and even philosophers and scientists in the West is not recognized as a valid form of knowing. Why? It must be because this form of knowing comes from a divine source, i.e. God, Whose existence Western science considers as unprovable.[56]

---

[53] "Everything We created is precisely measured." (Quran, 54:49) See also 41:9-12.

[54] "They care only about things of this world that are visible to them, while being totally oblivious of the Hereafter." (Quran, 30:7)

[55] "We did no create the heavens and the earth, and everything between them just for amusement. If we needed amusement, We could have initiated it without any of this, if that is what We wanted to do. Instead, it is our plan to support the truth against falsehood, in order to defeat it." (Quran, 21:16-18)

[56] Historical philosopher P. A. Sorokin is an exception. He recognizes the three integral forms of knowing: the sensory, the logical and the suprasensory. See his *Modern Historical and Social Philosophies*; pp 247-48.

Divine Judgement

Then comes the first difficult terminology: *Master of the Day of Judgement.* Three things should be noted here, namely (a) Man will be judged for everything he has done, and there is no escape from this judgement, (b) that judgement will be made on *a specific day* to come, and (c) the judgement will be made by God. However, the reward (of Paradise) and punishment (of Hell) are not mentioned in connection with this judgement.

For every human being to be judged for all his freely-made actions is logical and necessary. No rational person can gainsay this. But, what about *the Day*? It is on one human day of 24 hours? It cannot possibly be. It must refer to a period: one year, one generation, one century. The Quran informs us that a day with God is equivalent to a thousand or fifty thousand human years.[57]

The Day therefore refers to a period known only to God.[58] This is due to the fact that it includes man's input, man being free to act to re-make the world. Where will this judgement take place? In this world, or in some other place? The Quran informs us that we shall be resurrected in this world.[59] Therefore, the judgement will take place in this world. Has this divine judgement taken place and is on-going, or yet to take place? How can we differentiate between God's judgement from worldly secular judgement? Are the various conflicts, and wars, including the First and Second World Wars, and pestilences, earthquakes, big storms, great floods, great fires and so on (what we calls natural disasters), and starvation and widespread poverty -- are they to be understood as

---

[57] Quran, 22:47, 32:5, and 70:4.

[58] "The people will ask you about the Hour. Say, 'The knowledge thereof is only with God. For all you know the Hour may be close.'" (Quran, 33:63)

[59] "He said, 'Go down as enemies of one another. On earth shall be your habitation and provision for a while.' He said, 'On it you will live, on it you will die, and from it you will be brought out.'" (Quran, 7:24-25)

33

divine punishments. There seems to be no doubt about it, as they are the natural consequences of our actions direct or indirect actions. It is also stated that God's punishments are much more severe.[60]

The last question for us to answer is: What does it mean to say that, 'God is the Judge'? Is it to be understood literally, or figuratively? Taking other verses to explain this verse, this sentence should be understood figuratively. The judgement follows automatically, for man will judge himself.[61]

The next two verses regarding our object of worship and our source of help constitute the main principles of belief in absolute Divine Unity and absolute rejection of idolatry. These form the core of Divine Unity: absolute belief in it and absolute rejection of disbelief in it. As we shall show later, all the three Abrahamic religions, Judaism, Christianity and Muhammadanism (this term is used instead of Islam, as Islam would mean God's religion) have repudiated their original pristine monotheism by soiling it with some form of idolatry. Muslims are not even aware that they have idolized Prophet Muhammad through making his so-called *Hadith* (record of his sayings and doings) as an equal source of jurisprudence on par with and at times cancelling the Quran, as in the case of adultery.[62] Their writings in their homes and mosques of the names "Allah" and "Muhammad" on the same level are an indication of this idolatry, for which most Muslim are not even aware.

---

[60] Take this verse for instance: "This is to humiliate them in this life, then they suffer a far worse retribution in the Hereafter." (5:33)

[61] "We have recorded the fate of every human being; it is tied to his neck. On the Day of Resurrection, We will hand him a record that is accessible. Read your own record. Today you suffice as your own reckoner." (Quran, 17:13-14)

[62] See Kassim Ahmad, *Dilema Umat Islam – Antara hadis dan Quran*, (Pulau Pinang, 2002); p.25.

The straight path

Then comes the extremely important doctrine of *the Straight Path* for mankind to follow, the path that God favours and not the deviating paths taken by those on whom God is wrathful, and those who go astray. In other words, mankind is to choose the straight path of security and not the deviating paths of destruction. The idea of the straight path is an old idea. It was mentioned in Aristotle's *Nicomachean Ethics* as the "Golden Mean". It is the same as the Buddha's "Middle Path". In the Quran, Muslims are described as "The Middle Community."[63] This fact proves that God's teachings over the thousand years of civilization have been sent to every community, as the Quran tells us.[64]

No mention of predetermination, paradise or hell

Such is the meaning of this important chapter of the Quran. It stresses (a) God as the Ultimate Source of all creation, and man's absolute dependence and submission to this Ultimate Source, (b) Man's accountability to God for all his actions, (c) the importance of absolute belief in Divine Unity and absolute rejection of idolatry, (d) the importance of man following the Straight Path, and avoiding the deviating paths in order to find peace and security, avoiding self-destruction.

It should be noted that this chapter does not mention the doctrine of predetermination, of *qada* and *qadar*[65]; nor does it mention

---

[63] Quran, 2:143.

[64] "We have sent to every community a messenger saying : 'Worship God and beware of idol-worship' ...." (Quran, 16; 36)

[65] This is stated as the sixth Pillar of Faith. However, the Quran mentions only five and rejects the sixth. Quran, 4:136 and 4:78-79. It is preposterous to even think that God is the source of evil, as this so-called sixth pillar of the faith states. Verses 78-79 of Surah 4 state: "Say, 'everything is from God ...

Paradise and Hell. However, resurrection and afterlife are implied in the concept of the Day of Judgement. Afterlife has to be re-interpreted to mean further life in this world. The non-mention, or rather the rejection, of predetermination, as we have shown, must mean that it is a false doctrine. The non-mention of Heaven and Hell may be explained by the implied concept of reward and punishment linked to the Day of Judgement.

At this point, we want to introduce a verse (15:87) that has been wrongly translated in most traditional *tafsir*. Take the popular Marmaduke Pickthall's translation: "We have given you the seven oft-repeated verses (explained as the seven verses of the *Fateha*). Logically the *Fateha* is part of the Quran, and therefore the words "the grand Quran" cannot logically be there. According to Dr. Rashad Khalifa, it refers to the end of the world in A.D. 2280. I do not agree with this interpretation, as the end of the world is far, far into the future. The world will last as long as the energy it contains supports its continuing existence. This will be ten billion more years, according to the computation of scientists.[66] When this ceases, it will be destroyed. Only the Face of God remains.[67]

We shall deal with these topics in more detail in their appropriate chapters.

*****

Anything good that happens to you is from God, and anything bad that happens to you is from you.' "
[66] Frank Tipler, *The Physics of Immortality*, 1994.
[67] See 28:88.

CHAPTER 3

Definition of Divine Unity

- Meaning of divine unity
- Unity of being
- Perpetual fight
- Everything for the sake of man

Meaning of divine unity

As I said earlier, God is a great mystery. Yet the fact of His existence is implied in the objective existence of the universe. Without this mysterious self-existent power that we call God, there cannot be this universe. Thus the universe is a contingent being. Islam is designated as the religion of Divine Unity, because it is the creation of this One God. There logically cannot be two or many gods, as this would cause chaos in the whole universe. The universe, as facts have shown, is harmony, order, balance and lawful development.

Since the source of real power in the universe resides in this One God, the two major principles of Islamic monotheism, as mentioned in the Opening Chapter of the Quran, consist of the worship of Him Alone, and the supplication of His succour alone.[68] Any deviation from these two principles would bring loss.[69]

Idolworship, the worship of other than the One True God, is the only sin that is not forgiven by God.[70] The reason is that in worshipping idols, man acts against his own nature.[71] It is like committing suicide. The Quran mentions five forms of idolworship. I shall deal with this topic in the next chapter.

It is claimed by polytheists that they also worship the One God, but they use intermediaries to help them. The intermediaries may take the form of angels, prophets, saints, and leaders. This is false, since man cannot have anything except what he strives for. Only he can realize his true being; no one else can.

The doctrine of Divine Unity is the most important aspect of the religion of Islam, which the Quran states to be the religion approved by God.[72] Without it, Islam is nothing different from other polytheistic religions. However, the theologians of Islam of both the Sunni and Shi'ah denominations have made prayer as the pillar of the religion, not belief in and practice of Divine Unity.[73] This turned Islam from a revolutionary, life-affirming, death-defying, peace-and-justice-promoting religion into a quietist religion of withdrawal from the world and acceptance of slavery imposed by oligarchy! This is not Islam!

---

[68] See, Ch. 2.

[69] Quran, 103:2-3.

[70] Quran, 4:48.

[71] Quran, 30:30.

[72] Quran, 3:19.

[73] "God does not forgive idol worship, and He forgives lesser offences for whomever He wills. Anyone who idolizes an idol besides God has strayed far away." (Quran, 4:116) "As for those who lead a righteous life, male or female, while believing, they enter Paradise ..." (Quran, 4:124)

Belief in Divine Unity means (a) belief in one consistent lawful source of power in the universe, (b) belief that the Creator of universe being one, there is unity of laws throughout the whole multi-level structure, (c) therefore, man, to be successful must submit himself wholly to this one, and no other, source of lawful and consistent power, (d) this one lawful and consistent source of power, being the Truth,[74] Man must learn and uphold this truth in order to fulfill his role as the Divine vicegerent that he is, (e) rejection of this belief in Divine Unity and the embrace of many gods of various forms by disbelievers would bring failure and destruction to the human community.

The reason why total belief in one God and its corollary of total rejection of idolatry is so important has to do with human freedom. A human being is free only if he is not subject to any false power. The many gods besides God are false powers. If he subjects himself to any of these false powers, he automatically becomes their slaves and cannot exercise his God-given freedom to chart his destiny. Thus, his submission to the only true power, the One True God, and to no other, automatically confers on him freedom. This has been proved throughout history, in the cases of Abraham, Muhammad and the Republic of the United States of America, and in most other cases too.

Unity of being

Since God is One, it is also logical to assume that the whole universe constitutes one being that is linked together in a hierarchically-connected ascending evolutionary order. Thus unity of being constitutes another principle of Divine Unity. That is why respecting environment and kindness to animals form an ethical principle of good human behaviour. At the same time, in this chain of being, Man is recognized as the apex, the crown of

---

[74] "This is because God is the truth, while any idol they set up beside Him is falsehood, and God is Most High, Most Great." (Quran, 31:30)

creation, as he is sometimes called. Therefore, other creations logically serve him.[75] Hence the symbolism of the angels prostrating to Adam on God's order, as mentioned in the Quran.[76] Hence, in Islam, slaughter of animals to enable humans to eat their meat, except for the meat of pigs, is allowed.

Thus, at the end of this evolutionary process, Man becomes God: the Man-God or the God-Man. At this point, God attains His ultimate purpose in creating the universe, and Man fully realizes His mission of God's vicegerency on Earth.[77]

Although, in Islamic teachings, God is immanent in the world,[78] Islam should be distinguished from pantheism, which equates God with the universe. God is in the universe, but He is also transcendental.[79] He is Independent and Self-Existing, without beginning and without end.[80] In philosophical terminology, He is Necessary Being, while the universe is a contingent being.

Perpetual fight

The early monotheists and polytheists peopled Valleys of the Nile, Tigris and Euphrates, about 2,000 B.C. that the Bible and Quran narrate about. The polytheists fought the monotheists for control of the people and the land. Control of resources, physical and human, is the paramount aim – for the monotheists, to establish peace, justice and security; for the polytheists, to lord it over the whole of society.[81]

---

[75] See, Ch. 1, Note 41, 47.

[76] Quran, 2:34.

[77] Quran, 2:30.

[78] Quran, 57:3.

[79] Ibid., 57:3.

[80] Ibid., 57:3.

[81] The example of Pharaoh, the King of Egypt, and Prophet Moses provides a good example of this two opposing sides and their fate. Quran, 7:103 -29.

Thus the perpetual fight between good and evil, between what an American philosopher terms the oligarchical and humanist factions,[82] grew and developed down the centuries and millennia up to the present time when the world has become a Global Village. The fight is on all levels: ideological, political and military.

Everything for man

Where is God in this great fight? Of course, He is on the humanist side, as the story of the great fight between Pharaoh and Moses and human history show. Although God is a great mystery, and we shall never see Him[83], He is the Spirit behind the universe. He has made everything subservient to man[84], thus making man the measure of all things, and making humanism a relevant philosophy. The Medina Charter which Prophet Muhammad promulgated when he migrated to the town, referred by one writer as the first written constitution in the world, is a very important constitutional document that reflects this humanist philosophy.[85]

That is why the humanist faction will win. But the fight is wholly a human fight, with God inspiring the humanist faction, so to speak. Without doubt, the final victory will come soon, as the emergence of internationalist Global Village at the end of the 20th and the beginning of the 21st Centuries points to.

---

[82] See Lyndo H. LaRouche Jr., *The Secrets Known Only To The Inner Elites*, Campaigner Special Report, No. 11, New York, 1978.

[83] Quran, 6:103.

[84] "Do you not see that God has committed in your service everything in the heavens and in the earth, and has showered you with His blessings – obvious and hidden?" (Quran, 31:20)

[85] See Kassim Ahmad's article "A Short Note on the Medina Charter" on his website **www.kassimahmad.blogspot.com**

Remember that ever since Einstein, we know that time is relative. Had the human community fought their various oligarchical factions with greater unity and concentration, it would have won the final victory, much, much earlier. Take the case of 7th Century Prophet Muhammad of Arabia. He won this historic struggle in twenty-three long years. But soon after, less than a century after his death, his followers broke into political and theological factions that marked the beginning of the end, ending their tremendous upshot in becoming leaders in world science, technology, government and moral and military leadership.[86] Why? Because, as the Prophet said, military conquest is the easy part; moral conquest is the difficult part. Men must renew their moral commitment to good at every step of the way. They cannot and must not take a holiday from this continuous struggle.

The same thing happens to the American experiment. One may say that the United States' Constitution is the best republican-humanist constitution ever devised by man. It was a fine humanist document and produced such towering statesmen as Abraham Lincoln, George Washington, Franklin D. Roosevelt, and J. F. Kennedy, but, when the Republic comes under the influence of the British Empire, it becomes aggressive, cruel and oppressive, as when it dropped atomic bombs on Hiroshima and Nagasaki,

---

[86] "...If someone in the first third of seventh Christian century had had the audacity to prophesy that within a decade some unheralded, unforeseen power from the hitherto barbarous and little known land of Arabia was to make its appearance, hurl itself against the only two world powers of the age, , fall heir to ne – the Sassanid – and strip the other -- the Byzantine – of its fairest provinces, he would undoubted have been declared a lunatic. Yet that was exactly what happened. After the death of the Prophet, sterile Arabia seems to have been converted as if by magic into a nursery of heroes the like of whom both in number and quality is harder to find anywhere. The military campaigns of Khalid ibn-al-Walid and Amr ibn-al-'As which ensued in Iraq, Persia, Syria and Egypt are among the most brilliantly in the history of warfare and bear favourable comparison with those of Napoleon, Hannibal or Alexander." (Philip K. Hitti, *History of the Arabs*, 1970; p. 142.)

involved itself in countless coups and killings in Third World countries during the so-called Cold War[87] and brutally attacked Iraq and invaded it when it could not accept a firm anti-imperialist leader Saddam Hussein in an area where its surrogate nuclear-equipped country, Israel, lie!

We have to deal with a persistent question: why the relapse into polytheism so often happens. The answer, as the Quran puts it, is the pull of the earth.[88] The earth pulls the human being down to its level. Sociologically, it is cultural burden of the society's past, the various evil customs of generations, making their way back into the society, so as to make the new worldview of Divine Unity acceptable, as the turning Jesus into a member of the Trinity, to Roman paganism.[89]

Can this be stopped, and how? Of course, it can. We must remember that this is a *perpetual* struggle of human ascent on to higher and higher levels of existence. Once the socio-economic liberation is achieved, the society under the leadership of the humanist faction that has won the struggle must work out a methodology to educate and train society in its further upward journey. This methodology itself must be under constant revision so as to ensure its effectiveness. Such a society will be so inspired and achieve success after success that the enemy will not be able to do its work of destruction, as it has done in the past.

It will be remembered that Quran reveals to us that the religion of truth or the religion of God will triumph over all other false

---

[87] See William Blum, *Rogue State: A Guideto the World's Only Superpower*, 2000.
[88] "As for those who disbelieve, they enjoy themselves and eat as animals do, then end up in Hellfire. (Quran, 47:12)
[89] The doctrine of the Trinity was first promulgated as the official Christian doctrine at the Council of Nicaea in 325 A.D. This Council was presided over by the Roman Emperor Constantine (280-337 A.D.) who became the first Christian Roman Emperor.

religions in the future.[90] This religion of truth and of God will, of course, not be the present corrupted Islam. It will be the Islam as taught by Prophet Muhammad in the Quran. As the proverb says, the Truth wills out. The Truth is God[91], and God will certainly prevail.[92]

*****

[90] See, Ch. 1, Note 18.
[91] Quran, 22:45
[92] Quran, 58:21

CHAPTER 4

Idolatry and Its Implications for Human Society

- Definition of idolatry
- Five categories of idols
- Effects of idolatry on human beings
- Examples of slave-systems
- The ushering in the Age of True Freedom

Definition of idolatry

An idol is defined as an image of deity used as an object of worship, or a false god. Some human beings worship idols in order to gain power believed to be possessed by these idols. The Quran informs us there are five forms of idolatry, namely (a) worship of material objects, like stones, animals and tress,[93] (b) worship of the sun and the planets,[94] (c) worship of property and wealth,[95] (d) worship of leaders, like prophets, and religious and political leaders, and their attendant ideologies and systems,[96] and (e) worship of one's ego.[97] We have seen these forms of idolatry in many religions throughout history. The Jews idolized their religious leaders, Ezra being one of them. The Christians turned Jesus Christ, a great prophet and teacher of monotheism, into a

---

[93] Quran, 2:51; 6:74.
[94] Quran, 6:76-78.
[95] Quran, 18:42.
[96] Quran, 3:79; 5:17; 30:40-41.
[97] Quran, 25:43; 45:23.

begotten Son of God. The Muslims, unconsciously, idolized Muhammad, another great prophet, into a second god, besides the one true God. This they did by making his so-called Hadith/Sunnah a second principal source of Muslim jurisprudence, thus elevating him to a position equal to God.[98] The older religions of Hinduism, Taoism, and Zoroastrianism believe in a plurality of gods, although behind this plurality of gods, there remains a core belief in One God and the doing of good in all religions.

The Quran informs us that God All-Merciful forgives all sins, except the sin of idol-worship. Verse116 of Surah 4 categorically states: "God does not forgive the idolization of any idols besides Him, and He forgives all lesser offences for whomsoever He wills. Anyone who idolizes any idol besides God has gone far astray." Verse 65 of Chapter 39 states that: "It has been revealed to you and those before you that if you ever fall into idol-worship, all your works will be nullified, and you will be a loser." Further, Verse 22 of Chapter 17 ominously warns, "You shall not set up besides God any other god, lest you end up despised and disgraced." The disbelievers are also described as: "This s is because you were satisfied on earth with other than the truth. You only wanted to play." (40:75)

Effects of idolatry on human beings

Why is idolatry so severely condemned by God? To know the answer, let us see the status and role of the human being allotted to him by the God in His grand design. In a beautiful and profound metaphor, God offers all creations the responsibility of freedom to decide their own fate, thus to change the universe to

---

[98] See Kassim Ahmad, *Hadith: A Re-evaluation*, Monotheist Productions International, Tucson, Arizona, U.S.A., 1997. This book is a translation of the Malay original, *Hadis: Satu Penilaian Semula*, Media Intelek, Petaling Jaya, Selangor; 1986.

his taste. All of them, except man, refused for fear of being unable to bear this responsibility. Man alone accepted it, thus proving man's high status in the order of creation.[99]

The Quran assigns to man two complimentary roles. Firstly, he is the complete servant of the Lord, the true Creator and Sustainer of the universe. Man shall not serve any other master, but only this Lord. So idolatry, the worshipping of other false powers beside the true Power, is strictly prohibited, because it is self-destructive.[100] Secondly, man is, by Divine decree, ruler of the universe. He, like God, can change the earth and the universe to suit his purpose.

Of course, only the true believers can change the universe for the good, because only believers are the upholders and fighters for the cause of good.[101] But God has given this power to all men, regardless of whether they are believers or disbelievers! One can almost say that God is gambling! However, this is not true. Since He is All-Knowing, He knows that the believers will win. Thus, the Quran states unequivocally, "God has decreed, 'I and My messengers will most assuredly win.' God is Powerful, Almighty."[102]

Thus, it is of the utmost importance that man frees himself completely from any false powers: statues, planets, wealth, religious and political leaders, including false ideologies and systems, and egoism. These false powers, if he comes under any of them, would automatically rob man of his freedom, and render

---

[99] Quran, 33:72.

[100] Quran, 30:30.

[101] "God has bought from the believers their lives and their money in exchange for Paradise. Thus, they fight in the cause of God, willing to kill and be killed. Such is the truthful pledge in the Torah, the Gospel, and the Quran – and who fulfills His pledge better than God?" (Quran, 9:111)

[102] Quran, 58:21.

him unable to perform his God-given role of changing the earth into a Paradise of his own making and liking. This Paradise is to be distinguished from the Paradise of blissful innocence of Adam and Eve.[103] .

The slave systems

Man acquires this freedom by stages. He has gone through various socio-economic stages: the hunting phase, the various stages of agricultural phase, and the various stages of manufacturing phase. Each phase has taken many generations. We are now globally at a high stage of the manufacturing phase. We now stand at the dawn of a totally new era. Not only are we about to colonize space: we stand at the door of a just world.[104]

In past eras, the majority of human beings were slaves both to the system and to the master who owned the slaves. These slave-systems were run by the oligarchical factions, while the humanist factions fought to dismantle the slave-systems and free the human being. From the ancient Roman gladiator, Spartacus (d. 71 B.C.), who fought against the mighty Roman Empire and failed, or even earlier, from the time of Prophets Abraham and Moses, through to Prophets Jesus and Muhammad, and other humanist faction leaders, including Abraham Lincoln, and Mahatma Gandhi, who fought with varying degrees of success the oligarchies of their times, there is a vase gulf of time of 3,000 years or 100 generations. It is a long and continuing fight. At the end of the 20th and the beginning of the 21st Centuries, the fight is coming to a victorious end. The word "end" here is used not to mean that the struggle

---

[103] Quran, 9:111.

[104] " ... There will be no injustice on that day ..." (Quran, 40:17). This refers to a time when this world becomes a just world as a result of men's persistent struggles to bring it about. This, I believe, is what the Quran allegorically terms Resurrection.

stops. The struggle continues on higher psychological planes of existence.

The coming age of true freedom

Now, at the opening decade of the 21st century, with the help of the computer, the rocket and the Internet and a vastly awakened humanity, and with the American Empire, successor to the British Empire, disappearing before our very eyes – how many decades and generations do we need to bring into being the just world? I shall not speculate. I surmise it will not be too long.

Let us remind ourselves that God is Pure Spirit. He is Invisible and Unknown to us. "I was a Hidden Treaure. I wanted to be known. So I created the creation," a *Qudsi hadith* has it.[105] Another Qudsi hadith states that, "I was, and no one was with Me. I am now as I was before." The first statement tells us that God is immanent in creation, and that man is God's crowing glory. Man is, therefore, God-Manifested. The second statement tells us that the created universe is a contingent being, present and existing only as long as God manifests Himself. Once God ceases to manifest Himself, the universe ceases to exist, and God alone, the Pure Spirit, exists![106]

Thus, the Quranic statement that the whole universe was created to serve man is true, and realized at the end of time. The second Paradise, the first being the bliss of the Age of Innocence, is the result of men's struggles to achieve happiness.[107] It is not a Paradise to be achieved in a so-called After-life. The After-life is life in this world, for there is no other world, except this world,

---

[105] A Qudsi hadith is defined as a report whose idea is divinely-derived while the words are those of Muhammad. Like all hadith, it is conjecture and cannot be considered a religious source or authority besides the Quran.

[106] "Every thing perishes except His Presence." (Quran, 28:88)

[107] Quran, 9:111.

consisting of many levels, but one single unified, and multi-layered world.

The belief in individual physical resurrection is not reasonable. God is All-Powerful and is capable of resurrecting the individuals physically. But we should also know that the actions of God are not whimsical. They are in accordance to His qualities of being the Truth, Lawfulness, Harmony, Order, Balance, and Justice. We should know that God's Absolute Power does not make Him act unjustly, because that is contrary to His Nature. Hence, it is unreasonable to expect God to resurrect the human being *physically* and *individually*, because each human being is nothing but only a part of humanity (Ar. *nafsun wahidah*).[108] At the time of his physical individual death, he returns to God, and is resurrected in the next generation, as stated in many Quranic statements.[109] At the time of his physical individual death, he or she may be a baby, or a child, an adult, in a state of severe sickness, or may have died in war -- is he or she to be resurrected in a state exactly as at the time of death? This is unreasonable.

Again, at the material time of resurrection from the graves, very many people are still living, and going about their business in the world. What happens to them? Are they all to be struck dead by some terrible happening, and then resurrected as they lie dead wherever they happen to be? It can be seen how messy and illogical such resurrection is! It cannot be the work of a God whose universe is one of marvelous order and harmony, as testified by such famous self-confessed atheists as Einstein.[110]

Some believers are uncomfortable at this prospect, because they feel cheated that their works of worship are not rewarded, as they

---

[108] Quran, 4:1.

[109] Quran, 2:134; 10:13; 17:17; 77:16-17; 6:165; 7:137.

[110] Einstein is reputed to have said that God does not play dice with the universe.

have been promised by God. As we have pointed out, God does no do the slightest injustice to anyone. It is we who fail to understand God's teachings, preferring to rely on the teachings of our own created priesthood who sets aside reason. While we respect our scholars and learn from their works, we should not follow them blindly. Reward and punishment are natural consequences of our own actions. Moreover, we have also been taught to serve God, for the sake of God,[111] without expecting any reward, good being reward in itself. As it is, the reward (and the punishment), is there, as we experience it in our short span of individual life, and in the eternal span of our species life.

We are at the threshold of the Age of True Freedom and the Age of True Reason. That surely is enough reason to celebrate and welcome life.

*****

---

[111] Quran, 6:162.

CHAPTER 5

Religions in History

- Definition of religion,
- Purpose of religion,
- From pre-scientific to scientific,
- The uniqueness of Islam and plurality of religions,
- When science, philosophy and religion meet.

Definition of religion

Scholars have divided religions into three categories, namely (a) religions as social constructions,[112] (b) religions as progressing towards higher objective truth, and (c) a particular religion as absolutely true.[113]

---

[112] As Greek philosopher Xenophanes famously commented, "Men made gods in their own image; those of Ethiopians are black and snub-nosed, those of the Thracians have blue eyes and red hair." (Internet, Wikipedia.) The tradition of projectionist view of religion as a human product goes back in modern times to the seminal work of German philosopher Ludwig Feuerbach, who proposed that God was the extension of human aspirations, as is found in the works of Karl Marx, Sigmund Freud, and others. In ancient times, Sophist Critias (5th century B.C.) considered religion was invented to frighten men into adhering to morality and justice. Plato was not averse to providing new myths to perform this alleged function, as seen in his conception of the "noble lie" (i.e. the invention of myths to promote morality and order) in the *Republic*.

[113] Islam has made this claim (Quran, 3:19). However, this claim is conditional to the absolute adherence to the principle of Divine Unity.

When Adam and Eve were banished from the Garden of Eden to their new home on earth, God said,

> "Go down therefrom, all of you. When guidance comes to you from Me, those who follow My guidance will have no fear, nor will they grieve. As for those who disbelieve and reject Our revelations, they will be dwellers of Hell, wherein they abide forever."[114]

Thus the early primitive human community around Adam and Eve belonged to two religious types, i.e. believers and disbelievers. The believers were the righteous, upholding truth and justice, while the disbelievers were the evildoers, promoting falsehood and injustice. The breakup into the two groups is the result of the God-given freedom to men to decide their own fate. Those who freely decide to obey God succeeded in their life. Those who freely decide to disobey Him suffer. It is this rebellion that is the source of evil in the world. This profound truth is symbolized in the story God ordering the angels to prostrate before Adam, with one them disobeying God (implying man's freedom) and automatically becoming the Devil. The Devil (symbolizing evil) is the source of evil.[115]

The purpose of religion

The story of the human community from that time on is the story of the struggles between these two groups. The American philosopher, Lyndon H. LaRouche, has called the two groups as the *oligarchical faction*, representing the oppressors, and *the humanist faction*, representing the liberators.[116] This profound analysis is in accord with the teachings of the Quran.

---

[114] Quran, 2:38-39.
[115] We treat the problem of evil in Chapter 12.
[116] See, Ch. 3, Note 82.

Religion is, therefore, as old as the human community. It is a way of life, consisting of beliefs, rituals of worship, and a code of communal life, embracing communal cooperation, and ceremonies at birth, marriage, and death. The aim of the way of life is to promote communal cooperation and to guarantee the survival of the community. During the long childhood of mankind, from the time of Prophet Adam to the time of the last prophet, Prophet Muhammad, covering a period of more than 5,000 years, when man entered the Scientific Era and achieved adulthood,[117] he needed the close care and guidance of his parents. We may say that he needed the close guidance and care of his Creator and Preserver God. That is the function of prophets, philosophers, saints and sages, among whom number Abraham, Moses, Jesus and Muhammad in the Abrahamic tradition, and Gautama Buddha, Confucius, Lao Tzu and Zoroaster in the non-Abrahamic tradition. The Quran refers to this non-Abrahamic line as Sab'in.[118]

Note that the religion of Divine Unity, Islam, began as one, but along the way, due to regression, the pull of the earth, as the Quran puts it,[119] one became three, i.e. Judaism, Christianity and Islam. Outside the Abrahamic line, the same thing happened.

---

[117] It was Pakistani poet-philosopher See Mohammad Iqbal who pointed out that Muhammad's teachings stood between the ancient and the modern world. "In so far as the source of his revelation is concerned he belongs to the ancient world; in so far as the spirit of his revelation is concerned he belongs to the modern world. In him life discovers other sources of knowledge suitable to its new direction. ... In Islam prophecy reaches its perfection in discovering the need of its own abolition." (See, *The Reconstruction of Religious Thought in Islam*; p. 126.)

[118] Quran, 2:62.

[119] "As for those who disbelieve, they live and eat like the animals eat, then end up in hellfire." (Quran, 47:12)

From pre-scientific to scientific era

In that period of childhood, men had to be convinced of the teachings of God through miracles. That is why all the prophets had their miracles: Abraham survived the fire he was thrown into by the disbelievers, Moses with his famous stick turning into serpents which ate up the serpents of the magicians of the Pharaoh, Jesus with his ability to speak while he was a baby in the crib, to cure the leprous, as well as to revive the dead.[120]

Prophet Muhammad, however, according to the Quran, had no miracles.[121] Opening the modern era to mankind, he must appeal through knowledge and reason.[122]

That is why the first five famous verses of Surah 96 that he first received as revelation from God concern reading and teaching through the pen. Furthermore, the Quran claims not only to confirm, but supersedes previous scriptures.[123] That is why Muhammad ended the series of prophets.[124] However, by this

---

[120] These miracles are mentioned in the Quran in their appropriate places.

[121] "They said, 'If only miracles could come down to him from his Lord!' Say, 'All miracles come only from God. I am no more than a manifest warner.' Is it not enough of a miracle that we sent down to you this book, being recited to them. This is indeed a mercy and a reminder for people who believe." (Quran, 29:50-51). The Quran is, indeed, a miracle. It resides in its awesome 19-based mathematically-structured composition, known as the Code 19. See Rashad Khalifa, *The Computer Speaks: God's Message to the World.*

[122] "No one can believe except in accordance with God's will., and He places a curse on those who will not use reason." (Quran, 10:100)

[123] "Then We revealed to you this scripture, truthfully, confirming previous scriptures, and superseding them." (Quran, 5:48)

[124] "Muhammad was not the father of any man among you. He was a messenger of God and the final prophet. God is fully aware of all things." (Quran, 33:40)

statement, God's communication with human beings does not stop, but continues.[125]

All prophets had their interims. Although their basic teaching of Divine Unity is the same throughout,[126] their laws differed from one another. The laws of Jesus differed slightly with the laws of Moses, although both were sent to the Jews. Muhammad differed from Moses and Jesus in that he was sent to the whole of mankind.[127] His laws, taken in the universal perspective, are much more humane than previous laws.[128] So, there will come a time when Muhammad's interim will come to an end and the Quran will have fulfilled its function as a guide to mankind. At that time, mankind will no doubt, according to God's will, find new guidance for their onward journey.

4. The uniqueness of Islam and plurality of religions

Islam's uniqueness lies in its total adherence to the principle of Divine Unity. Two of these major principles are mentioned in the Opening Chapter of the Quran, namely, the worship of God alone and of none other, and recourse for help to God alone, and to none other.[129] Without this absolute adherence to Divine Unity, Islam becomes another of the many religions, belief in many gods, and practicing many bad customs. One of the bad customs is

---

[125] "No human being can communicate with God, except through inspiration, or from behind a barrier, or by sending a messenger through whom he reveals what He wills. He is Most High, Most Wise." (Quran, 42:51).

[126] "We did not send any messenger before you except with the inspiration: 'There is no god except Me; you shall worship me alone.'" (21:25)

[127] "Say, 'O people, I am God's messenger to all of you.'" (Quran, 7:58)

[128] Although the Quran came down to an Arabia of early 7th Century Arabia and has a historical context, its teachings embrace a universalism that is humane. Take an example. The cutting of the hand for a thief (5:38): the verse is immediately followed by a verse that advocates lightening of the punishment, and even pardon.

[129] Quran, 1:5.

exclusivity. "I am better than you. My nation is superior to you. I therefore have a divine right to dominate you." This exclusivity, latterly clearly shown by the United States of America under the two Bush presidencies, has not brought peace to the world, but disaster of the worst kind.[130] "The greatest country in the world" will have to change.[131]

When science, philosophy and religion meet

There is no doubt true knowledge of life, science taken at its best (i.e. in congruence with religion and philosophy at their best), not arrogant science, thinking that it can solve all questions, as in the 19th century, will bring peace, plenty, justice and happiness to the world in this 21st century. The West considers modern science and technology as "the be all and end all" of existence, making science and technology a dictator, dictating life for us. As a result, we do not have peace, security and justice, but instead, self-destruction. The First and the Second World Wars bears testimony to this self-destruction. What may come in the future is more and worse self-destruction. The human community must put a stop to this.

This can be done when we temper science with higher reason – compassion and wisdom – philosophy and religion at their best. In the past, religion has been a good as well as a bad influence. Practiced as a disciplined way of life dedicated to finding peace and cooperation among mankind, religion has been a tremendous good. Practiced in the form of fanaticism, it has been a great curse. The human community has reached a point where truth must be

---

[130] Bush Junior who illegally invaded and occupied Iraq, and murdered its president Saddam Hussein, must be hauled to be tried by the International Court of Justice and shot.

[131] As I write this sentence (5th November, 2008 at 12.0 noon, Malaysian time.), news came on the wires that Democratic presidential candidate Barrak Obama, who has promised change, has won the election. He must bring about the change.

57

sought in a healthy debate, and naked power must give way to right reason and compassion. The United Nations Organization, with all its weaknesses, provides the framework of debate and discussion that are necessary for the further development of human civilization, indeed for further human survival. We either destroy ourselves totally and completely, or choose to let ourselves be ruled by higher reason and compassion. The first is the way for complete and total self-destruction; the second is for survival and further development. The choice is clear.

We have no other option but to take the second road. When we do that, and I believe we are already on the road to doing that, we shall be ready to climb the next ladder of our unending evolution to higher and higher states of being.[132]

*****

---

[132] "That We may change your state and make you grow into what you do not know." (Quran, 56:61)

CHAPTER 6

Components of Religion

- Religion as a way of life
- Components of religion
- Philosophy and metaphysics
- Rituals of worship and socio-economic doctrines.

Religion as a way of life

Religion, as a way of life, does not include just the rituals of worship. It includes every aspect of human life, from a worldview (which includes metaphysics, cosmology, epistemology, and eschatology), to law, politico-economic and social doctrines, customs and rituals of worship. Of these, the worldview is the most important component and controls the other aspects. The worldview of Islam is the concept of Divine Unity (Ar. *tawhid*). Without belief in and affirmation of this concept, other elements, including the ritual of prayer, becomes null and void.[133]

Take the case of Islam. We should discard the wrong view of Islam as the religion brought by Prophet Muhammad. In God's

---

[133] "God does not forgive idolatry, but He forgives lesser offences for whomsoever He wills. Anyone who sets up idols beside God, has forged a horrendous offence." (Quran, 4:48)

sight, Islam is the religion approved by Him for mankind.[134] It started as early as the rise of human society. Although Adam is considered the first prophet, he did not yet have a clear conception of Islam. Following him, we have prophets Idris and Noah mentioned in the Quran as believers and muslims. Their localities are not clear. These and subsequent prophets, including Moses and Jesus, were spiritual teachers of the religion of Islam of their communities and times. They were national prophets, teachings national religions.[135] With Prophet Muhammad, mankind entered the internationalist era. He was sent to the whole of mankind.[136]

The various components of religion

When it comes to Abraham of the Chaldeans, the picture becomes clearer. He was definitely a believer and a muslim. The Quran informs us that with him, God gave mankind the rituals of worship of prayer, fasting, and pilgrimage to the House of God in Becca.[137] Later traditions that credit Prophet Muhammad with ascent to Heaven to receive the five prayers from God were simply fabricated stories to amuse audiences of that time as we amuse ourselves with various television entertainment programs today.

It was this clearly defined Islam brought by Prophet Abraham that was passed down through the various prophets, including Moses, Aaron and Jesus to the Jews, and lastly through Muhammad to the Arabs and to the whole of mankind,[138] each time with the

---

[134] Quran, 3:19

[135] See *The Holy Quran with English Translation and Commentary*, Islamic International Publication, U.K., 1988, Vol I; pp. v-vi & x-xxii.

[136] See, Ch. 5, Note 127.

[137] Another name for Mecca.

[138] Muhammad, unlike the other prophets, was sent to the whole of mankind. See, Ch. 5, Note 127.

teachings upgraded to suit changing times. Muhammad is the *last* of the series of divine teachers sent to teach the right way of life, the *Straight Path* of the Quran. The Quran, guaranteed as to its purity by God Himself, is His final and completed message to mankind.[139] The Quran contains all the teachings that men need to complete his journey in the modern world. According to the Pakistani philosopher Muhammad Iqbal, with Prophet Muhammad's advent, mankind enters a new era – the Age of Science and Technology.[140]

Philosophy and metaphysics

The Quran states that no vision comprehends God, but God comprehends all vision.[141] Thus the meeting with God on the Day of Judgement means His judgment rather than meeting with Him. This judgement means the application of the natural law of good for good and bad for bad. This judgement is actually made by man himself.[142]

However, this original religion of strict submission to the One True God, called Islam, each time deteriorated into some form of polytheism due to the re-entry of popular culture bearing many polytheistic practices that nullify the monotheistic belief in Divine Unity, thus turning the majority into disbelievers.[143] The idolization of prophets and of religious leaders happened to all groups, including Jews, Christians and Muslims. The present state

---

[139] Quran, 15:9.

[140] See, Ch. 5, Note 117.

[141] "No vision can encompass Him, but He encompasses all visions. (Quran, 6:103)

[142] "We have recorded the fate of every human being; it is tied to his neck. On the Day of Resurrection We will hand him a record that is accessible. Read your own record. Today you suffice as your own reckoner." (Quran, 17:13-14)

[143] "The majority of those who believe in God do not do so without committing idol worship." (Quran, 12:106)

is as described by Verse 62 of *Surah Al-Baqarah* that there exists a small group of true believers in all the religions. This follows logically from the fact that God sends His messengers to all national communities.

As we stated above, the most important component is the worldview of *Tawhid* or Divine Unity. Without this, the monotheism of Islam is nullified.[144] This is the only universal component of the religion; the rest belong to the world of relativity. Take the case of law. God commands us to rule men justly, while He recommends us to be also humane. The laws of various nations vary from nation to nation and from time to time. In other words, there is plurality of laws. So is also true with politico-economic systems. Men have lived under various forms of politico-economic systems: nomadism, feudalism, capitalism, socialism-communism and religious theocracy. There is thus plurality while at the same time adhering to unity.[145]

The same is true when we deal with the customs of various nations. How each nation has its own customs when it comes to eating and dressing, how each nation has customs relating to births, deaths and to marriages. Again here there is pluralism.

When we come to rituals of worship, we also notice pluralism with each religious community having their own rituals.[146] This is to be expected, as vast times and spaces separated the human communities that originally came from one community.

---

[144] "It has been revealed to you and to those before you that if you ever commit idol worship, all your works will be nullified, and you will be with the losers." (Quran, 39:65)

[145] "For each of you, we have decreed laws and different rites." (Quran, 5:48)

[146] "For each congregation, We have decreed a set of rites that they must uphold. Therefore, they should not dispute with you. You shall continue to invite everyone to your Lord. Most assuredly, you are on the right path." (Quran, 22:67)

Rituals of worship and socio-economic doctrines

The belief in an afterlife too share the same characteristics. There is plurality, the basic core being a belief in a Final Judgement with its appropriate rewards and punishments coming in the form of a Perfect World, or God's Kingdom, or Paradise. It must be pointed that the human community is actually one being (Ar. *nafsun wahidah*)[147], the myriad physical forms do not count. Afterlife must mean life in this world that comes later, not another different world, although changed due to men's creative activity. We have come a long way from primitive life and barbarism, given to barbaric practices, to a modern civilized life with a humane international law under United Nations Organization where we discuss and deliberate on the affairs of the human community.

Since Man the vicegerent of God creates his own world, the resultant world only comes into being through his own efforts. He is logically there in every generation. He exists in his children's generation, in his grand-children's generation, and so on. Thus, he is ever-present, and never absent. That is how man is resurrected.

Thus, there is a plurality of methods and ways. We cannot say there is only one right way in terms of laws, politico-economic doctrines, customs and even rituals of worship. The only exception is the worldview of Divine unity. It is this that separates God-approved religion of monotheism from other forms of polytheism. This goes to prove that religion is a way of life, designed to promote good and prevent evil in the human community, thus to ensure its survival, with the scientific worldview of Divine unity guaranteeing the greatest possible success to that community. *****

---

[147] Quran, 4:1.

CHAPTER 7

Metaphors and Allegories

- A correct understanding of the Quran
- The use of metaphors and allegories
- Man must change psychologically and morally
- The coming era of conscious evolution.

A correct understanding of the Quran

The Quran is unique in the sense that it gives its own principles of interpretation. A first principle is that it contains two types of verses, namely the clear straightforward verses (Ar. *muhkamat*), and the metaphorical and allegorical verses (Ar. *mutashabihat*)[148]

While the classical methodology of *hadith* explaining the Quran was inadequate even then, it is more so now. I have offered, as an addendum, a scientific methodology in the English translation of my *Hadith* book.[149] I was happy to discover in a website recently that a Muslim American scholar has commented quite lengthily on it. I was disappointed that no Muslim scholar from any part of the Muslim world, especially in my own country, has commented

---

[148] "He sent down to you this scripture containing straightforward verse – which constitute the essence of the scripture – as well as multiple meaning or allegorical verses. Those who harbour doubts in their hearts will pursue the multiple-meaning verses to create confusion and to extricate a certain meaning. None knows the true meaning thereof except God and those well founded in knowledge. They say 'We believe in this – all of it comes from our Lord.' Only those who possess intelligence will take heed." (Quran, 3:7)

[149] See *Hadith: A Re-evaluation*, Monotheist Production International, Tucson, Arizona, U.S.A., 1997; pp 126-151.

on it. I shall publish his comments and my rejoinder in Appendix I of this book.

In that proposed scientific methodology, I mentioned nine principles of interpretation. They are (1) the principle of two types of verses, (2) the principle unity of Quranic verses, (3) the principle of congruence of Quranic teachings with truth and logic, (4) principle of self-explanation, (5) the principle of good intention, or objectivity, (6) the principle of topical context (obvious enough for any reader of any book but I have included it to offset the wrong interpretation given to verse 7 of Chapter 59), (7) the principle of historical context, (8) the principle of easy practicability, and (9) the principle of distinction between principle and method. I have also tested the efficacy of this methodology in this addendum.

The use of metaphors and allegories

Metaphors and allegories are to be found in abundance in the Quran. As far as I know, no systematic study of these has been made. Some useful explanations are to be found in some translations.[150] The excellent reference volume of our veteran scholar, Fathi Osman, *Concepts of the Quran* (1997: Kuala Lumpur) should have dealt with Quranic metaphor and allegories. Unfortunately, it did not. But their usage in the Quran is very effective in explaining the meanings of certain concepts. Take the case of the Arabic term *khalifa*,[151] meaning vicegerent. It refers to a special creation of God, the *Homo sapiens*, who, by his rational and creative capabilities, is given the role of ruling and re-making the world. The metaphor of God teaching him names refers to his capability of knowing the world; the metaphor of God ordering the angels to prostrate to him, showing that the whole of God's

---

[150] See especially Maulahum Muhammad Ali, *The Holy Quran – Arabic Text with English Translation and Commentary* (Lahore:1917, New Edition 2002)
[151] Quran, 2:30-34.

creation is put to his service; the metaphor of rebellion against God's order by one of the angels, symbolizing man's freedom as well pointing to rebellion against God, as the source of evil; and the metaphor of God advising Adam and Eve against approaching "This Tree"[152] symbolizing man's achieving self-consciousness. All these great and profound concepts are depicted in these metaphors.

The same with the allegories. Allegories are used to refer to events and entities that cannot be described literally. For instance, God, Whose majestic descriptions in the famous Throne Verse[153] or in the equally famous Light Verse...[154] The Day of Judgement, Heaven and Hell are also described allegorically. Look, for instance, at the fearful description of the Day of Judgement: -

> *Your Lord's requital is unavoidable. No force in the universe can stop it. The day will come when the sky will violently thunder. The mountains will be wiped out. Woe on the day to the disbelievers -- who are in their blundering, heedless. They will be herded into Gehanna forcibly. This is the fire in which you used to disbelieve. Is this magic or do you not see? Suffer the burning. Whether you are patient or impatient, it will be the same for you. This is the just requital for what you did. The righteous have deserves gardens and bliss. They enjoy what their Lord has reserved for them; their Lord has spared them the retribution of Hell. Eat and drink happily in return for your works.[155]*

On the other hand, the Day of Judgement or the Resurrection is also described as a time when the world undergoes major changes. For instance, look at these verses:-

---

[152] See Quran 2, 35.
[153] Quran, 2:255.
[154] Quran, 24:35.
[155] Quran, 57:7-19.

66

To Him is your ultimate return, all of you. This is God's truthful promise. He initiates the creation then repeats it, in order to reward those who believe and lead a righteous life equitably. As for those who disbelieve, they incur hellish drinks and a painful retribution for their disbelieving.[156]

On that day, We will fold the heaven like the folding of a book. Just as We initiate the first creation, We will repeat it. This is Our promise; We will carry it out. We have decreed it in the Psalms as well as in the other scriptures that the earth shall be inherited by My righteous worshippers.[157] (21:104-05)

When we compare these verses to other verses which states that resurrection is a natural process, like the change of seasons,[158] or like sleeping and waking[159], and further take note of the verse that inform us that men at that time automatically judges himself,[160] then we get a clearer picture of the meaning of the Day of Judgement or the Day of Resurrection.

Man must change psychologically and morally

It should be noted that these changes cannot come about unless there is a change in the psychological and moral state of the human being. He must rise above his animalistic, cannibalistic and barbarous beginnings.[161] It should be noted also that these

---

[156] Quran, 10:4.

[157] Quran, 21:104-05.

[158] Quran, 30:19. See also 30:50; 50:99-11; 21:104; 35:9.

[159] Quran, 25:47.

[160] See, Ch. 6, Note 142.

[161] The Quran mentions three psychological states: *nafs'ul-amarah* (12:53: the lowest animalistic stage where the human being thinks that only he is right while others are wrong), *nafs'ul-lawwah* (75:2: the second higher stage where he concedes that he may be wrong while others may be right, and lastly *nafs'ul-mutmainnah* (89:37: the highest stage where he achieves peace with his external and internal selves) At the moment, the human

changes comes not as an external pressure but as an internal development.

The British historical philosopher, Robert Briffault, correctly stressed that ethical evolution follows in the steps of rational evolution. He says in his excellent book, *The Making of Humanity*, "The decay of human sacrifice and cannibalism was not the effect any mysterious and uncaused 'development of moral sentiment', but a beginning of religious skepticism. Moral progress has in every case consisted not in a development of feeling but in a development of thought; the rational evolution has preceded and brought about the ethical revolution... nothing is more conspicuous than the feebleness, the impotence of abstract moral sentiment as such. Unless there is a real material interest disguised under it, or it is the expression of a clear rational process, mere moral principle has scarcely achieved anything at all in the betterment of the world. All history bears witness to the tragic futility of pure abstract moral principle."[162]

The coming era of conscious evolution

The American futuristic writer, Barbara Marx Hubbard, writes about the internal pressure of the changes that are coming. She says, "Occasionally, in the course of history a new worldview emerges that transforms society. It happened when Jesus's disciples were inspired by his life to believe in radical transformation through love. It occurred in the Renaissance when the idea of progress through knowledge was born. It happened in the United States when the ideas of freedom and democracy became institutions through the Constitution and the Bill of Rights, and again among the transcendentalists, such as Ralph Waldo Emerson and Walt Whitman, who believed that each

---

community is on the road from the first to the second stage. When the last stage comes, we shall achieve peace and justice.

[162] See *The Making of Humanity*, p. 300.

individual is an expression of the divine, a free and sovereign person. Now, once again a new worldview is arising. This idea is the culmination of all human history. It holds the promise of fulfilling the great aspirations of the past and heralds the advent of the next phase of our evolution. It is the idea of *conscious evolution.*" (Italics given.)[163]

What these writers have said have been stated in the Quranic metaphors and allegorical verses that we have quoted above. As regards the importance of reason and truth, we want to call our readers' attention to the verse that states that, in Islam, faith and right reason compliment and do not contradict each other.[164] As to truth, the Quran informs us that God is the truth.[165]

******

---

[163] See her book *Conscious Evolution,* (California, 1998); p. 1.

[164] "None can believe except with God's leave, and He bars those who do not use reason." (Quran, 10:100).

[165] "On that day, God will requite them fully for their works, and they will find out that God is the Truth." (Quran, 24:25)

CHAPTER 8

God, the Pure Spirit, and Man, The *Homo Sapiens* and God's Vicegerent

- Who or what is God?
- Is the world eternal or created?
- God is both transcendental and immanent
- What is man, the *Home sapiens*?
- Man will colonize space.

Who or what is God?

Who or what is God? Obviously, this is the most difficult question anyone can be confronted with. God is a Great Mystery. As the Quran says, no vision can comprehend Him, while He comprehends all vision. He is different to different peoples: remember the proverbial blind men describing an elephant![166]

> God, there is no god besides Him, the Ever-Living, the Self-Subsisting by Whom all subsist. Never a moment of unawareness or slumber overtakes Him. To Him belongs everything in the heavens and everything on earth. Who could intercede with Him, except by His leave? He knows their past and their future. No one attains any knowledge, except as He wills. His dominion encompasses the heavens and the earth, and

---

[166] See, Forward, Note 2.

ruling them never burdens Him. He is he Most High, the Great.[167]

God is the light of the heavens and the earth. The allegory of His light is that of a concave mirror behind a lamp that is placed inside a glass container. The glass container is like a bright pearl-like star. The fuel thereof is supplied from a blessed oil-producing tree that is neither eastern nor western. Its oil is almost self-radiating, needing no fire to ignite it. Light upon light. God guides to His light whomever He wills.[168]

He is the First and the Last, and the Outward and the Inward. He is fully aware of all things.[169]

He is the One God; there is no other god besides Him. Knower of all secrets and declarations. He is the Most Gracious, Most Merciful. He is the One God; there is no other god besides Him. The King, the Most Sacred, the Peace, the Most Faithful, the Supreme, the Almighty, the Most Powerful, the Most Dignified. God be glorified, far above having partners. He is the One God; he Creator the Initiator, the Designer. To Him belongs the most beautiful names. Glorifying Him is everything in the heavens and the earth. He is the Almighty, Most Wise.[170]

No vision can encompass Him, but He encompasses all visions. He is he Compassionate, the Cognizant.[171]

This proves that God is the Truth, while any idol they set up beside Him is falsehood, and that God is the Most High, Most Great.[172]

---

[167] Quran, 2:255
[168] Quran, 24:35
[169] Quran, 57:3
[170] Quran, 59:22-24
[171] Quran, 6:103

The above verses inform us that God is Power, Knowledge, Life Ever-living, Self-subsisting, Eternal, Creator, Designer, Preserver and Sustainer of the universe, Transcendental as well as Immanent as regards the world.

As we have seen, there are many religions in the world: monotheistic like Judaism, Christianity and Islam; polytheistic like Hinduism; and atheistic like Buddhism and Confucianism. This proves that the idea of God or the sacred reverence of life expresses itself in many forms. There is not one form. Although there is one Truth and one true religion,[173] men are unable to comprehend it fully. God is the Great Unknown. He is Pure Spirit. Just as we cannot place where our own soul or spirit (which comes from God, the *min ruhi* of the Quran[174]) lies in our body, so we cannot place God behind the phenomenal universe. He is hidden from us, as our soul is. Just as we do not exist without our souls, so this universe does not exist without God.

The unbelievers deny the existence of God because they cannot see Him. They only see the world.[175] Can they see the roots of a tree? But without its (hidden) roots, there can be no tree.

Is the world eternal or created?

The Greek philosophers wrestled with the problem of creation, because they could not visualize a time when he universe was not, since a Creator-God had to be simultaneous with His creation. But, obviously, the universe, being of decaying matter, could not exist by itself. A Self-Existing, Creative Power, whom we call God,

---

[172] Quran, 31:30

[173] Quran, 3:19

[174] "Your Lord said to the angels, 'I am creating a human being from aged mud, like the potter's clay. Once I perfect him, and blow into him from My spirit, you shall prostrate before him.'" (Quran, 15:28-29)

[175] As the Quran states, "They only care about the things of this world that are visible to them, ..." (30:7)

must bring it into being. How did He do it? Did he create it from nothing? Creation *ex-nihilo*, as Christian theologians believed?[176] The Quran informs us that God's order of creation is to say to *it*, "Be!" and it complies. According to Muslim philosophers,[177] the object *it* is to the potential matter of the universe that is from God Himself. Thus, there was nothing with God before creation; the universe came later after the order of creation was issued by God. To God, time is instantaneous. It is the eternal now.

God is both transcendental and immanent

God is outside or transcendental to the universe which He created. At the same time, He is immanent in it, because the world is His manifestation. A Qudsi hadith[178] has it that "I was a hidden treasure and I wanted to be known, so I created the creation. I am now as I was before." This proves that God cannot be known. As the Quran states, vision cannot comprehend Him, but He comprehends all vision.

Who or what is man?

Man, the *Homo sapiens*, is the crown of God's creation. He appeared on Earth later, about a million years ago, after the mineral, the vegetable and the animal kingdoms have come into being. The Quran refers to him as a new creation.[179] With his appearance, a new dimension was added to the universe. Being endowed by God with the ability to be a ruler and a creator of his own destiny, he participates in the growth of the universe. This ability of his is symbolized in the Quran by the angels bowing

---

[176] St. Thomas Agustine (354-430) in New Encylopaedia Britannica

[177] See Dr. Jamila Khatoon, *The Place of God, Man and the Universe in the Philosophic System of Iqbal*(Pakistan:1963); pp. 43 on.

[178] See Ch. 4, Note 105.

[179] Quran, 23:12-14.

down to him on God's order.[180] The Quran further states that everything in the universe is made to serve the humans.[181]

Although man, in his already long history in the world, (actually very short compared to the age of the universe[182]) has left a trail of blood, he has progressed from barbarism to civilization, ascending yet higher and higher. However, the progress is not nonlinear, but multilinear, "creatively recurring and integralist."[183] At times, he ascends; but at many times also he descends. However, on the whole, he ascends. One can say that greater glory awaits man. Remember the symbolism mentioned in the Quran of only man, of all created beings, accepting the awesome trust of responsibility offered by God?[184] The great dramatist, Shakespeare, even goes poetic about man.[185] I can say man will justify God's optimism about his capabilities.[186]

Man will colonize space

We have seen how man has created and gone through various socio-economic systems. First living in the caves, he began as a hunter hunting for food. He then developed low agriculture, farming land as he went from one area to another. Then he developed higher agriculture, improving the land and the yield through fertilization and through machinery, from simple to more complex machinery. We are now at the higher stage of agriculture. At the same time, he creates the industrial society by making tools

---

[180] Quran, 2:34.

[181] See Quran 45:13.

[182] Man has been on Earth for 1 million years. Compared to the age of the Universe (20 billion years) it is very brief indeed!

[183] See P. A. Sorokin, Modern Historical and Social Philosophies (New York:1950); pp. 291-92.

[184] Quran, 33:72.

[185] See, Ch. 1, Note 43.

[186] Quran, 2:30.

and products from simple things as eating plates to bicycles, cars, trains, airplanes, ships and rockets.

Man is now colonizing outer space. Soon he will be living in all the planets. This is indicated in the Quran when it says that men will live in paradise that is as wide as the heavens.[187] Thus, there is no limit to men's development, although a time will come, a hundred billions of years from now, when the energy in the universe will have been used up.[188] At that time, as the Qudsi hadith we have quoted says, only God remains.[189]

*****

---

[187] Quran, 3:133.

[188] See Frank J. Tipler, *The Physics of Immortality* (New York: 1994).

[189] "Everything perishes except His Presence." (Quran, 28:88)

CHAPTER 9

The Individual and the Collective

- Mankind is of one selfhood, the individual does not count except as part of that one selfhood,
- Creativity of the Individual,
- The emergence of Man, the *Homo sapiens*,
- Man's mission in the world.

1. Mankind is one

The Quran informs us that mankind, although consisting of many individuals, is actually oneself (Ar. *nafsun wahidah*). Note that the word used is not soul or spirit (Ar. *ruh*)

> O people, observe your Lord, the One who created you from one being, and created from it its mate, then spread from the two many men and women.[190]

> The creation and resurrection of all of you is the same as that of one person.[191] (31:28)

This pronouncement about mankind is not only interesting, but extremely important. It carries many meanings. Firstly, it is the universal selfhood of man, *the One* that is of paramount importance. Secondly, the particular selfhood of many individual men, like Moses, Jesus or Muhammad, *the Many*, is not important.

---

[190] Quran, 4:1.
[191] Quran, 31:28.

Thirdly, mankind as a whole has *a historical mission*, and this historical mission is accomplished by *any* leading individual, not necessarily the ones that have played that role, like Moses, Jesus and Muhammad.[192] Thus if there were no such Moses, Jesus or Muhammad, other creative individuals with like missions would have been raised to take their places.

2. Creativity resides in individuals

However, creativity and leadership reside in individuals. There would have been no scientific, or artistic progress, or any type of progress, and hence, no civilization, without those creative and leading individuals. Through 5,000 years of civilization, the human family, from generation to generation, has carried forward human progress, the latter generations inheriting from the earlier generations, till the emergence of the precarious global community that we are now living in. I say precarious, because the nuclear sword of Damocles that hangs over us, threatening us with total destruction. Consider this verse from the Quran:

> We have adorned everything on earth in order to test them, and thus distinguish those among them who work righteousness. Inevitably, We will wipe out everything on it, leaving it completely barren.[193]

This has been the result of mankind's excessive belief in modern science and technology in the 18th and 19th centuries to the neglect of the moral and spiritual sides of his being. The destruction wrought in the First and Second World Wars grimly proves the picture depicted by the verse , and the new call for "sustainable

---

[192] "Muhammad was no more than a messenger like the messengers before him. Should he die or get killed, would you turn back on your heels? Anyone who turns back on his heels, does not hurt God in the least." (Quran, 3:144)
[193] 18:7-8.

development"[194] shows that world leaders are now ready for a radical socio-economic change. For the last several decades after the Second World War, two models of development were implemented: the Western liberal-capitalist system of free market, and the Eastern socialist-communist centrally-planned system. Such is the dire state of the human community that both these systems have as good as collapsed (the Eastern one in 1989-90 when the Berlin Wall crumbled bringing the so-called Cold War phase of our history to an end, and the Western one in an on-going process of complete collapse from July, 2008). Consider this verse from the Quran:

> *There is not a community that We will not annihilate before the Day of Resurrection, or inflict severe retribution upon them. This is already written in the book.*[195]

Further consider this:

> *If God were to punish the people for their sins, He would not leave a single creature on earth. But he respites them for a predetermined interim. Once their interim is fulfilled, then God is Seer of His servants.*[196]

I remarked earlier that God took a calculated risk against the objections of the angels[197] in trusting to Adam the dangerously high position of His vicegerency on earth, with the mission to rule

---

[194] The Brundtland Report of 1987, released by the United Nations, defines sustainable development as "development which meets the needs of the present without compromising the ability of future generations to meet their own needs." This Report, however, has its critics. "Limited Growth" is countered with "Unlimited Growth". The point to note is that a new concept of development is being sought to replace the above-mentioned two failed ones..

[195] !7:58.

[196] 35:45.

[197] Quran, 2:30.

and change it. God, of course, being Omniscient, knows that man will ultimately succeed.

3. The emergence of Man the *Homo sapiens*

It was a momentous event in the universe, this emergence of the *Homo sapiens*. In the world of relativity it took eons, a hundred million years of evolution.[198] There was nothing like it before. The event shook the heavens and elicited strong objections from the angels, as stated above – the angels who know only wild animals, but know nothing of this new being, Man, a being capable of knowing the world and of changing it, a being with self-consciousness, knowing what to and how to do it. Thus it was that God Himself orders the angels to prostrate to Adam, an unheard-of thing – blasphemous -- since God has decreed that man should prostrate to no one except to Him Alone. Now the order has come out for the whole of creation to serve Adam![199]

4. Man's mission in the world

God assigned to man the role of *khalifa*, i.e. ruler in the world, in fact, in the whole universe (implying that man will in future also live in outer space). Remember the time when God offered this responsibility of rulership to the whole of His created order and it was refused by all (out of fear of not being able to shoulder it), except man who accepted it! God's comment on man's acceptance

---

[198] See Frank J. Tipler, *The Physics of Immortality* (New York: 1994).

[199] "God promises those among you who believe and lead a righteous life that He will make them sovereigns on earth as He did for those before them and He will establish for them the religion He has chosen for them and will substitute peace and security for them in place of fear. All this because they worship Me alone: they never set up any idols beside Me. Those who disbelieve after this are the truly wicked." (Quran, 24:55) While this verse that we have quoted refers to believers, this one refers to mankind in general, "He has made subservient to you whatever is in the heavens and whatever is in the earth all from Himself." (Quran, 45:13)

of the responsibility was that he was a little ignorant and unjust.[200] Looking back over five thousand years of human civilization, this comment is more than appropriate.

As human beings fall into two types: the believer, i.e. the upholder of truth and justice, and the unbeliever i.e. the upholder of falsehood and injustice there has been a perpetual fight between the oligarchical faction and the humanist faction.[201] In spite of the wars and other evils inflicted on humanity by the oligarchical factions over three millennia, we can say that humanity has not only survived, but made great progress, in scientific and technological fields, in the fields of art and culture, as well as in the field of administration and human rights. Once we cross the threshold of our present great crises of systems and possible nuclear annihilation, the promise of a coming new just world is very real indeed.[202] Again we must recall God's amply-justified optimism about man's future.

All these go to prove the correctness and profundity of the Quranic metaphors about man's ability to know the world,[203] denied by modern skeptical philosophers like Kant, and of man's superiority over other created orders, as symbolized by the angelic prostration to Adam.[204]

*****

---

[200] See Ch. 4, Note 99.
[201] See, Ch. 3, Note 82.
[202] "There will be no injustice on that day." (Quran, 40:17)
[203] Quran, 2:31-33.
[204] Quran, 2:34.

CHAPTER 10

The Problem of Creation

- The creation of the world,
- Emanation or evolution?
- Fixed and open laws
- Life is a miracle of creation

1. The creation of the world

Why and how did God create the world? A *Qudsi hadith* has it that, "I was a hidden treasure. I desire to be known. So I created the creation.[205] The Quran informs us of God's serious intention in creating the world in the following wonderful words:

> *We did not create the heavens and the earth, and everything between them, for amusement. If We wanted to make up an amusement, We would have done it on Our own. But We wanted to set up the truth against falsehood in order to expose it and render it obsolete.[206]*

> *It was God's will to establish the truth with His words and to punish the disbelievers. For He causes the truth to prevail and falsehood to vanish, despite the evildoers.[207]*

---

[205] A Qudsi hadith is defined as the idea being from God, while the words are Muhammad's. See Ch. 4, Note 105.

[206] Quran, 21:16-18.

[207] Quran, 8:8

God created the heavens and the earth for a specific purpose, to repay every soul for whatever it did, without the least injustice.[208]

Thus, God's creation of the universe not only has a purpose, but a very serious one at that – to eliminate falsehood and advance the truth, and to repay justly the works of men, i.e. to give success to human endeavour to create civilization and to advance along men's journey to higher and higher states. These statements and their realization put paid to those skeptics who attribute whimsicality and purposelessness to God.[209]

God created the world, we are told, just by saying: "Be!" to the world:

All He needs to do to carry out any command is to say to it, "Be!" and it is.[210]

Say, "You disbelieve in the One Who created the earth in two days and set up idols to rank with Him, though He is the Lord of the universe" He placed on it stabilizers (mountains), made it productive, and He calculated its provisions in four days, to satisfy the needs of all inhabitants. Then He turned to the sky, when it was still gas, and said to it and the earth, "Come into existence, willingly or unwillingly." They said, "We come willingly." Thus He completed the seven universes in two days, and then set up the laws for every universe. And We adorned the lowest universe with lamps, and placed guards around it. Such is the design of the Almighty, the Omniscient.[211]

---

[208] Quran, 45:22.

[209] See quotation from Logical Positivist philosopher, Bertrand Russell, Chapter 1, Note 40.

[210] Quran, 36:82.

[211] Quran, 41:9-12.

Notice that God gave the order to an object, "it" (Ar. *lahu* = to it). Does this mean that something already exists, besides God, at the time of the creation of the universe? If so, what is this "it"? Logically, there cannot be anything else, since the existence of something else would beg the question of who created that something else. As another *Qudsi hadith* puts it, "I was, and there was nothing with me. I am now as I was before." Therefore, there was nothing except God before creation. The emergence of the universe is due to its creation by God. That means God created the universe from Himself, in the same way, as one would say, an artist creates a work of art from himself.

The theory of creation *ex nihilo*, i.e. that God created the world from nothing is variously interpreted, to mean He created it from Himself, or out of some preexisting mater called chaos, or that it creates itself. The famous Malay world Sufi figure of the 16th century, Hamzah Fansuri, rejected this theory of creation.[212] So did the Pakistani philosopher Muhammad Iqbal.[213] However, it is clear that the universe was created by God from Himself . God is a Necessary Being (the *Wajib'al-Wujud*), existing by Himself, while the universe is a Contingent Being (the *Mumkin'al-Wujud*), existing only as long as God manifests Himself.

The scientists postulate the existence of matter and energy, which, at what is known as the Big Bang singularity, the galaxies were formed, forming the universe, which is expanding. Of course, they do not include a Creator-God behind the formation of the universe, making the universe physical. This is at odds with the concept of Reality being spiritual. But Reality includes God, i.e. that God is immanent in the universe, although He is also transcendental. Thus the universe will last only as long God

---

[212] See Syed Muhammad Naguib, *The Mysticicm of Hamzah Fansuri* (1970), pp.
[213] See Dr. Jamila Khatoon, *The Place of God, Man and Universe in the Philosophic System of Iqbal* (1963), pp.

manifests Himself in it. When God ceases to manifest Himself, the universe collapses and die.[214]

2. Emanation or evolution?

God, being free and unbounded by time and space, issued the order of creation, which appeared to Him instantaneously. In actual fact, as the history of the universe has shown, it took eons for life to appear on earth, and later still for man, the *Homo sapiens* and God's vicegerent. Before man, the evolution of the earth takes place in accordance with certain fixed laws. With man, however, this evolution takes place with inputs from man's freely chosen activities, thus taking him higher and higher in the ladder of evolution and existence.[215]

Man, not being perfect, cannot advance along a straight line. At times, he regresses; at times, he progresses, but, in the long run, man progresses upwards, proving God's seriousness in His purpose of creation. The regression serves to teach him to avoid further regression. Thus, in the long run, man progresses along the ladder of unending creative evolution of the French philosopher, Henri Bergson (1859-1941). This at once rejects the Neoplatonic notion of emanations, with God descending in gradations from Logos to matter.

As a wise saying goes, "Whoever knows himself, knows his Lord." We can, therefore, view creation from two poles: the poles of microcosm and macrocosm, microcosm representing man, and macrocosm representing the universe. In this way, we argue for the existence of a Creator-God. The intelligent creative activities of man, like speech, thought, and creative ideas, are only possible if he possesses a soul. Remember the Quranic metaphor of God

---

[214] Quran, 28:88.

[215] "That We may change you from state to state and make you row into what you know not." (Quran, 56:61)

blowing a spark of His Soul (Ar. *min ruhi*) when He completes the creation of man.[216] Without this soul, his physical body is only a corpse. Can we locate this soul? We cannot, but it is certainly there. So also the physical universe would be a huge corpse without the creative Divine Spirit that is behind it.

3. Fixed and open laws

With man with his creative freedom in the equation, the laws of the universe cannot be fixed. Prior to that, with existence before the appearance of man, the *Homo sapiens* and God's vicegerent, the laws are fixed. We call this predetermination (Ar. *taqdir*). The opposite of this is freedom. That is why no one knows when the Day of Resurrection will be.[217] It depends on the activities of men. The law governing this field is called in Arabic *sunnat'ul-Lah*,[218] that may be translated as "God's system".

If the universe is ruled by laws, how to explain the suspension of such laws through man's supplication of His Lord.[219] The answer is, obviously, Divine freedom. God's omniscience must be distinguished from predetermination. Although He knows from all eternity the past, the present and the future, it does not mean that men's actions are predetermined. Man is free to act. Divine foreknowledge does not constitute Divine intervention. Of course, at many times, God, being All-Merciful, intervened in answer to men's supplications to Him.[220]

---

[216] Quran, 15:29; 38:72.
[217] Quran, 79:42-46.
[218] Quran, 17:77.
[219] Quran, 2:186.
[220] "When My servants ask you about Me, I am always near. I answer their prayers when they prey to Me. The people shall respond to me and believe in Me in order to be guided." (Quran, 2:186)

4. Life is a miracle of creation

What about miracles? Miracles are extraordinary events, events that happen under a different set of laws, but laws nevertheless. A certain set of laws are suspended, replaced by a different set of laws – that is when miracles happen. Take the case of the computer. Its coming into being in our life is a miracle. Now that it has entered our lives and become ordinary, it is no longer a miracle.

The coming into being of a new life into the world (a baby) is a miracle. Such a tender and precarious thing – its coming into the world, alive and kicking, is a miracle! Russian biochemist, Aleksander Ivanovich Oparin (d. 1980), are among those scientists who consider the emergence of life a miracle. It is not possible by ordinary physical laws. It is the result of a supernatural event, which is one permanently beyond the descriptive powers of physics and chemistry.[221]

Despite studies in various fields, it is a remarkable fact that that no general statement exists on what life is. There are four hypotheses. Hypothesis One is the one just mentioned. Hypothesis Two: Life - particularly simple forms – spontaneously and readily arises from non-living matter in short periods of time, today as in the past. Hypothesis Three: Life is coeternal with matter and has no beginning; life arises on Earth at the time of the origin of the earth or shortly thereafter. Hypothesis Four: Life arose on early Earth by a series of progressive chemical reactions. Such reactions may have been likely or may have required one or more highly improbable chemical events.

The Quran states that the creation of Man is a new creation.[222] Therefore, at the stage of Man, the *Homo sapiens*, life takes a new

---

[221] Dipetik dari New Encyclopaedia Britannica.
[222] Surah 23:12-14.

turn. It is the emergent evolution of philosopher Bergson that I referred to above.

*****

CHAPTER 11

The Divine Method

- What is the Divine method?
- The problem of evil,
- The persistence of man's struggles for freedom,
- Who decides?
- God's multiple methods – His "inscrutable" ways.

1. What is the Divine method?

We have heard people speak of the "inscrutable ways" of God. What does the phrase mean? It seems to mean that God does what He wants and succeeds in getting them done by ways that are strange, contradictory, many and varied. One of the qualities of God mentioned in the Quran is that He is Rich, and not restricted in His Richness.[223] Take the case of the creation of Man, the *Homo sapiens.* It is the end result of a long evolutionary process from the earth, from amoeba. Life itself, as we have shown in a previous chapter[224] is a complex process. One of the four hypotheses is that life is a miracle.[225]

2. The problem of evil

The existence of evil has been an argument against the existence of a Beneficent and a Merciful God. This is a false argument. God, being Beneficent and Merciful, cannot give rise to evil. Evil actually arises out of rebellion against God. If man is not free to

---

[223] Quran, Surah 112:1-4.
[224] See, Ch. 10, Note 221.
[225] See, Ch. 10, p. 4.

rebel against God, then he is not the master of his own destiny. Being the vicegerent of God on Earth, he is master of his own destiny.

God has in fact put his faith in man. In a parable in the Quran, God offered the entire creation the task of administrating the universe; only man accepted it, the rest cringe from the task for fear of not being able to do it. This shows that God has put His faith in man.

I shall deal more fully with this problem in the next chapter.

3. The persistence of man's struggles for freedom

The long history of life on earth, from lifeless matter (the mineral kingdom) through the vegetable kingdom, then the animal kingdom, then to man, the *Homo sapiens*, proves that life is a creation of a Beneficent and Merciful God. It has a serious and lawful aim. As the Quran variously puts it, it is to elevate truth over falsehood, to pay everyone justly, and to see who is best in works.[226] Of course, God knows what everyone is capable of doing. The phrase means each one's works are witnessed by everyone else and thus contribute to the growth of civilization.

The French atheistic philosopher, Jean-Paul Sartre (1905-80), was so pessimistic about men's freedom that he wished them not to be free: he cursed this freedom! His famous statement "Man is condemned to be free." implies that he wished him to act, as animals do, by instinct, not by reason, as reason would compel him to choose, and this would lead him to error. Or, he might mean that man has no choice but to be free, and he might as well learn to use his freedom wisely. Definitely freedom is fraught with danger, because man might misuse it. Precisely because of this God cautioned Adam against this danger when He counseled

---

[226] Quran, 21:35.

Adam against approaching "this tree" (of freedom) in the Quran.[227] However, God's plan is that man is His vicegerent on earth, ruler and determiner of his own fate. Thus, man is God's co-worker and his freedom is necessary to realize God's will.

4. Who decides?

In the end, it is God who decides. But God is the Great Unseen." Vision does not comprehend Him, but He comprehends all vision."[228] However, as all rational people believe in a Creator-Fashioner-Guider God, although they do not see a Creator-God creating the world, they are bound to know that in the end, everything happens as God desires it. It is God's will.[229] But no one knows God's will except through His signs or through His manifestation in the world. His crowning manifestation is Man, the *Homo sapiens*. Through man, through the activities of man, who is free (symbolized in the Quranic metaphor of man's acceptance of the trust of freedom)[230], God realizes His will.

5. God's multiple methods and "inscrutable" ways

The other side of man is that he is God's servant, as all created things are. All of us do His bidding, one way or another, willingly or unwillingly. The planets, the galaxies, the mountains, the oceans – everything in the created order – including humans, do His bidding. The small mosquito as well as the ferocious lion does His bidding. If there were no mosquitoes to harass us, if there were no lions to terrify us -- and such-like negatives – we would not have developed mentally. In Malaysia, we have the *durian* (the King of Fruit), the *rambutan* and hundreds of other delicious fruits

---

[227] Quran, 2:35
[228] Quran, 6:103
[229] Quran, 4:78-79
[230] Quran, 33:72

that we wonder at the richness of God. Thus, His ways are multiple, both positive and negative.

Then He makes us fight one another in wars that, so far have not wiped us out, but almost nearly so, in order to teach us the benefits of peace and cooperation. This is not to say that these wars have been pre-determined. They were not. They occurred due to our errors or free choice. Thus, God is teaching us through our errors. Thus, God's ways are "inscrutable".

*****

CHAPTER 12

The Problem of Evil

- The problem of evil
- The source of evil
- Categories of evil
- The difficulty in resolving the problem
- Can evil be eliminated? Man's three psychological states

1. The problem of evil

The problem of evil has been advanced against a belief in God. Athenian philosopher Epicurus (341-270 B.C.) is generally credited with first expounding the problem, called "Epicurean paradox" or the "The Riddle of Epicurus". He said, "Either God wants to abolish evil, and cannot, or He can, but does not want to. If He wants to, but cannot, He is impotent. If He can, but does not want to, He is wicked. If God can abolish evil, and God really wants to do it, why is there evil in the world?"[231]

The modern version of this argument was given by David Hume (d. 1776) in his *Dialogues Concerning Natural Religion*. This argument assumes that man has no responsibility to eliminate

---

[231] As quoted in *2000 Years of Disbelief.*

evil. It further assumes that man is not free to reject evil and to choose the good. Both assumptions are false.

Let us consult the Quran:-

> *Wherever you are, death will catch up with you, even if you live in formidable castles. When something good happens to them, they say, "This is from God," and when something bad afflicts them, they blame you. Say, "Everything comes from God." Why do these people misunderstand almost everything? Anything good that happens to you is from God, and anything bad that happens to you is from you. We have sent you as a messenger to the people, and God suffices as witness.*[232]

The above verses seem to contain two contradictory statements. One states that *everything* comes from God; the other that only good comes from God, while evil is the result of man's own action.

2. The source of evil

There is a deeper problem. How does evil arise? One trend of thought attributes the creation of evil to God, God being the Creator of all things. This argument contradicts the All-Perfect nature of the Divine Being that is upheld by all monotheistic religions. The answer to this mystery is revealed in a profound metaphor found at the beginning of the second chapter of the Quran. It refers to the divine intention to create Adam, Adam standing for man, the *Homo sapiens*, whom God named *"khalifa"*, an Arabic term meaning "vicegerent" or "ruler" or "successor". To this divine intention, all the angels without exception objected, saying "Why do You want to create ones who will spread evil and shed blood?" To which God replied that He knew better. God then taught all knowledge to Adam and challenged the angles to

---

[232] Quran, 4:78-79.

inform Him of this knowledge. The angels were dumbfounded, not being able to answer God's challenge. Forthwith, God ordered them, one and all, to bow down to Adam -- a mark of subservience to Adam for his superior knowledge. All, except one, did the bowing of subservience. That one automatically became the Rebel-in-Chief, the *Iblis*, the Satan, the Seducer of men to evil. This horrible, unheard-of act of rebellion against the All-Powerful God shook the heavens. But this profound metaphor refers to the birth of man's freedom to choose between good and evil.[233]

In other words, God the creator of all things does not create evil, evil being the consequence of men's own actions. The freedom given to men must, *ipso facto*, include the freedom to oppose God. Hence, the automatic emergence of the Devil, who heads the opposition.

3. Categories of evil

Let us analyze evil in more detail. Evil can be simple or complex. There is evil committed by an individual, as in the case of a drunkard who knocks an electric pole and kills himself while driving home. In this case, only a single individual is involved. It is a clear-cut case which does not involve any other person.

There is the complex case which involves more than *one* person, as in the case of a road accident involving, let us say, four motor vehicles, in which three motorcars are smashed and one driver is killed and four others are seriously injured, and three escaped unhurt. Whose fault is that? Was the first car driver who got knocked by an in-coming lorry and killed himself at fault? Or were both, the car and the lorry drivers at fault? This case shows that we cannot separate individual humans. Individual humans are engaged in a single human endeavour to promote a free and

---

[233] Quran, 2:30-34.

safe society. Each has to play his or her part responsibly. Any failure on anyone's part will put the collective in jeopardy.

This complex case includes wars and widespread diseases. Wars are of two types, (a) wars in self-defense, like Prophet Muhammad's great Battle of Badr, the only wars allowed in Islamic Law, and (b) wars of aggression. Aggressive wars are caused by individual leaders who want to increase their power over mankind illegally, by a failure of rational diplomacy among leading nations, and by the populations' failure to discipline their leaders, in the inimitable words of the Quran, "to enjoin good and forbid evil". In a major war, like the First World War or the Second World War, almost every one of the human community is involved, especially the European nations. Thus the destruction wrought by these two wars were colossal and universal, including the deaths of non-combatant men, women and children, old and young! If one were to ask: Why the young who just come into the world with no responsibility whatsoever for the wars, what will be the answer? Obviously, it is a collective punishment. Is it consistent with our belief in a Merciful God? It should be consistent. The ways of God are many and at times inscrutable! We find the Quran informing us that if God were to punish men for all their wrong-doing, He would not leave anyone on the face of the earth![234]

The case of widespread diseases, like the 14th Century European Black Death, which killed an estimated 25 million Europeans, is also a case of human error, occurring over a long period, involving hygienic and related neglect, on the part of those entrusted with looking after the health of the population.

There is the more complex case of what we call *natural disasters*. No doubt, it is an evil – a huge one! Volcanoes, earthquakes,

---

[234] Quran, 35:45

floods, hurricanes and storms – the wrath of the Earth, we might almost call them – taking toll of many human lives, young and old, from time to time. What do we make of these in terms of divine punishment or divine mercy? Many of these disasters hit the poor, while the rich are spared in their big mansions! Again the Quran informs us that God does not punish except the disbelievers.[235] The Quran mentions the Great Flood of Noah's time as a divine punishment for the disbelievers of that community. So were many other divine-inflicted disasters on the ancient disbelieving communities of Lot, 'Aad and the rest.

The Quran also informs us that the good and the bad that happens to us are a test.[236] The good is a test to see whether we are grateful for it and use it to good purposes, and not boast about it. The bad is a test to see whether we are patient in the face of it and persevere to use the bad to overcome it in the future.

4. The difficulty in resolving the problem

The modern Pakistani philosopher, Muhammad Iqbal, made the following tentative remarks regarding this difficult problem, "How is it, then, possible to reconcile the goodness and omnipotence of God with the immense volume of evil in His creation? This painful problem is really the crux of Theism. ... The paradox cannot be finally decided at the present stage of our knowledge of the universe. Our intellectual constitution is such that we can take only a piecemeal view of things. We cannot understand the full import of the great cosmic forces which work havoc, and at the same time sustain and amplify life. The teaching of the Quran, which believes in the possibility of improvement in the behaviour of man and his control over natural forces, is neither optimism nor pessimism. It is meliorism, which recognizes

---

[235] Quran, 34:17.
[236] Quran, 2:155.

a growing universe and is animated by the hope of men's eventual victory over evil."[237]

5. Can evil be eliminated?
The three psychological states of men

According to the Quran, there will be a time in the future when there is no injustice in human society.[238] How will this come about? It will come about because of the change in men's psychological-moral make-up. There are, according to the Quran, three psychological-moral states.[239] The lowest is the state of the angry self, which is the animalistic state. Then by training and experience, the self moves up to the second state, called the self-critical state, which is properly the human stage. Lastly, the self enters into a state of blissful harmony with itself, with the finite world, and with God. It is at this psychological-moral state that man enters Paradise. We are, of course, referring to men in the collective, not individual. Note that all types of mysticism aim at *individual* improvement of the self. What humankind is aiming at is the collective improvement of the human community so that it can bring about the just world. This is evident in the setting up of various international organizations that have reached their summit in the formation of the United Nations Organization after the Second World War. It has been a very slow process – remember the lowest psychological state of the self we were and are in, and we are still not over the danger zone (the danger of a thermonuclear war, the systemic collapse of the Anglo-Dutch liberal system that is occurring now), but we can safely say that we are heading towards the birth of a new just world – a world

---

[237] See *The Reconstruction of Religious Thought in Islam*, pp. 80-81.
[238] Quran, 40:17.
[239] The Quran mentions three psychological-moral states: the lowest (Ar. *amarah*) (12:53), the second higher stage (Ar. *lawwamah*) , and the third highest stage (Ar. *mutmainnah*) (89:27)

where men and women can act justly towards one another. I shall deal with the question of a just world in a later chapter.

*****

CHAPTER 13

The Problem of Freedom and Determination

- Is man free, or not?
- What is the meaning of freedom and determination?
- The distinction between God's comprehensive knowledge and His actions,
- The meanings of God's "leave" (*bi izni'l-Llah*) and His pleasure (*masya Allah*),
- The terms *qada* and *qadar*, and God's system, *sunnat'ul-Lah*

1. Is man free?

To appreciate the difficulty of this problem, let us quote from the Muslim philosopher Ibn Sina (known to the West as Avicenna). When he was asked to explain the meaning of the Sufi saying "To make known the secret of predetermination is an act of heresy," his reply was as follows:

> "This is an extremely recondite problem and one which cannot be put on paper save in the language of a cipher, a matter which may not be made known except as a hidden mystery: to disclose it in full would work mischief to the people at large. The fundamental text in this connection is the saying of the Prophet: 'Predestination is the secret of God: do ye not disclose God's secret.' It is related that a

man asked the Caliph Ali about predetermination, and he answered: 'Predetermination is a deep see: do not embark upon it.' Asked a second time, he replied: 'It is a hard road: do not tread it.' A third time asked, he retorted: 'It is an arduous ascent: do not undertake it.'"[240]

The above answers are not much of a help. The reason given for not discussing predetermination ("would work mischief to the people at large.") is, of course, unacceptable.

Ibn Sina, in that short essay entitled "Predestination", did not actually discuss predestination, or man's freedom. Arguing why men should do good and avoid evil, he concluded, "Moreover men must be bound by one kind of fetter or another – either of the sacred law, or of reason – in order that the order of the world may be maintained in full perfection: it is a matter of common observation that if any man were loosed from both sets of chain, the corruption he would commit would be quite intolerable, and the entire order of the world's affairs would be impaired as a result of his release from both kinds of fetters."[241] In short, it is good social convention to believe in predetermination; it is not connected to problem of truth or falsehood.

The problem of freedom and determination occupied the minds of early Muslim philosophers and theologians. They fell into two groups: the determinists called *Jabariah*, and the upholders of men's freedom, the *Qadariah*. These two contradictory streams were later "resolved" by the great Sunni theologian, Hassan Ash'ari (d. 935 A.D.), into a half-way house between freedom and determination. Men's attempt to choose freely, he asserted, exists, but the attempt itself is God-given, whatever this means! This is stated in the sixth pillar of orthodox faith as "belief in predetermination, i.e. good and bad ends are from God." This, as

---

[240] See *Avicenna On Theology*, p. 38.
[241] *Ibid*. p. 41.

it can be clearly seen, undermines men's freedom completely, and throws the ball back to God's feet!

In an essay entitled "Ultimate Responsibility: Man's 'Free' Will and God's Absolute Sovereignty", Ken Eckerty wrote, " The subject of man's "free" will in relation to God's absolute sovereignty is a doctrinal dilemma that is just as controversial today as it has been in past centuries. Many believers do not understand how the choices of men can be reconciled with the plans of God, and so it is often dismissed by the average Christians as being too hard a subject to comprehend."[242]

One writer informs us that, "Quranic passages in favour of free-will far outnumber those which are suggestive of determinism. According to the Quran, man is free to choose his actions and beliefs, and he merits punishment or reward according to whether his choice is right or wrong. It is for God to show the right path and for men to follow it or not to follow it. Everything is predetermined in the sense that it is predetermined by man's nature and known as such to God from eternity. The eternal knowledge of God does not interfere in the least bit with man's choice."[243]

When discussing the problem of evil, we refer to the profound metaphor of the angels submitting to Adam, by order of God Himself, mentioned at the beginning of the second chapter of the Quran.[244] This refers to the *absolute potential power* of man over the whole universe. Man is here declared to be free to chart his own destiny, although this freedom is fraught with the greatest danger. This danger to man's own safety prompted God to advise Adam and Eve against approaching "this Tree" (of knowledge and moral consciousness). We shall have ample time to relate this danger,

---

[242] http://www.savior-of-all.com/freewill.html
[243] Kenneth W. Morgan (Ed.) *Islam – The Straight Path*, p. 157
[244] Quran, 2:30-34

which capped in two World Wars in the 20th Century! No wonder, the anguish of the famous French atheist philosopher, Jean Paul Sartre, himself a great champion of man's freedom, made him declare that man's freedom is a curse!

2. Modern Muslim philosophers' views.

Even modern Muslim philosophers, like Shah Waliullah (1702-1763) and Muhammad Iqbal (1877-1938), find this problem of man's freedom quite irksome. Let us listen to both. In one of his books, Shah Waliullah said: -

> "There is no doubt that man feels he has a free will to choose any of the alternative courses at his disposal. Though he seems to choose one particular course and discard the rest with freedom and without any external coercion or compulsion yet in reality he has *no freedom* (Italics given) of will in making a particular choice. His choice is natural and essential consequence of a series of courses which lead the mind to decide on a particular course. Neither the series of causes that affect the particular choice, nor the faculty of choice itself, are subject to the control of man. They are all determined and created by God."[245]

Iqbal, however, weighs on the side of freedom by arguing, based on Quranic verses, that a thing, including man, is made according to an eternal unchanging nature made by God.[246] Therefore, man

---

[245] Quoted in A. J. Halepota, *The Philosiophy of Shah Waliullah,* p. 237.

[246] "Therefore, you shall devote yourself to the religion of strict monotheism. Such is the natural instinct placed into the people by God. Such creation of God will never change. This is the perfect religion, but most people do not know." (Quran, 30:30) "Recall that your Lord summoned all the descendants of Adam, and had them bear witness for themselves: 'Am I not your Lord?' They all said 'Yes. We bear witness.' Thus you cannot say on the day of Resurrection, 'We were not aware of this.'" (Quran, 7:172) See M. Ikram

is free to act within that nature and will be rewarded or punished, as he chooses to do good (i.e. obeying God), or to do bad (i.e. obeying the Devil and disobeying God).

3. The stand of modern science and philosophy

Modern Western philosophy can be divided into two main streams, namely the mechanistic empirical stream beginning with Newton, with one ending in a cul-de-sac of Logical Positivism of the Vienna school led by Ludwig Wittgenstein after the First World War, and the other developing into an evolutionary rationalist stream of the humanist philosophers, like Henri Bergson, Spinoza, Leibniz, Samuel Alexander and Alfred North Whitehead.

The mechanistic physics of Newton started the science of determination of matter. But this science, adhering closely to scientific methodology, meets its opposite in the famous "uncertainty principle" propounded by the German physicist Werner Karl Heisenberg in 1925. "...That principle is generally considered to be one of the most profound and far-reaching principles in all science. What the uncertainty principle does is to specify certain theoretical limits on our ability to make scientific measurements. The implications of this principle are enormous. If the basic laws of physics prevent a scientist, *even in the most ideal circumstances* (Italics given), from obtaining accurate knowledge of the system that he is attempting to investigate, it is obvious that the future behaviour of all that system cannot be completely predicted. According to the uncertainty principle, no

Chaghatai (compiler, annotator and translator), *Iqbal: New Dimensions*: "Iqbal and the Problem of Free Will" by Raziuddin Siddiqi, pp. 319 onward.

improvement in our measuring apparatus will ever permit us to surmount this difficulty."[247]

However, many eminent physicists, including Einstein, have not accepted this indeterminacy. As W. C. Dampier said:

> "The principle of indeterminacy seems to introduce a new kind of incalculability into nature. The uncertainties hitherto described might possibly be due to ignorance, and might pass into determinism again as knowledge increases. It is dangerous to build on them a philosophy of free-will. But ... the work of Schrodinger and Bohr indicates that there is an uncertainty in the nature of things. The alternative uncertainties that, if we try to calculate the position of an electron its velocity becomes indeterminate, have been thought by some to indicate that, in the ultimate analysis, the scientific argument for determinism breaks down. But others hold that this indeterminacy merely expresses the inadequacy of our system of measurements to deal with problems outside the realm of physics."[248]

He further said, "And of these [mental] sensations, one of the most vivid and most persistent is that of volition and free-will. Hitherto the strongest argument against its validity has been the mechanical determinism which seem to some to follow inevitably from physical sciences. But Eddington holds that if philosophic determinism is still to be defended, it must now be on metaphysical evidence. Its advocate can no longer call science to witness in its favour. Scientific determinism has broken down, and broken down in the very citadel of its power – the inner

---

[247] See Michael H. Hart, *The 100 – A Ranking of the Most Influential Persons in History*, p. 242.
[248] See *A History of Science*, pp. 480-81.

structure of the atom."[249] In spite of indeterminacy, it looks as though the evidence of science for the freedom of the will is not conclusive.

4. The meaning of freedom

Let us analyze the various meanings of freedom. As in the case of evil,[250] we shall group men into individuals and collective. Again we should remind ourselves that man is actually *one person*.* The individual is *part of the collective* and the *collective consists of individuals*. One can also say that the *whole* human family, the family of the *Homo sapiens*, is *One Life*, as God's whole created universe is one unified Being.

An individual is free in so far as his socio-economic and intellectual environment allows him to exercise that freedom. The freedom is conditional and grows as men change the over-all environment they inherit from their ancestors. The main conditions are the existence of intellectual and of socio-economic freedoms. Take the case of the migration of the little band of Prophet Muhammad's followers from the oppressive conditions in Quraishy-oligarchical control of the city-state of Mecca to the more free city-state of Medina in 7th Century Arabia. There they were free to practice their Abrahamic legacy of monotheism, now replenished by new revelations of God to Prophet Muhammad. There they were free to arrange their socio-economic life under Muhammad's leadership. It was this leap into freedom by this little band of Muslims that created the Arab Renaissance, bringing in for the first time a scientific culture and civilization opening the way to modern civilization.[251]

---

[249] *Ibid.* p. 483.
[250] See chapter 12.
[251] See, Ch. 5, Note 117.

The second example of the lunge of freedom is the European immigration into the New World that started with the famous Pilgrim Fathers in 1620, the English and the Europeans fleeing from political and religious persecution, the same as happened to Arab Prophet Muhammad's followers in the 7th Century Arabia! The Thirteen Colonies declared independence from England on July 4, 1776 and formed the United States of America, the new beacon of freedom for the world.[252] It was and is in this reformed and revolutionary Europe and America that modern science and technology quickly developed and flourished until we are now in the Age of Space Colonization and the amazing cyber communications.

Even before Muhammad, it is stated that man made a historic attempt to institute freedom in Prophet Abraham's fight against the then oligarchically-imposed paganism of his times in 2,100 B.C. in ancient Mesopotamia, that is, present-day Iraq. One can say that this historic fight between the humanist and the oligarchical factions in human society is an ever-recurring thread from very early times down to the present-day. The fight has now become global. It is obvious that we shall realize this free society, the fruit of long human struggles and endeavour, in the coming years, one, or two or three generations at the most.

5. Confusion between God's Omniscience and God's Action.

That is on the one pole. There is, of course, the other pole. In the created world of relativity, we have pairs of everything.[253] We have God in one hand and we have the created universe on the

---

[252] It was Abraham Lincoln, 16th President of the United States of America, who said, "Freedom is the natural condition of the human race, in which the Almighty intended man to live. Those who fight the purpose of the Almighty will not succeed. They always have been, they always will be beaten."

[253] "And of everything We have created pairs that you may be mindful." (Quran 51:49).

other. We have life and we have death. We have death and we have resurrection after death. This occurs throughout the created universe.

The compliment of freedom is determination. To God the Absolute, everything is known and, therefore, determined. The Quran informs us that not a leaf falls, but He knows it.[254] God, being All-Knowing, knows everything from start to finish. Does he therefore determine each thing's occurrence? In the case of man, the answer is: No. God, as we have seen, has given him freedom to chart his destiny. Man chooses his own destiny, but what he chooses is known to God, and symbolically kept in a record.[255] In the case of lower forms of life, like minerals, vegetation and animals, God has given them their designs and they behave instinctively thus.

Take the simple case of a glass of milk and a glass of liqueur. God says, "Take the milk. It is good for you. Do not take the liqueur. It is bad for you." If we follow God's advice by taking the milk, the good therefore comes from God. If we ignore God's advice and take the liqueur, the evil that ensues is therefore the result of our own rebellious action. Let us refresh ourselves with the verses of the Quran on this matter:

> Wherever you are death will catch up with you if if live in formidable castles. When something good happens to them they say, "This is from God," and when something bad afflicts them, they blame you. Say, "Everything comes from God." Why do these people misunderstand almost everything? Anything good that happens to you is from God, and anything bad that happens to you is from you.[256]

---

[254] "Not a leave falls without His knowledge." (Quran, 6:59)
[255] I.e. "Guarded tablet" (Ar. *Lawhun mahfuz*). Quran, 85:22.
[256] Quran, 4:78-79.

The above verses point to two different things. Taken together, firstly, it states that everything, including man's freedom to choose evil, comes from God. Secondly, it asserts that only good comes from God, thus denying that evil comes from God. Thus, it should be clear that evil comes from rebellion against God. Freedom is meaningless unless one is able to oppose. Recall that the angel that refused to obey the divine order to the angels to prostrate to Adam automatically became the Rebel-in-Chief, the Devil,[257] an enemy of God.

The Quran informs us that God created the universe with a purpose. It is to make truth prevail over falsehood.[258] As we have seen, the Devil was given power to seduce men away from Divine guidance, which was to take men out of darkness to the world of light, of enlightenment -- the Abode of Bliss, that is Paradise. God's foreknowledge, which humans has no excess to, must not be confused with determination. Man is free to chart his own destiny -- this awesome freedom being granted to Him by God Himself. But God's foreknowledge of everything makes the course of things seem determined. This is, of course, not the case. Thus freedom and determination are not contradictory; they are complimentary. As the Quran puts it, they are pairs.[259]

Man is free to create his Abode of Bliss. Remember that his first abode of bliss was the bliss of innocence. This time the Abode of Bliss is Man's own creation, created, of course, according to the Divine Plan. Thus freedom and determination is a unified whole.

*****

---

[257] Quran, 2:34.
[258] Quran, 21:16-18.
[259] Quran, 43:12.

CHAPTER 14

Prophecy, Prophets and Miracles

- What is prophecy?
- Prophets and miracles: why Muhammad is the last prophet?
- How do we know? A question of epistemology.
- The link between God and Man.

1. What is prophecy?

Obviously, prophecy is a special method of knowing, given to certain individuals. These individuals, like Moses, Jesus and Muhammad, through prophecy, had brought scriptures into the world – teachings that have become the religious and moral foundations of mankind.

What exactly is prophecy? Consulting the Quran, we get the following answers:-

> *No human being can communicate with God except through inspiration, or from behind a barrier, or by sending a messenger through whom He reveals what He wills.*[260]

In the case of Prophet Muhammad, the Quran is three things to him, namely (i) a revelation (Ar. *ayat*), (ii) God's word (Ar.

---

[260] Quran, 42:51.

kalimatu Rabbik),[261] and (iii) the utterance of an honourable messenger (Ar. *qaula rasulun karim*),[262] or (iv) as in (iii) words coming out of the Prophet Muhammad's mouth (Ar. *ahsan'al-hadith*).[263] Note that the first two show that the Quran comes from God, whereas the last two show that the Quran is the product of Muhammad's consciousness. The Quran, therefore, informs us that there is a close connection between Divine Consciousness and the prophet's (i.e. man's) consciousness. Considering the verse we quoted earlier (42:51), the process can be called either inspiration, which is common, or the hearing of a voice from behind a veil, as in the case of Moses, when he heard God talking to him from behind a bush.[264]

Modern psychology has investigated this phenomenon. Let us hear some results from its investigations. A Marxist writer, Maxim Rodinson, dismissed Christian writers' rejection of Muhammad as fraud, wrote:

> "A study of Muhammad's earliest messages, coupled with a perusal of accounts of the crises of doubt or despair which preceded or accompanied them, can only produce a skeptical attitudes towards the theories which see them as evidence of a coolly calculated plan carried out ruthlessly from motives of either ambition or philanthropy. And these accounts do seem to be authentic. Tradition, concerned to stress the supernatural affiliations of Muhammad's personality, would not have invented from scratch such very human traits. *A genuine Muhammad is*

---

[261] Quran, 6:115.
[262] Quran, 69:40 and 81:19.
[263] Quran, 39:23.
[264] Quran, 28:30.

much less difficult to explain than a fraudulent one. (Asterisk added)[265]

Rodinson continued:

> "Muhammad was not a *kahin*. He did no find lost camels or interpret dreams. Nor did he set himself up as a professional seer, adviser in supernatural matters to a particular tribe or prince, although such a post might carry a good deal of prestige. But again, this would have been to associate himself and his particular psychic gifts with the whole social and intellectual framework of Arab society, which, unconsciously, he was trying to transcend. He remained an ordinary trader, a good husband and father and a prudent sensible man; but he was learning and thinking all the time. *Little by little his spirit was advancing along the road which was to lead him far beyond the limits of his own time and place.*" (Italics added.)[266]

Some traditions describe the state he was in when he received the revelation. Let us look at one.

> "… As the months went by the revelations continued, now causing less surprise and terror. But it was still a painful an agonizing experience. We are told that Muhammad's face was covered with sweat; he was seized with a violent shuddering and lay unconscious for an hour as though in a drunken stupor. He did not hear what was said to him. He perspired copiously even in cold weather. He heard strange noises, like the sound of chains or bells or rushing wings. 'Never once did I receive a revelation,' he said, 'without thinking that my soul had been torn away from

---

[265] *Mohammed* (trans. From French by Anne Carter), Penguin Books, Great Britain, 1971; pp. 77-78.

[266] Ibid. p. 58.

me.' For the most part, at first, he felt something like an inward inspiration not expressible in words; and then when the crisis was past, he uttered words which obviously corresponded for him to the inspiration he had received..."[267]

During the long childhood of mankind, form the time Prophet Adam right up to Prophet Muhammad, the human communities everywhere had their prophets and messengers sent them by God to teach the right religion. As pointed out earlier, the original one religion of divine unity, in the case of the Abrahamic line, became three: Judaism, Christianity and Islam. One can infer that the same thing happened with the non-Abrahamic line, the religions of Hinduism, Buddhism, Taoism, Zoroastrianism, Manichaeism and Confucianism.

2. Prophets and miracles. Why Muhammad is the last prophet

These many prophets, with the exception of Prophet Muhammad, needed their miracles to convince their peoples of the truth of their missions. Modern skeptical philosophers, like David Hume, throw doubts on causality and on the possibility of miracles. Throwing doubt on causality undermines science itself, while the happening of miracles is entirely within the laws of science. Miracles mean the suspension of ordinary laws in place of extraordinary laws, but laws, nevertheless. When God issued the order of creation: "Be!" to the universe, the universe automatically came into being. That is a miracle, if ever there was one! But it took eons for universe to form, as we know.

With Prophet Muhammad, however, mankind entered a new era, both internationalist and scientific in character. Muhammad, therefore, was a prophet for the whole international community,[268]

---

[267] Quoted in *ibid.* p. 74.
[268] See, Ch. 5, Note 127.

which now had to be convinced of the truth of his mission through scientific and rational methods.[269]

3. How do we know? A question of epistemology

How do we know? When one is a child, one does not know. One's parents teach him/her this and that, and then one goes to school. During the whole of this period, one gets full guidance from one's parents and teachers. This can be likened to mankind's period of prophethood. When one reaches adulthood (spiritual adulthood is forty years),[270] one wants to break out of one's parents' apron-strings. One wants to be free. At this crucial time, one has to assume full responsibility.

Thus to know is extremely important. A Muslim researcher concluded that no thorough work has been done on Muslim epistemology.[271] However, the Quran has casually, as is usual with the Quran, introduced the phrases regarding our methods of knowing. Firstly, it is through sensory evidence (Ar. *'ain'ul yaqin*)[272] ; secondly, through logical evidence (Ar. *ilm'ul- yaqin*);[273] and lastly, through direct evidence (Ar. *haq'al-yaqin*).[274]

Take the case of a fountain pen. You can see and feel a fountain pen in front of you. You obtain certainty about the fountain pen through sensory evidence. You then logically deduce that it was made by a craftsman from certain materials derived from the earth. This is logical evidence. In the third step, the question is asked where the craftsman and the materials for the fountain pen come from. In the truncated empirical epistemology of Western science, the question is simply not asked, as it cannot be

---

[269] See, Ch. 5, Note 117.
[270] Quran, 46:15.
[271] See Syed Muhammad Dawilah al-Edrus, *Islamic Epistemology* (1992); p. xi.
[272] Quran, 102:7.
[273] Quran, 102:5.
[274] Quran, 56:95.

answered![275] Therefore, for Western empirical epistemology, evidence from inspiration is rejected, because it sees only part of the world, the visible part.[276] It therefore assumes the eternity of the world and rejects a Creator-God, Nourisher and Fashioner of the world without any evidence. This is a failure of Western science, making a god of the world, elevating machine to be God, and disposing of the good character of the material world that is the divine manifestation. For this error it has paid dearly, the two horrible World Wars being the obvious consequences of this materialistic worldview.

4. The link between God and Man

The Quran describes Man, the *Homo sapiens* as God's vicegerent on Earth (Ar *khalifa*.) Thus, between God and Man there is a very close link. God, being immanent in the universe, becomes manifested in Man, the crown of His creation. Remember that God made man His vicegerent on Earth and entrusted Him with the responsibility to chart his own destiny to and the destiny of the universe. Man's consciousness is the motive force of his slow evolution. From childhood to adulthood, from earth-bound to higher regions of morality and spirituality, man ascends higher and higher in the ladder of evolution, driven by his own consciousness. The power of his consciousness naturally comes from God-consciousness.

God's plan is for man to create his own Paradise on Earth. Naturally, this has to happen in accordance with God's Laws. The verse stating the exchange made between believers and God in Surah 9, Verse 111 clearly points to this fact. The term 'believers' in this verse, does not refer exclusively to any nominal religious group (Jews, Christians. Muslims, Hindus, etc.); it

---

[275] See Errol E. Harris, *Nature, Mind and Modern Science*, (London:1954); p. 3.
[276] Quran, 30:7.

refers to those who actually believe in God and fight in His course.

******

CHAPTER 15

Muhammad and the Era of Internationalism

- Prophet Muhammad: his life and mission,
- The divinely-protected Quran,
- The idolization of Prophet Muhammad,
- The loss of the original Quran and its restoration

1. Prophet Muhammad: his life and mission

Muhammad is the last prophet of completed and perfected Islam, God's religion, the religion of truth that will prevail over all false religions.[277] Unlike other prophets before him, Muhammad was sent by God to the whole of mankind.[278] His advent was foretold in the Old as well as the New Testaments.[279] He was initially

---

[277] "He is the One who sent His messenger with the guidance and the religion of truth, to make it prevail over all other religions." (Quran, 48:28) See also 9:33 and 61:9.

[278] See, Ch. 5, Note 127.

[279] There are several prophecies about the coming of Prophet Muhammad in both the Old and the New Testaments. Here we give two. "So the Lord said to me (i.e. Moses), 'I will send them a prophet like you from among their own people; I will tell him what to say, and he will tell the people everything I command. He will speak in My name and I will punish anyone who refuses to obey him.'" (*Deuteronomy*, 18:17-19) "(Jesus said): 'I still have many things to say to you, but you cannot bear them now. However, when He, the Spirit of Truth, has come, He will guide you into all truth; for he will not speak on his own authority, but whatever he hears, he will speak; and he

rejected by the "People of the Book," i.e. the Jews and the Christians, his rejection being for no other reason than that of jealousy.[280] That is Muhammad, who, if he were to appear among present-day "Muslims", would be rejected by them too, because they, along with disbelievers among Jews, Christians and others, have deviated from the original teachings of God's messengers, which is to believe in God's Oneness and to live righteously.[281]

Prophet Muhammad's history is well-known. He came at the end of a long series of divine prophets, beginning with Adam, and going through the major prophets, such as Abraham, Moses and Jesus. All of them, except Muhammad, were sent to teach their national communities. These prophets are mentioned in the Quran, but many more (for the Quran informs us that to all human communities had divine prophet-messengers sent to them[282]) are not mentioned.[283]

He was born in Mecca on 29th August, 570. His father, Abdullah, died a few days before he was born, at the age of 25. His mother, Aminah, died when Muhammad was six, making him an orphan. After this, he was in the care of his grand-father Abdul Muttalib. After his death three or four years later, his guardianship fell to his uncles Abu Talib.

He married his first wife Khadijah (a highly-respected lady in Mecca and a business woman for whom Muhammad became a partner), in 595 A.D. at the age of 25 (Khadijah was a widow, aged 40 then) in a long and happy 25-year monogamous marriage until Khadijah died in 620 A.D. The many wives he married after her

---

will tell you things to come. He will glorify me, foe he will take what is mine and declare it to you.'" (John, 16:12-14)

[280] Quran, 2:109.

[281] Quran, 12:106 and 2:62.

[282] Quran, 10:47.

[283] Quran, 4:164.

death were done so for political alliances. He was an active and responsible youth. He set up a Youth League to help oversee the peace and security of Mecca, which was deteriorating at that time. An obvious intelligence, a profound and critical observer, and an extremely honest man, with a deep sense of responsibility for the welfare of his people – that was Muhammad.

He was called to prophethood at the age of 40, the age of spiritual maturity,[284] when he first received divine revelation while in seclusion in a nearby cave called the Cave of Mt. Hira. His wife Khadijah was the first to believe in him. For 12 years he and his small band of followers in Mecca were persecuted by the Meccan Quraisyh aristocracy. It was at this time that he received the divine call to migrate to Medina, a town some 300 miles north of Mecca. Here he was well-received by the inhabitants of the city, known as the Helpers (Ar. *Ansars*), those migrating became known as the Immigrants (Ar. *Muhajirin*). Here he set up the city-state of Medina, to which he gave the first written constitution in the world, known as the Medina Charter.[285]

He continued to receive divine revelation, over a period of 23 years: (13 in Mecca and 10 in Medina) until he died two years after he liberated Mecca from idolatry and from religious and political persecution of the Muslims in 630 A.D.

2. The Divinely-protected Quran

He had about 40 scribes to take down the revelations as they came down. Not all, of course, were present to take down the revelations at any one time, but more than two. These writings were annually recited by him and his followers during the fasting month, and they were memorized by his followers. Before his death, he had the whole Quran collected and arranged in the

---

[284] Quran, 46:15.
[285] See, Ch. 3, Note 85.

order that we have today.[286] At the time of his death, Muhammad manuscript was given to his wife, Hafsah, for safe keeping.

That is the outline of his life and work that any reader can find in his biography. The earliest and most consulted biography is the *Sirah* ("Life of the Prophet") of ibn Ishak (d. 767 A.D.)

Sixty years after his death, the Arab armies, fired by the liberating message of the Holy Quran, went to liberate the oppressed peoples under the Persian Empire, and most of the Byzantine Empire. The British historian Philip K. Hitti wrote, "If someone in the first third of the seventh Christian century had had the audacity to prophesy that within a decade some unheralded, unforeseen power from the hitherto barbarous and little known land of Arabia was to make an appearance, hurl itself against the only two world powers of the age, fall heir to one – the Sassanid – and the other – the Byzantine – of its fairest provinces, he would undoubtedly have been declared a lunatic. Yet that was exactly what happened. After the death of the Prophet sterile Arabia seems to have been converted as if by magic into a nursery of heroes the like whom both in number and quality is hard to find anywhere. The military campaigns of Khalid ibn-al-Walid and 'Amar ibn-al-As which ensued in al-Iraq, Persia, Syria and Egypt are among the most brilliantly executed in the history of warfare and bear favourable comparison with those of Napoleon, Hannibal or Alexander."[287] .

Another European writer remarked, "Islam penetrated into the neighbouring lands like a trident bolt of lightning. One of the most inexplicable chapters of world history was beginning... The irresistible Arab armies won battle after battle. An astonishing number of countries and cities were conquered in incredibly short

---

[286] Quran, 5:3. This famous verse was revealed 81 or 82 days before the Prophet's death.
[287] *History of the Arabs*, (10th Edition) 1970; p. 142.

time. Damascus (635), Jerusalem, Mesopotamia and Babylonia, Hulwan (640), Nihawand (642), Isfahan (643), and Persia fell into Arab hands. Then Alexandria (642), Egypt (639-641), Tripoli (647), and Cyprus (649). A vast area, 2500 miles long and between 300 and 650 miles across, fell to Islam. Centuries-old empires, like Persia and Egypt, once the glory of antiquity, had ceased to exist, and mighty Byzantium was pressed back to the Taurus, the barren mountain chain that separates Asia Minor from the mother continent. Islam had in one mighty burst altered the course of history. Faith, courage, boldness and luck, combined with the inner weakness of its opponents had made possible the unbroken success of the first onslaught."[288]

Arab Renaissance inherited the knowledge of antiquity, made its own original contributions, and passed this on to Europe and the West during the centuries of European Renaissance. Of this, the British historian of science, G. Sarton, said, "The main task of mankind was accomplished by Muslims. The greatest philosopher, al-Farabi, was a Mulsim; the greatest mathematicians, Abu Kamil and Ibrahim ibn Sinan were Muslims, the greatest geographer and encyclopedist, al-Masudi, was a Muslim; the greatest historian, al-Tabari, was also a Muslim."[289] Unfortunately, apart from a few who acknowledge Europe's debt to Arab-Islamic science, the majority of Western scholars conspire to erase this portion of their intellectual history.

3. The idolization of Prophet Muhammad

As is wont, even with Prophet Muhammad, described by the Quran as "a mercy to all mankind"[290], his followers soon deviated, and created a corrupted version of "Islam" about 250-350 years after his death. The power struggles and the beginnings of

---

[288] *A Concise History of Islam*, Djambatan/Amsterdam, 1957; p. 10.
[289] *Introduction to the History of Science*, Vol. I, Baltimore 1927; p. 642.
[290] Quran, 21:1107.

political and, therefore, theological factions already started during the time of the third and fourth republican Caliphs Uthman (644-56) and 'Ali (656-61), thirty years after the Prophet's death! But it took about 200 years for Imam Shafi'e (d. 820 A.D.) to come up with a new doctrine, acceptable to the majority of the Muslim community, that the so-called Prophetic traditions, i.e. *Hadith/Sunnah*, is equally incumbent upon the Muslims to believe in, on par with the Quran, at times even overturning the Quran.[291] It was precisely after the acceptance of this illegal doctrine by the Muslim community that *hadith* collectors, (Bukhari, Muslim, Abu Daud, Ibn Majah, Tirmidhi and al-Nasai, for the Sunni sect, and Al-Kulaini (d. 329 A.D.), Ibn Babuwayh (d. 381 A.D.), Jaafar Muhammad al-Tusi (d. 411 A.D.), and al-Murtada (d. 436 A.D.) for the Shiah sect) arose with their *official* collections of *Hadith*. Note that during the period after the death of the Prophet till the acceptance of the official collections, the status of Muhammad's meager non-revelation speech was at best a precedent. It is a far cry from the status that Imam Shafi'e conferred on it – a principal source on par with, and at times canceling even, the Quran!

Fast on the heels on this new illegality, other deviations crept in. I shall enumerate these: the setting up of a priesthood to dictate on religion upon the people; the division of knowledge into secular and religious knowledge and giving priority to religious knowledge; the promulgation of a so-called divine-based law, called the *Syari'ah* that is at variance with the teachings of the Quran; the growth of a new mysticism relegating "Muslims" into a withdrawal into a cave-like existence; the turning of the Quranic revolutionary conception of life as active, dynamic and creative, fighting to build a just world in the here and now, into a reactionary conception of passive life given to false worship, and waiting for death and an imaginary reward of an imaginary

---

[291] See Kassim Ahmad, *Hadith: A Re-evaluation*, (1997: Arizona); Ch. IV.

121

Paradise; and, last but not least, the turning of the Quran into a song-book to induce a false sense of solace and tranquility.

Although a tomb was erected by the scholars to prove the meticulousness in their methodology of the study of the *Hadith*, it boils down to nothing more than an apology to make the so-called hadith (many of which were clear fabrications, as they are not only against the teachings of the Quran,[292] but also blasphemous to the Prophet himself[293]), acceptable. In fact, they become a vehicle for the idolization of Prophet Muhammad – an unforgivable sin, in the sight of God.

4. The loss of original Quran and its restoration

So it was that the "Muslims" were relegated to the "dustbin of history" and replaced by the divine law of replacement by the Europeans as the new torch-bearers for mankind. But God's religion is not about to become irrelevant, in spite of "Muslims" deviation and infidelity. Of all the scriptures in the world, the Quran is the only one to be accorded divine protection.[294] It is proved by a highly sophisticated, miraculous mathematically-structured composition of the Quran based on what is called Code 19.[295] This Code exposes a horrendous crime against the Quran by an illegal insertion by the Uthman Commission of two additional verses (128-129) at the end of Surah 9 in idolization of Prophet Muhammad.[296]. This event causes the wars that ensued during the

---

[292] See above, Note 291.

[293] As in the case of the so-called hadiths about his cruelty and his sexual prowess. For the first, see *Sahih Muslim*, Book 16, No. 4131. For the second, see *Sahih al-Bukhari*, Vol. 1, Book 5, No. 268. This information was supplied to the writer by Syed Akbar Ali of Malaysia.

[294] Quran, 15:9; 56:77-80.

[295] See Kassim Ahmad, *Hadis: Jawapan Kepada Pengkritik*, (1992: Media Indah, Kuala Lumpur), Ch. 6.

[296] This is a horrendous crime. The two verses (128-129) were added ostensibly to give credit to the Prophet. They were added on the testimony of

time of the caliphates of Uthman and Ali. The crime of the Uthman Commission, recorded in several documents, caused the loss of the original Quran to the Muslims and to the world until it was discovered and restored recently, thanks to the work of Dr Rashad Khalifa.[297]

Of course, some of Dr. Rashad Khalifa's views are controversial. My attitude is to leave aside the controversial parts, but take those that restore the genuine Quran to us. This extremely important act will cause the original Quran to re-enter the consciousness of mankind in the near future. This is very important because mankind has no future, except under the guidance of the One True God. That is when God's religion, the religion of truth, will triumph over all false religions.[298]

This will be a major event in the history of mankind, an event that will take men to higher levels in the long journey of his evolution to become the Man-God that he is destined to be, the crowning glory of this God-created universe.

******

Khuzaimah alone. Later, Muhammad's copy of the Quran that was in the safe-keeping of his wife Hafsah was ordered to be burnt by Caliph Marwan bin Hakim (d. 65/684). If Hafsah's copy was the same as Uthman Commission's new copy, why must it be burnt? (See Ahmad von Denffer, *Ulum Al-Quran* (1983: The Islamic Foundation, United Kingdom). Also see Rashd Khalifa, *Quran – the Final Testament*, Appendix 24).

[297] See his translation of the Quran, *Quran: Final Testament,* (1989: Tucson).

[298] Quran, 48:28; 9:33; 61:9. ......

CHAPTER 16

The Noble Quran

- What is the Quran?
- History of Quranic revelation,
- The difference between the Quran and other scriptures,
- Uthman's "authorized" version: a horrendous crime,
- The Code 19,
- The *muqatta'at* letters or the Quranic initials,
- Islam's final triumph.

1. What is the Quran?

The Quran is, according to Islam, God's final scripture that was revealed to His last prophet, i.e. Prophet Muhammad. It is believed to be the speech of God (Ar. *Kalamul*lah),[299] delivered by Angel Gabriel to Prophet Muhammad. It is the only scripture protected by God from human corruption,[300] as happened to previous scriptures. Islam did not begin with Muhammad, as many people, including Muslims, erroneously believe. It began with Prophet Adam, going through many prophets (every community was sent a messenger[301]), including Abraham, Moses, Jesus, and ending with Muhammad. The core teaching of Islam is the same throughout, namely: "There is no god, but God. Worship Him alone." The laws differ. For instance, there were no religious rituals or code until Prophet Abraham.[302]

---

[299] Quran, 6:115.
[300] Quran, 15:9.
[301] Quran, 35:24.
[302] Quran, 2:128.

The Quran mentions the Old Testament (the *Taurat*) given to Moses and the New Testament (the *Injil*) given to Jesus. The Jews and the Christians, when they became separate religious communities, are termed as "People of the Book" in the Quran, meaning communities that have received scripture from God. However, it does not specifically mention communities outside the Abrahamic line, except by the general term *Sabi'in*.[303] By implication, this includes the major religious communities of Hinduism, Buddhism, Taoism, Confucianism and Zoroasterism and their scriptures.

It is the belief of Muslims that these very ancient scriptures had been corrupted through time in the basic belief in One God, and that a final scripture, protected by God, was necessary to set the errors right. The Quran is described by God as confirming what is right in the previous scriptures, while at the same time, superseding them.[304]

All divine scriptures, including the Quran, were meant to teach mankind, firstly through the many individual communities, spread over many cultural areas, and finally the whole of mankind, the right guidance, i.e. how to live righteously. As men have freedom of choice, some followed God's teachings, while others did not and followed their passions instead. Thus arose the believers in God, the monotheists, and the unbelievers or the misbelievers, the polytheists.

The Jews and the Christians failed to believe in Prophet Muhammad when he appeared to them as the last prophet, due to jealousy, wishing everyone else to follow them.[305] It is most revealing to know what British Prime Minister Gladstone said in the British Parliament in the early days of British colonial

---

[303] Quran, 2:62.
[304] Quran, 5:48.
[305] Quran, 2:109.

penetration of Islamic societies about the Quran. "As long as this Quran is among them, nothing can be accomplished."[306]

2. The history of Quranic revelation.

As is well-known, the Quran was sent down to Muhammad over a period of 23 years when he received the call to prophethood at the age of 40, first in Mecca (10 years), then in Medina (12 years), and again in Mecca (1 year). The first revelation, the famous five "Iqra'" verses, which later formed the 19-verse Surah 96 (*Al-'Alaq*), came to him while he was meditating in the cave of Mt. Hira. It is stated in the *Sira* (ibn Ishaq's biography of Muhammad) that he could neither read, nor write at that time, even though his cousin Ali, and his companions Abu Bakr and Uthman ibn Affan could. However, his contemporaries accused him of writing down what was dictated to him,[307] proving that he could read and write. This is more likely, because Muhammad was at this time a successful merchant. Moreover, the Arabic word *ummi* here means 'gentile', i.e. non-Jew.

It is stated that Muhammad himself was fearful when he first received the revelation, and he did not believe himself. His wife Khadijah, however, believed in him and took him to her cousin, a *hanif* (i.e. a follower of the religion of Abraham), named Waraqah ibn Naufal, who was learned in the scriptures. Waraqah told her the meaning of the momentous event, i.e. that Muhammad was the prophet then being awaited.[308]

Then followed a period of persecution of him and his few followers during which however, a stalwart of Mecca, Omar Ibni

---

[306] Quoted by Ali Shari'ati in his book *What Is To Be Done*, p. 41.

[307] Quran, 25:5.

[308] See *The Life of Muhammad – A Translation of Ishaq's Sirat Rasul Allah* (1974); p.83. See also Karen Armstrong, *Muhammad: A Biography of the Prophet* (1992); p. 80.

Khattab, went to see Muhammad with the intention of killing him, but ended up believing in Muhammad.[309] Muhammad went to Taif, a town nearby where he was pelted with stones by the boys there. He also sent a delegation to the Christian ruler Negus in Abyssinia where the ruler, in spite of the Quraishy representatives' opposition, received the delegation with respect and courtesy and heard their leader pronounce Prophet Muhammad's mission as well as Islam's view of Prophet Jesus. The ruler was overwhelmed to tears by what he heard, and accorded them his protection.[310]

The revelations that Muhammad received during this early Meccan period took on the character of ideological exhortation. When he migrated to Medina twelve years later after receiving support and invitation from its inhabitants, he gave to the city a Charter known as the Medina Charter, the first written constitution in the world.[311] During this Medina period (12 years), the revelations took on the character of laws. The laws are of two dimensions, namely historical and universal. This is a very important distinction which the early classical jurists did not notice and thus committed an error which gave a bad name to Islamic law, the *Shari'ah*. It fell to a Sudanese republican leader, Mahmoud Mohamed Taha who pointed out this distinction in his thesis, *The Second Message of Islam*.[312]

Although the Quran is generally regarded as revelations from God to Muhammad, described as "God's word", it is also described as the "utterance of a noble messenger,"[313] or "the best hadith".[314] Thus, it is a two-way communication. Muhammad is

---

[309] *Ibid.*; pp. 156-157.
[310] Ibid., pp. 146-153.
[311] See M. Hamidullah, *The First Written Constitution in the World*, (1981).
[312] See Abdullahi Ahmed An-Na'im, *Towards an Islamic Reformation*, pp. ix ff.
[313] Quran, 69:40.
[314] Quran, 39:23

not just a passive recipient; his consciousness also played a creative role. As is known, God's language is not a human language. The fact that the Quran is in the Arabic language is due to its recipient being an Arab.

3. The difference between the Quran and other scriptures.

The verses of the Quran were written down as they were being revealed to the Prophet. Muhammad had about forty scribes who took down the revelations when they came to him. They were also committed to memory by his companions. It is reported that during every fasting month he would recite the revelations, arranging them in the order that it would assume later. Before he died, the whole Quran, thus arranged, is in the hands of many scribes.

All other prophets before Muhammad had their own God-given miracles to prove their divine missions. It is stated in the Quran that Muhammad had no miracles. His only miracle is the Quran.[315]

The Quran, being the last divine scripture to mankind, confirms the teachings of previous scriptures (those that are true) as well as supersedes them.[316] The Quran has also to be protected against corruption by human hands, as happened in the past. This is achieved through what is known as Code 19. Code 19 stands for an awesome mathematically-structured methodology of composition, rendering it impossible to be authored by any except God.[317]

---

[315] Quran, 29:51.

[316] Quran, 5:48.

[317] See Quran 10:37. For Code 19, see Appendix 1 of Rashad Khalifa's translation. See also Kassim Ahmad, *Hadis – Jawapan Kepada Pengkritik*; ch. 6.

4. Uthman's "authorized" version of the Quran – a horrendous crime

During the time of the Caliphate of Uthman (644-650), different readings of the Quran arose and there was a need to streamline and systematized them. He formed a Commission to execute this extremely important task. Every scribe, every manuscript of the Quran and every memorizer was called to give evidence. The rule followed by the Commission was that every verse of the Quran had to have two or more witnesses Such reports in Hadith literature is called *mutawatir*, meaning multiple witnesses. However, the Commission committed a horrendous act by adding two verses (verse 127 and 128) at the end of *Surah Al-Taubah*, in order to give credit to Prophet Muhammad.[318] This fact is recorded in Suyuti's *Al-Itqan* and also in Bukhari.[319] Furthermore, this surah is not prefixed by the *Basmallah*, a sign of God's foreknowledge of the horrendous crime, making Him withhold His official chop, so to speak. It is also reported that these two verses only had one witness i.e. Khuzaimah, whose witness, according to a hadith is equivalent to two! Moreover this chapter is labeled Medinan, while the two verses are said to be Meccan. Verse 128 also contains a phrase ("compassionate and merciful") referring to Muhammad, whereas it always applies to God alone. Moreover, the ever-vigilant Code 19 rejects these two verses.[320]

There is another evidence to this crime. Hafsah's manuscript, entrusted to her by her father Omar Ibn Khattab, was ordered to be burnt later by Caliph Marwan Ibn Al-Hakam (d. 65 A.H./684 A.D.) thus obliterating the only authentic manuscript of the Quran from Prophet Muhammad's days!

---

[318] See Appendix 24 of Rashad Khalifa's translation of the Quran.
[319] Lihat Kassim Ahmad, *Jawapan Kepada Pengkritik* (1992); p. 60.
[320] As in Note 317 and 318 above.

It was reported in Suyuti's *Al-Itqan,* that Ali Abi Talib vehemently objected to this addition.[321]

5. The Code 19

As I have stated earlier, the divine protection of the Quran lies in an intricate, sophisticated and mathematically-structured composition of the Quran. This makes it impossible for any human being to author it. The researches of Dr. Rashad Khalifa revealed that it is based on a code called Code 19. This number 19 is found in verse 30 of surah 74, which goes, "Over it is nineteen." In verse 35 of the same surah, this allegory is describes as "one of the greatest miracles".

Code 19 requires that every surah, every verse and every letter conform to the number 19 or multiples of 19. For example, the first verse (1:1) known as *Basmalah* consists of 19 letters. The Quran consists of 114 chapters. 114 is 19x6. The total number of verses in the Quran is 6346, which is 19x334. The word God (*Allah*) occurs 2698, which is 19x142. Numerous other examples can be shown.[322] Any addition or subtraction of chapters, verses, words or letters would immediately be exposed by this code.

Why did God choose 19 to be the basis of this sophisticated system? According to ancient Arab numerical system, 19 is the numerical value of the Arabic word, *wahid.* In other words, the basic theme of the Quran and its message is that GOD IS ONE.[323]

---

[321] *Ibid.*

[322] See Appendix 1 of Rashad Khalifa's translation of the Quran. Also See, *Nineteen: God's Signature in Nature and Scripture*, Edip Yuksel, Brainbow Press, 2011.

[323] See Kassim Ahmad, *Hadis – Jawapan Kepada Pengkritik* (1992); Ch. 6.

6. The *Muqatta'at* letters or the Quranic initials.

What is known as *muqatta'at* letters or Quranic initials appear at the beginning of 29 chapters of the Quran. These make up 14 sets, such as A.L.M in surah 2 (*Al-Baqarah*) and surah 3 (*Ali-Imran*), A.L.M.S. in surah 7 (*Al-A'raaf*), till the end (the letter N), totaling 14 sets. These *muqatt'at* letters reveal a major secret embedded in the Quran, i.e. the date of the "end" of the world. Verse 15 of surah 20 states: "The Hour is surely coming. I will keep it almost hidden. For each soul must be paid for its works." The Hour refers to Resurrection or the "end" of the world. Verse 87 of surah 15 further gives the date. To cut the matter short, since Muhammad's interim is 1709 years, the end of the world is 309 years from the date when Dr. Rashad Khalifa made the discovery (in 1400 A.H.). The figure 309 is found in the Quran (18:25) in the context of Resurrection. Thus we get the date of Resurrection as 1710 A.H. or 2280 A.D.

The Quran states that God's religion, Islam, will rise again. This will happen in the 21st and 22nd centuries. We have 270 years more to that date, counting from 2010. It is highly reasonable that Islam will have completed its mission by then, and the world is ready for the establishment of God's Kingdom. This is what Resurrection means. It is not the end of the world, for the world has many millions of years more to go. It means a major revolution in the life of mankind. It is the bringing into being of a Paradise which generations of believers had struggled and sacrificed for since the beginning of history.[324]

7. Islam's final triumph

Twenty-two days before Prophet Muhammad died, he received the famous revelation "Today I have completed your religion perfected My blessing upon you and I have decreed Submission

---

[324] See Quran 9:111.

(Islam) as the religion for you."[325] Only the 3-verse surah Al-Nasr came after that – that was the last revelation to him.

It should be noted that this verse pronounced unequivocally about the completion of the religion of Islam, and about God's pleasure that Islam becomes the believers' religion. In spite of this clear pronouncement, Muslim scholars later claimed that the Quran must be coupled with the Hadith in order to make its teachings complete. This was the beginning of the end of Islam in the world. After this, deviation after the deviation crept in, bringing Islam down and giving rise to its replacement by a reawakened Judeo-Christian Europe to lead and define the modern world and modern civilization. Subsequently, the total failures of the three world systems (Theology, Communism and Capitalism) points to the truth of the "Straight Path" system of the Quran. It is this Straight Path, this Golden Mean, that mankind must now seek to avoid his total destruction and ensure his fullest salvation.

*****

---

[325] Quran, 5:3.

CHAPTER 17

The Problem of the So-called Prophetic Traditions

- What are Prophetic traditions?
- The canonization of the Hadith and Shafie's role,
- Their effects on Muslim society,
- Criticism of Hadith and the possibility of reform.

1. What are Prophetic traditions?

Also known as the *Sunnah* or *Hadith*, the Prophetic Traditions are records of what Prophet Muhammad was alleged to have said or done during his career of prophethood and messengership of God. In the earlier period before their canonization (the officially recognized reports by the two major sects, the Sunnis and the Shi'ahs spanning over a period of 250 to 350 years after the death of the Prophet) , they were personal notes kept by his Companions, Abu Bakr and Omar Ibn Khattab. However, these personal notes were later destroyed for fear that they might be false, or they might be confused with the Quran.[326]

Why this long lapse of time? The answer must be that it was prohibited by the Prophet.[327] However, Muhammad's name has already begun to be used by the political factions of Abu Bakr and

---

[326] See Kassim Ahmad, *Hadith: A Re-evaluation*; pp. 52-53.
[327] See M. M. Azmi, *Studies in early Hadith Literature*, (Beirut:1968); pp.22-23

Ali in order to strengthen their cases for the leadership of the nascent Community after the death of the Prophet. This bad practice widened and extended into other than political areas: into theology, into rituals of worship, including the influencing of so-called righteous living by fabricating hadiths.[328]

It was perhaps this division that prompted Imam Shafi'e (d. 820) to create for the first time what later became the basis of Muslim jurisprudence. Raising the so-called Hadith/Sunnah to the same level of the Quran on the basis of Verse 59, of Surah 4,[329] which he subjectively and arbitrarily translated as upholding the Quran for the "obeying of God" (note that the word 'Quran' is not mentioned in the text) and upholding the Hadith for "obeying the messenger" (note also that the word 'hadith' is not mentioned in the text). His jurisprudential theory states that there are two principal sources and three secondary sources. The two principal sources are (a) the Quran and (b) the Hadith, while the three secondary ones are (a) *Qias*, or Analogy, (b) Consensus of religious scholars, and (c) *Ijtihad*, or creative attempt by individual leaders or scholars to arrive at solutions to new problems. For instance, the famous Medina Charter promulgated by Muhammad when he and his followers migrated to Medina twelve years later can be described as Muhammad's *ijtihad* at promulgating a constitution.

Shafi'e's placing of the Hadith on par with the Quran is fraught with danger. Firstly, many hadiths neither fulfills the need to be in line with reason, nor with the teaching of the Quran, two criteria agreed to for choosing the authentic hadiths.[330] Secondly, Shafi'e also introduced the theory of the congruence of the Hadith with

---

[328] See Ahmad Amin, *Fajar Islam,* Dewan Bahasa & Pustaka, Kuala Lumpur (1980); pp. 291-96.

[329] "O you who believe, you shall obey God, and you shall obey His messenger and those in charge among you..."

[330] See Fazlul Karim, *Mishkat-ul-Masabih*, Vol I, pp. 21-22

the Quran,[331]and concocted the notion of hadiths sometimes cancelling the Quran![332] These things later threw the Muslim Community into irrevocable divisions and into intellectual stagnancy, bringing about its downfall.

2. The canonization of the hadith and Shafi'es' role

It was after Shafi'e introduced this new doctrine, that the Hadith/Sunnah is a primary source on par with the Quran and must be adhered to, that the Hadith collectors collected their hadiths. The Sunnis came up with their "Six Authentic Collections", made by Bukhari (d. 870), Muslim (d. 875), Ibn Majah (d 886), Abu Daud (d. 888), al-Tirmidhi (d. 892) and al-Nasa'i (d. 915). The Shi'ites had their own collections, by al-Kulaini (d. 962), Ibn Babuwayh (d. 1013), and Ja'afar Muhammad al-Tusi (d. 1043)

The top Sunni Hadith collector, Bukhari, is reported to have collected 600,000 hadiths, from which he only selected 7,275 to be included in his so-called authentic collection.[333] Ibn Hanbal is reported to have stated that there were 7,000,000 'authentic' hadith.[334] If these reports are true, and one is inclined to say that they are, it only goes to show the extent of the fabrication of hadith. Bukhari's rejection of almost 99 % of his total collection shows his extreme care in selection.

One peculiar feature of the Hadith collection was its heavy reliance on the *isnad* or string of narrators, whether they were trustworthy persons or not. How that could be established for persons three generations away from the collector, not to say six

---

[331] See *Shafi'es' Risalah*; p. 184. Also see, *Hadith as Scripture: Discussions on the Authority of Prophetic Traditions in Islam*, Aisha Musa, Palgrave, 2008.

[332] *Ibid.*; p. 184

[333] See *Miskat-ul-Masabih*; p. 38.

[334] See M.M. Azmi; *Ibid*, p. 301

or more,[335] is beyond comprehension. It was reported that the venerable Bukhari rejected a narrator because he cheated when calling the hens to him by throwing sands at them rather that some cereal! The collector should concentrate more on the *matn*, i.e. the content of the report. Many hadiths fail on this score, because they do not tally with reason, logic and the teachings of the Quran.[336]

3. Their effects on Muslim society

As I have stated, the effects of the Hadith on the Community were to create irrevocable political and theological divisions, as well as to render intellectual stagnancy, using the great name of the Prophet. Following Christianity, it further created a clerical class with the function and role of interpreting religion for the masses. It also separated knowledge into two divisions, the religious and secular, with the former being given a higher status. The elevation of Prophet Muhammad and members of the religious class into idols for the Community is another serious deviation. Further, the Quran is turned into a text to be memorized and recited without understanding throughout the Muslim world, thus rendering it not as a text for its guidance, but into a song-book! By the time of al-Ghazali (1058-1111), 450 years after the death of the Prophet, all these things had happened to the Community. Plus the hypocrisy and the corruption practiced by both the secular and the religious establishments – ingredients for the downfall of Islam – the actual downfall dates from the destruction of Baghdad by the Moghul barbarians in 1285. In the West, the Kingdom of Granada in Spain fell to the Christians in 1492.

---

[335] See Kassim Ahmad, *Ibid.*; p.88.

[336] In a simple survey, we estimate that 40% of the so-called authentic hadith clearly contradict the teaching of the Quran. See Kassim Ahmad, *Delima Umat Islam: Antara Quran dan Hadis* (Malaysia:2002)

All these happenings had taken place by the end of the 15th Century. They rendered the once-invincible, Quran-inspired, Muslims into another religious community that is no different from the others.[337]

4. Criticism of hadith and the possibility of reform

Due to the above-mentioned weakness of the Hadith/Sunnah, criticism against it arose early. The Mu'tazilites' criticism took two forms: outright rejection as well as partial rejection. Early in the 20th Century, streams of criticism arose in Egypt and India.[338] The modern reformist movement of Muhammad Abduh, although adhering to the two-primary-source doctrine of Shafi'e, sought a tighter selection for authenticity. Thus, the present writer's criticism of the Hadith is nothing new. However, he makes bold to say that his criticism is comprehensive and systematic.[339]

It looks as though that reform, i.e. to make present-day "Muslims" give up the Hadith or to re-evaluate it, is a near impossibility. It has become part of their psyche. Paradoxically, the liberation of the Community might come from the more intellectually free West once enough of its population embraces Islam. It seems certain that this will happen in this century, within the next few decades.

*****

---

[337] "Surely, those who believe, those who are Jewish, the Christians, and the Sab'in -- anyone who believes in God and believes in the Last Day, and leads a righteous life – will receive their recompense from their Lord. They have nothing to fear, nor will they grieve." (Quran, 2:62). This verse clearly indicates that whoever is a true believer from among the religious groups are guaranteed salvation by God. It is noteworthy that the verses predicting the latter triumph of Islam all refer to the Religion of Truth or the Religion of God, not Islam. The religion of Islam has long been corrupted by the Muslims themselves!

[338] See Kassim, *Hadith – A Re-evaluation*; pp. 78-79.

[339] See Kassim Ahmad, *Hadis – Satu Penilaian Semula* (1986); p. 22.

CHAPTER 18

Shari'ah – The Divine Law?

1. What is Shari'ah?
2. Its development from the early period till today;
3. Fixed penal punishments – the *Hudud*;
4. The failure of reforms;
5. Where lies the solution?

1. What is Shari'ah?

Law, or *Shari'ah*, in Islam is only secondary to faith, which is belief in the One True God. After this faith, Law is the all important thing. Verses from the Quran stipulate that those who do not rule by God's law are simultaneously unjust, wicked or unbelievers.[340] Law in Islam is therefore the command of God. However, the famous jurist, al-Shafi'e (767-820) who laid down the foundation of Muslim jurisprudence, 200 years after the death of the Prophet, subjectively and arbitrarily interpreted the verse "Obey God and obey the messenger"[341] to mean not only to uphold God's message, i.e. the Quran, but also the *Sunnah* of the Prophet. The two are termed primary sources in his jurisprudential theory. Then comes two other supplementary sources of *Ijma* or Consensus of the Community, and *Qias* or Analogy.[342]

---

[340] Quran, 5:45, 44 and 47.

[341] Quran, 4:59.

[342] See N. J. Coulson, *A History of Islamic Law* (Edinburgh:1964); Ch. 4. See also Ahmad Ibrahim, *Islamic Law in Malaya*, (Singapore:1965); Ch. 1.

Muslim law is conceived to be different from Western law in the sense that the latter is secular and undergoes changes according to times and places. The classical Muslim jurists before the modern period when Western civilization came to clash with the Muslim Community had no historical sense, and were elevated by that Community to be above criticism, the so-called *taqlid* (blind following) period and its corollary of the "closing of the door of *Ijtihad*" beginning from the 12th Century.

In actual fact, a right understanding of the Quranic text would distinguish between the historically-bound verses from the universal ones.[343] Above and beyond that, there is the philosophical question of the nature of human existence: do we exist for God, or for ourselves? In other words, is our life (the human collective life) to be based on humanism and secularism, or is it to be submerged in slavery to God and then to get His rewards and punishments?

Metaphor is littered throughout the text of the Quran. In its first Surah, verse 2, we find the sentence "Master of the Day of Judgement.", meaning that God will judge us on that Day. In

---

[343] In 1967 the leader of the Sudanese Republican Brotherhood, Mahmoud Mohamed Taha, published his booklet, *The Second Message of Islam*, in which he distinguished the historically-bound verses of the Quran from the universal ones. (See Abdullahi Ahmed An-Naim, *Towards an Islamic Reformation*; p. x) Although M. M. Taha seemed to have made a very important discovery, a close look at the verses concerning punishments for thievery and others would have made this obvious. Listen to this: "The man or woman, addicted to theft, cut off their hands ... But whoever repents after his wrongdoing and reforms, God redeems him. God is Forgiver, Most Merciful." (5:38-39) Note that in all cultural areas, ancient punishments were severe. In this and similar other verses, the severe punishments are followed by forgiveness and mercy from God, if the wrongdoer repents and reforms. This means that the punishments can be lessened or even forgiven. Strangely, the classical lawyers ignored these verses, and stranger still, later generations of scholars accepted their interpretations without question.

actual fact, it is the individual and collective human being who will judge himself.[344] That judgement will, of course, be in accordance to God's Laws; that is why God takes final responsibility for the judgement. Moreover, one of the qualities of God is that He is Absolutely Independent and does not need anything from the human being, or from any of His creations. That means His scriptures to mankind, including the Quran, is meant for the good of mankind. He states it so in several *muhkamat* (clear by itself) verses.[345]

2. The development of the *Shari'ah*

The Quran, by its own definition, is a guide to those who are righteous, or rather who choose to be righteous.[346] It guides through moral and ethical teachings, through historical examples of past communities, through cosmological insights into the creation and evolution of the universe, through biological insights into Man's creation, development and evolution, and through philosophical insights of the truth of God's creation. It is God's Final Scripture to mankind, and contains His comprehensive teachings, confirming and superseding His previous scriptures to the various communities.[347]

In terms of law, the Quran contains very few legal injunctions. Moreover, distinction must be made between the historically-bound verses and those that are of universal application. However, what is called universal is also historically-bound, since even the so-called Global Village is bounded by its period. All periods are, therefore, contextual.

---

[344] Quran, 17:13-14.

[345] One of them goes thus: "Those who strive for their own good. God is is no need for anyone." (29:6)

[346] Quran, 2:2.

[347] Quran, 5:48.

But men have always conspired to understand the "divine-inspired" texts in ways quite different from what the text actually means. The case of the divinity of Jesus Christ is a case in point. The same happened to the followers of Muhammad. It is clear that nothing can supersede or be on par with the Quran, yet two hundred years after the death of the Prophet, their Master Jurist al-Shafi'e did precisely this by putting the so-called *Sunnah* of the Prophet as a primary source of Muslim law, that can at times abrogate the Quran![348] In time, it is the *Ijma'* , the Consensus of the Scholars, that decides everything, from the authenticity of the Sunnah to the correct interpretation of the Quran.[349] This doctrine spells doom to the Muslim Community, because the closing of the door of creative thinking means thinking is banned in the Community.

3. The so-called fixed punishments

I want to take the case of the fixed punishments, the so-called *hudud* punishments, to illustrate the illogicality of the Law worked out by the classical jurists. In the first place, logical thinking cannot accept any idea of a fixed punishment for anything. A punishment, to be effective, must be equivalent to the crime, and there are all sorts of crimes, and they are of different magnitudes. So, how can any punishment be fixed?

Moreover, the Arabic word *hadd* (pl. *hudud*), which occurs 14 times in the Quran, does not refer to punishment at all. The word means 'limit' or 'bounds', and in the Quran it is used to mean a metaphorical boundary beyond which men should not trespass. A man needs to eat and sleep; if he does not eat and sleep, he will die of hunger and fatigue. If, on the other hand, he eats and sleeps

---

[348] See *Islamic Jurisprudence: Shafi's' Risala* (trans by Majid Khadduri); pp 184-187. Also see, *Hadith as Scripture: Discussions on the Authority of Prophetic Traditions in Islam*, Aisha Musa, Palgrave, 2008.
[349] See Ahmad Ibrahim, *Islamic Law in Malaysia*, p. 25.

too much, he will also die from over-eating and over-sleeping. This is what the word means – never pass the boundary of appropriateness. How our clever classical jurists made this mistake is beyond our comprehension. It only shows that critical thinking is a "must" for any society wanting to progress so that correction can be made by the following generation. But the doting public erected a "beyond criticism" board for these master jurists, turning them into idols that are clearly forbidden by the Islamic faith. In practice, it prevents the Community from progressing.

4. The failure of reforms

Thus, when the Community came face to face with Western civilization and with values that are different, during the Colonial Interregnum, it faces a crisis – modernize or die! Take the ideas of historical development, evolution, and secularism. Volumes have been written by Muslim scholars against these ideas during the last hundred years, thus causing stagnation in Muslim society, pulling it down to the lowest rung of human progress.

Take another case: woman's liberation and welfare. It can be said that Prophet Muhammad was the first world leader to liberate women from their bondage to men, to give them equal rights with men and to guarantee their welfare. Yet, today Muslim women in most Muslim countries are far from attaining the position the Quran has elevated them to. Why? Because what the clever classical jurists had assigned to them in their legal manuals, based on their limited, historically-bound understanding, is considered sufficient by the Community, and cannot be improved!

4. The solution to the impasse

Can the Community get out of its dilemma without going back to the teaching of the Quran? Will it criticize its Master-Jurist Shafi'e and accept only one principal source of Law, i.e. the Quran, one

142

general subsidiary source, i.e. the practice of those in charge? Under the second source, fall all other teachings, both Islamic and non-Islamic. For instance, *Hadith* falls under this category, as do Greek, Hindu and modern philosophies. The Community will not be able to do this unless it adopts the absolute belief in the One True God and throws out the false gods, i.e. the false sources. Can and will it do this? Can it forego the sectarianism and unite on the basis of Quranic teaching? Can it do away with its priesthood? Will it allow its scholars the freedom to criticize our intellectual inheritance?

All these the Community must do in order to recover its lost position and regain the position of "the best community" ever raised up for mankind, "because you enjoin good and forbid evil, and you believe in God."[350] Can it do it? This is a task like the fabled cleansing of the Augean stables by Hercules. It is well-nigh impossible! The "Muslim" Community is too deep in its cesspool it throws itself into to get out quickly. By the divine law of replacement,[351] God will select other communities to do His bidding. Comparatively, it is the Western world, particularly the United States of America, is intellectually free to accept Islam without its intellectual baggage. The time is ripe for that, because of the current systemic collapse of its free market ideological system of Capitalist-Liberalism, the other major world ideological system of Marxist-Communism having already collapsed. Reality will force not only the West but the whole world to seek the "Straight Path" alternative system recommended by the Quran. .

*****

---

[350] Quran, 3:110.
[351] Quran, 47:38.

143

CHAPTER 19

Mysticism –
A Deviation from the Straight Path

- What is mysticism?
- How did mysticism originate in Islam?
- Islam upholds the middle path against extreme
- The "terrorist" revolt of Islam against the West

1. What is mysticism?

It is better that we define the meaning of mysticism precisely, because the entirely human tendency to isolate oneself to reflect on the meaning of life, on God's creation and on man's role in this life may also be described as mystical. Prophet Muhammad, before he became prophet, often did this in the month of Ramadan in the cave of Mt. Hira near Mecca. While alone here, he used to pray and contemplated on those questions, until one day it is reported that the Angel Gabriel came to him with the first revelation from God. Was Muhammad a mystic? We must unequivocally answer "No!" to this question.

Mysticism refers to a very personal and individualized experience of the Reality, of God, that cannot be proved as to its truth. This is the distinct difference between the rational results of contemplation, and the unprovable, sometimes irrational, claims of the mystics.[352] Faced with such claims on matters spiritual, the

---

[352] For instance, the famous Master Sufi, Ibni Arabi, claims that his *Fusus al-Hikam* ('The Bezels of Wisdom') was copied word for word from a book

oppressed people have no defense, except a resort to the truth. That means finding definite answers in the Quran and in the truly authentic practice of the Prophet.

In the case of Ibni Arabi, the claims that he made regarding his famous work, *Fusus al-Hikam*, is difficult to believe, because, as his translator said: "... the work apart from its arrangement into twenty seven chapters lacks any real system or organization of its subject matter."[353] Further, this translator says, "... the subject matter of most of the chapters bears little or no relation to the name of the prophet in the title. Indeed, there is often scant connection between the subjects discussed in a chapter and the particular Wisdom of the title. Within the chapters there is often a considerable measure of discontinuity in the topics dealt with. The main themes of his thought occur again and again from chapter to chapter in a rather haphazard way..."[354]

Resorting to testing its truth against the Quran needs to be done, because no less than scholars like Fazlur Rahman and Seyyed Hossein Nasr have inveighed their weight on the side of mysticism.[355] Today it is almost taken for granted that mysticism

---

granted to him in a visitation by Prophet Muhammad. (See *Ibn Al'Arabi – The Bezels of Wisdom*, Translated & Introduced by R. W. J. Austin (1980); p. 17.

[353] *Ibid.*, p. 18.

[354] *Ibid.*, p. 20.

[355] In his classic book, *Islam* (Second Edition), Fazlul Rahman stated, "Muhammad's Prophetic consciousness, which issued in his mission, was founded upon very definite, vivid and powerful mystic experiences briefly described or alluded to in the Quran ... (From this point of view, the claims of later Sufis, that in practicing mysticism they are only following the spiritual legacy of the Prophet, is not altogether fanciful even if it may be questioned on historical grounds.) ..." (p. 128) Seyyed Hossein Nasr, in his book *The Three Muslim Sages* is even more equivocal. "Sufism as a spiritual realization and the attainment of sanctity and gnosis is an intrinsic aspect of the Islamic Revelation ... For a person who participates in Sufism, who lives the life of a 'follower of the Path', the most perfect Sufi was the Prophet

(its name in Islam being Sufism) is part of Islam. I think this is wrong, as I shall show.

2. How did mysticism originate in Islam?

The Quran warns the "People of the Book", i.e. the Jews and the Christians, of relapse into cross materialism over the moral life of enjoining good and preventing evil – an active dynamic life to remake the world.

A perpetual deterioration -- a relapse into cross materialism -- seems natural to man, because it is animalism from which man arose, and God warns Jesus's followers from withdrawing into a solitary life of hermitism. The Quran says;

> "Subsequent to them, We sent Our messengers. We sent Jesus the son of Mary, and We gave him the Gospel, and We placed in the hearts of his followers kindness and mercy. But they invented hermitism which We never decreed for them. All We asked them to do was to uphold the commandments approved by God. But they did not uphold the message as they should have. Consequently, We gave those who believed among them their recompense, while many of them were wicked."[356]

It is obvious that the Quran teaches us to balance between a life of extreme materialism and a life of extreme mysticism. As a matter of fact, the whole tenor of the teachings of the Quran, as reflected in the life of Prophet Muhammad, is one of a revolutionary, active and dynamic conception of human life aimed at re-making the world.

Muhammad ... and after him the representative *par excellence* of Islamic esotericism, Ali ibn Abi Talib." (p. 83.)
[356] Quran, 57:27.

A Prophetic tradition, reported by Bukhari and Muslim, runs thus:

> "Once after the Prophet delivered a lecture on the truth of Judgement Day and Judgement before God, a number of Companions met at the house of 'Uthman bin Maz'um and stated their resolve to fast every day, to pray every night, to refrain from sleeping on beds, to refrain from eating meat and fat, refrain from having contact with women and avoid the use of perfumes; to wear only course clothes, and in general to reject the world. When the Prophet heard this, he said to them, 'I have not been ordained by God to adopt this life-style. Your body has rights over you: so, fast, but also cease from fasting; pray at night, but also sleep. I fast, but I also do not fast. I take meat and fat, and I also marry. Whoever turns away from my way, is not of me.'"

3. Islam upholds the middle path against extremes.

It is clear that Islam rejects a solitary life-style of cave-like existence, because man has a mission to re-make the world into a better place through active, creative, revolutionary action, as shown by the example of Prophet Muhammad. That is the meaning of man as vicegerent of God. The Hereafter, much urged on us by the Quran, is actually this world raised to higher moral, intellectual and spiritual levels. This is to be achieved by a perpetual and relentless struggle upward of Man, the *Homo sapiens*, the vicegerent of God on earth. The believers, i.e. the upholders and doers of good must defeat the unbelievers, i.e. the upholders and doers of evil, and turn the entire universe into a Paradise.[357]

---

[357] "God has bought from the believers their lives and their money in exchange for Paradise. Thus, they fight in the cause of God willing to kill and get killed.

However, the law of deterioration came to intervene even in Prophet Muhammad's struggle. We can say that he was the only prophet who completed his mission successfully during his life-time. He re-entered Mecca, his birth-place, triumphant, as a liberator on 30th January, 630 A.D. He died on 8th Jun 632 after being a Messenger of God for 22 years and leaving a Book – the Quran - for the guidance of the whole of mankind.

Yet, hardly thirty after his death, the seeds of destruction were sown in his community: civil wars between various theological sects and political factions broke out. Between 250 and 300 hundred years after his death, new juristic doctrines (*Hadith* elevated to a level on par with the Quran and consensus of scholars (*Ijma*) created to make laws) purportedly aims at eliminating divisions, the rise of a clerical class of *Ulama* to interpret religion for the masses, imitating Christians and Hindus; the division and separation of knowledge into religious and secular knowledge and the elevation of the former to higher position for the community to acquire, thus ignoring science and mathematics – all these deviations came hard and fast, following one another. They became the bane of Muhammad's Community and led to its complete downfall with the fall of Baghdad to the Mogul hordes in 1258, in the east, and the fall of Granada to the Christians in 1492, in the west, and finally the abolition of the Ottoman Caliphate in Istanbul in 1924.

All these things need not happen, if the Community had been vigilant. But the earthly pull downwards, wallowing in wealth and ostentatious living, it seems, is part and parcel of mankind's animalistic heritage in its ceaseless struggle to ascend to higher

Such is His truthful pledge in the Torah the Gospel and the Quran – and who fulfills His pledge better than God? You shall rejoice in making such an exchange. This is the greatest triumph." (Quran, 9:111) "Therefore, you shall race towards forgiveness from your Lord, and a Paradise whose width encompasses the heaven and the earth." (Quran, 57:21)

levels of existence. Already beginning under Uthman ibni Affan (Caliph 644-56), a contrary mode of life of mysticism, a rejection of worldly ostentation developed with Companions like Abu Dharr (d. 652) and Hudzaifa (d. 657) and al-Hasan of Basra (d. 657) and later to be joined by many others culminating in Ibn al-Arabi, called the Great Sheikh (d. 1240). This mystical withdrawal from society into a specialized personal world of private piety caused the stagnation and deterioration of the Community.

According to S. H. Nasr, in the 19th century, a rejection of mysticism even to the extent of accusing it to be a Western colonialist conspiracy, developed in a section of Muslim society.[358] However, after the First and Second World Wars, not only in the Muslim but also in the Western worlds, certain sections of them looked again at mysticism and Sufism for a spiritual vision of the world to replace the dry so-called scientific rationalist vision that has failed them. We are at this point now, a cross-road between a scientific-rationalist path that has failed, and a religious-mystical path that has also failed.

It must be mentioned that the Sudanese mystic, Muhammad Ahmad Ibn As-Sayyid Abdullah (1844-1885), who claimed to be the divinely-appointed leader of Muslims at the end of times, rose to successfully challenge the Egypt-controlled Sudan and to take over its administration and set up a theocratic state there. The so-called Islamic Revolution in Iran in 1979, carried to success by all the democratic and revolutionary forces against the Shah was later taken over by the clerical class. Mysticism, a withdrawal from public life, however, must be distinguished from the clerical class, which, as European and Islamic history has shown, is an interested political class.

---

[358] See *Living Sufism*, p. 2.

I shall also mention the case of the Quranic story of the encounter between Prophet Moses and the legendary Khidr, referred to in the Quran as "one of Our servants whom We bless with mercy and bestowed knowledge from Ourselves."[359] Was he a mystic? The wording of the Quran would make him a prophet, one who received revelation from God, but was not bound to deliver it to his people. Therefore, he is not an example for people to follow. The two good examples to be followed, mentioned in the Quran, are Prophets Abraham and Muhammad, both of whom, especially Muhammad, showed an active revolutionary character.

4. The "terrorist" revolt of Islam against the West

After its own deterioration – a relapse into over-materialism and its opposite of mysticism – Islam must return to the "Straight Path" that the Quran teaches. On September 11, 2001, the rebels in the Muslim world launched a "terrorist" attack against the economic and military citadels of the West. Although this was not the beginning of Islam's revolt against the injustices of the West, it marked the beginning of Islam's new urban guerrilla war against the West, well displayed in the case of U.S.-occupied Iraq.

The concept of *jihad*, a revolutionary struggle "to enjoin good and forbid evil" is mentioned in the Quran.[360] It is derived from the Arabic root word *jahada* meaning 'to strive' or 'to struggle'. Thus

---

[359] Quran, 18:65.

[360] Quran, 3:110, although this verse does not use the word. The word is used in many verses, e.g. "O you who believe, let Me inform you of a trade that will save you from painful retribution: believe in God and His messenger and strive in the cause of God with your money and your lives. This is the best deal for you, if you only knew." (61:10-11) In other places, the word 'fight' or 'kill' is used, as in this: "God has bought from the believers their lives and their money in exchange for Paradise. Thus they fight in the cause of God, willing to kill and get killed. Such as his pledge in the Torah, the Gospel, and the Quran – and who fulfills His pledge better than God? You shall rejoice in making such an exchange. This is the greatest triumph." (9:111)

'jihad' means 'a struggle in the cause of God'. The phrase 'in the cause of God' simply means 'in the cause of goodness'.

Needless to say, this fighting in the cause of God must be undertaken only in self-defense without involving unnecessary loss of lives and property. The Muslims have ample reasons to fight against multiple Western aggressions, but their disunity and technological backwardness leave them no means to do so effectively. Hence their resort to this "terrorist" warfare.

This "terrorist" warfare, curiously, is having and will continue to have the effect of the West's intellectual and philosophical scrutiny of Islam. The West's long-held animosity against Islam was the result of envy-born prejudice and misunderstanding – "Islam is a heresy of Christianity".[361] The current failure of the Western ideologies and their systems is driving the West to look for a new world-outlook that can solve theirs as well the world's problems. In this way, the world will find the truth that is to be found in God's Final Scripture, the Quran, that Prophet Muhammad bequeathed to the world.

******

---

[361] See Hilaire Belloc, *The Great Heresies* (1936); Ch. 4.

CHAPTER 20

The Non-Abrahamic Line: Other Scriptures

- Non-Abrahamic religions (the *Sabi'in*),
- Their scriptures and the common ideas,
- Similarities and dissimilarities with the Quran,
- The problem of religious exclusivity.

1. Non- Abrahamic religions: (the *Sabi'in*)

The Quran calls the Jews and the Christians as "People of the Book",[362] as they received revelations from God contained in the Torah and the Gospel. As has been pointed out earlier,[363] every community has had its messenger or messengers. The twelve tribes of Israel had many messengers, among whom were Moses and Jesus. Outside of these, as we know, there are many other religions or religious communities, such as Hindus, Buddhists, Confucians, Taoists, Zoroastrians, and others, with scriptures of their own. I think that the term *Sabi'in* in the Quran[364] refers to

---

[362] Quran, 3:64 etc. The Arabic term is *Ahlu'l Kitab*.

[363] See Ch. 16, Note 301. Quran, 35:42; 16:36.

[364] This word occurs thrice in the Quran: here and in 5:69 and 22:17. Commentators are not in agreement as to the meaning of this word. The context in which this term occurs warrants us to attribute this meaning to it. This verse and 5:69, include all religions. Since Judaism and Christianity of Abrahamic Tradition are mentioned by name, the term Sabi'in must mean other religions, i.e. the Non-Abrahamic Tradition.

these other religious communities. They form the Non-Abrahamic Traditions, whereas the Jews, Christians and Muslims form the Abrahamic Traditions.

Religions before Prophet Muhammad were for a particular community. They were national in character. For example, both Moses and Jesus were sent to the people of Israel. So were the others – the spiritual teachers of Hinduism, Buddhism, Confucianism and Zoroastrianism. Their scriptures stated them as such.[365]

Historical circumstances -- limited means of transportation and communication -- determined them to be so. Not only that, however. The mental, emotional and spiritual growth of man and the human family dictates the necessity for a universal religion. That historical juncture came with Muhammad.[366]

2. Their scriptures and the common ideas contained in them

Not all revelations from God have been preserved in scriptures. For example, we have no scriptures handed down from the religious communities of Prophets Adam, Idris and Noah. It seems that the earliest scripture is the scripture of Abraham.[367] Some authorities[368] say that Hinduism is the oldest religion in the world. According to this, the Hindu scriptures, the Vedas and the Bhagavad Gita are, therefore, the oldest scriptures. The Buddhists, who have no concept of God, have their scriptures. So do the others.

There are many common ideas in these scriptures that are common also in the Abrahamic tradition. It is difficult to arrange

---

[365] See, Ch. 6, Note 135. *The Holy Quran* -- with English Translation and Commentary, 1988: U.K., Vol. 1; pp. v-vi & x-xii.

[366] See, Ch. 5, Note 6. Quran, 7:158.

[367] Quran, 87:18-19.

[368] See Bansi Pandit, *The Hindu Mind* (New Delhi: 2001); p. 21 & 37.

them in order of importance, but I list below the three major ideas in all religions.

Firstly, the idea of the Divine, the idea of the existence of a Reality that precedes all existences... That is the idea of God. He (actually this Reality is genderless, and the term 'He' shows the inadequacy of human language to express the Divine world) has many names. In the Quran, it is stated that all the beautiful names belong to God.[369] He is the Truth, the Perfect, the All-Powerful, the Beneficent, the Merciful, the Just, the Creator, the Fashioner, the Preserver and so on. It is commonly but inaccurately stated that He has ninety-nine names.

In Christianity, He is the Logos, God the Father, Son and Holy Spirit. In Judaism, He is Yahweh, Elohim, and the God of Israel. In Hinduism, He is the Brahman, Lord Krishna, and so on. However, in Buddhism, the idea of the Divine is implied rather than expressly stated.

The second common idea is the idea of Afterlife, or the Hereafter. This idea expresses the belief that a human being is part of the larger humanity, the Human Family, in other words. The immortal part of a human being, the soul, has existences in other worlds when he dies. Depending on his or her actions in this life, he or she will reap the harvest. The good will go to Heaven; the bad will go to Hell. Hell, however, is not permanent. After the soul is cleansed, it will go to Heaven.

The third common idea is that a human being should serve God, in the words of the Quran, "enjoining good and preventing evil".[370] This is to ensure that truth and justice prevail, and falsehood and injustice defeated, in the world.

---

[369] Quran, 7:110.
[370] Quran, 3:110.

There are many other common ideas. Their aim is strengthen and enforce those three common ideas above. It is for these that there has arisen a belief that all religions teach goodness, and no religion teaches evil. But as we have seen, fanaticism in people, promoted by vested-interest groups, is what makes religion dangerous and evil.

3. Similarities and dissimilarities with Islam

It can be seen that the teachings of the Non-Abrahamic religions has many similarities with the teachings of the Quran, God's final scripture. The three common ideas of the Divine, of Afterlife and of Final Judgement, i.e. the consequences of good and evil works, of reward in Heaven and punishment in Hell, are to be found in all religions. The language used may be different, as metaphors and allegories are much used in all religions. //

However, it cannot be said that Islam, or to be more precise, the teachings of the Quran, are similar to those of other religions, including Christianity and Judaism. Firstly, Islam, as taught in the Quran, is a *universal* religion. It is to be distinguished from all other religions, in the sense that is not a *national* religion for any group of nations. Prophets Moses and Jesus were sent to the Twelve Tribes of Israel. The prophets of Hinduism were for the Hindus; so were the prophets of other national religions. This is the first point.

The second point is that the idea of the One True God, of pure and strict monotheism is to be found only in the Quran. However, the concept of man as the crown of God's creation, God-manifested, and vicegerent of God on Earth, is to be distinguished from the idea of the incarnation of God in Jesus Christ and in the many Hindu and other religions' deities.

155

It is also stated in the Quran that it confirms and supersedes other scriptures,[371] and that other scripture contains only a tenth of the Quran.[372] What does this mean? In spite of several books that have written on this, I believe that our study of the Quran is still at an infant stage. The Quran is a profound book. Its depth is fathomless.[373]

4. The problem of religious exclusivity and how to solve it

Religious exclusivity, or fanaticism, is always the great danger posed by religions. We have seen how religious wars in Europe[374], the Christian crusades against Islam for two centuries from 1095 to 1291, as well as its animosity against science and learning.[375] In recent times, we saw how the Christian Right in America influenced the American Administration to launch its aggressive wars against Iraq and Afghanistan. It is not that Islam is not at fault. This disease has infected Islam as well when the equivalent of priesthood, the *ulama* class, emerged about three hundred years after Prophet Muhammad's death to dictate religion on the Muslim masses.

However, it should be clearly pointed out that in all these instances, it is the subjective interpretations of the religion by vested-interested groups that are to blame, not the religion itself. In general, religion has a great and important role to play in the life of individual nations, as well as the whole of mankind. It forms the basis of moral life in all societies, and it should form the moral basis of the entire world, if we want peace, security and

---

[371] See, Ch. 16, Note 316.

[372] Quran, 34:45.

[373] Quran, 18:109.

[374] A series of European wars that began about 1524 till 1648, the basis of which was religion. It consisted of seven wars affecting most European countries, including England, France and Germany.

[375] See A. D. White, *A History of Warfare of Science with Theology in Christendom*, Vol. I & II 1895, Canada.

justice to prevail in the international system and in our international relations.

Take the case of Israel, for instance. Firstly, it was a mistake of the British imperialists to arbitrarily allot "in Palestine a national home for the Jewish"[376] just because the Jews had been brutally slaughtered by the Germans in the Second World War, an event that has come to be known as "The holocaust". Secondly, the Arabs and the Muslims, divided and weak at the time of the formation of the Israeli state, did not have a common policy towards this question. Thirdly, the Western powers unjustly supported the Jewish state in their quarrel with the Arabs and helped Israel to become an undeclared nuclear power in West Asia. Fourthly, Israel took advantage of its military superiority to act unjustly against the Palestinians and to occupy more and more lands belonging to Palestine. Last but not least, many of the resolutions of United Nations regarding this question were never implemented due to Israeli intransigencies, knowing that the United States is behind them.

As a result of all these, this problem festered without solution for more than six decades. A major war, possibly the Third World War, may result from this long drawn-out impasse.

The Western bias in the international system, the United Nations Organization, must be quickly reformed to provide universal justice for all nations. Unless this is done soon, the U.N.O., like its predecessor the League of Nations, is doomed, and universal chaos that has reigned since the illegal US-led occupation of Iraq will inevitably lead to universal destruction and death – the so-called Apocalypse and Doomsday, in religious literature. Mankind must act to avoid and stop this senseless destruction.

******

---

[376] The Balfour Declaration of 1917.

CHAPTER 21

The Straight Path

- What is the Straight Path?
- The Post World War II Period
- The Period of Universal Chaos and Disorder
- Seeking the Straight Path

1. The straight path versus the deviating ways

The concept of the straight or right path, the middle road or the golden mean is an ancient one. It was mentioned by Aristotle (384 – 3222 B.C.) in his *The Nicomachean Ethics* , and by the Buddha (563 – 483 B.C.) in his teachings. It refers to a way or a mode of life that avoids excesses or extremes. In the Quran, it is also referred to as God's 'boundary', the *had*[377] and man is told not go beyond God's boundary in doing anything. The ancientness of the idea implies that it is a teaching from God to man in the earliest times in order to guide him to attain success and happiness in his life.

In the Quran, this idea is found in the Opening Chapter. The straight path that God blesses is differentiated from the two deviating paths that are followed by those upon whom falls God's

---

[377] See Kassim Ahmad, *Kontroversi Hukum Hudud* (2002: Penang); pp. 2-3.

wrath, because of their rebellion, and those who stray away from it without wanting to rebel.[378]

Although this path is of limited width, not unlike Jesus's narrow path mention in the Gospel,[379] yet it is a wide one, in order to provide for mankind's many differing national characteristics. The path is defined by the principles of truth, justice and compassion, whereas the deviating paths go against these principles. It applies to all departments of life: politics, economy and finance, education, the arts, philosophy, religion, science and technology, and customs and rituals.

Communities and nations of the past rose to prominence or fell to disgrace according as they conducted themselves righteously or otherwise. This law, which is in concert with nature, is natural law, religiously termed 'God's system' (Ar. *Sunnatullah*)[380] This law is immutable. It favours no one community. We have seen the rise and fall of nations of various religious denominations, including Islam.

2. The post-World War II period

In modern times, we have seen the rise and fall of the Muslim community, the rise and fall of feudal-colonial-capitalist nations, like Spain, Portugal, Dutch, France, Italy England, Germany and Japan. We have also seen the rise and fall of communist nations, like Russia and China. We have also seen the rise and fall of the United States of America. In all these cases, without fail, when they acted according to the principles of justice, truth and compassion, they rose. But when they violated these principles, they fell. Some of these nations rise again after their fall. These include Japan and China.

---

[378] See verses 6-7.
[379] See *Matt.*, 7:13-14
[380] Quran, 35:43.

As a whole, the period immediately after the Second World War, we experienced a period of universal renaissance. Colonial nations became independent: India, Indonesia, Egypt, and Malaysia, to name a few. There was economic boom. America and Russia sent man into space, and there was landing on the moon, a historic event, marking the start of man's colonization of outer space. All these took place in spite of the Cold War between the so-called Western capitalist-democratic camp, and the centrally-planned economies of the Eastern non-democratic communist camp.

3. The period of universal chaos and disorder

When the Cold War was over towards the end of the Twentieth Century, the euphoria of the so-called peace dividend soon evaporated to be replaced by the so-called War against Terrorism. A U.S-led coalition of Western nations illegally attacked and occupied Iraq. Afghanistan went into another period of war with American-led N.A.T.O forces fighting the War Against Terror. Western capitalism went into another acute crisis, with the U.S. becoming a trillion debtor- nation, with many European countries becoming bankrupt. We are into a period of universal chaos, affecting all countries, thanks to the emergence of a usurious global economy.

Who are behind this universal chaos? The same old hegemonic forces that we referred to earlier.[381] As a result, humanity is living in Chaos Universal, Mao Tse-Tung's "Great Disorder under Heaven". It has given rise of a general feeling of a universal doom, the Apocalypse, prophesied in the Bible, the "End of the World" scenario. Prophets of Doom abound even in a mainly science-and-technology-driven world.

What has gone wrong?

---

[381] See, Ch. 3, Note 81.

4. Seeking the straight path to solve the problem of world peace and security

Many things have gone wrong. Measured against the "Right Path" or the "Straight Path" of the Quran, and the "Golden Mean" of Aristotle and the Buddha that we mentioned at the beginning of this chapter, how does our global system fare? We have seen that capitalism has gone to the extremes of individual freedom. On that score, even sodomy have be practiced and legalized in some countries. Usury is practiced on a large scale, albeit under different guises. Aggressions have been justified at the highest international level, the Security Council of the United Nations. Extreme injustices have been committed by so-called democratic powers. On the pretext of national security, so-called War Against International Terrorism has been launched.

All these excesses have turned the world into a chaotic state. How can we get out of? To say that the world now lacks intelligent leaders who do not know what should be done is unimaginable. But obviously they lack the moral courage to do the right things. Do they not know the right things that they should do? Why do they not put their heads together to find the solutions? Cannot the annual General Assembly of the United Nations find the solutions? We believe the solutions have been put forward in magazines, journals and books, and in the many international discussions. The problem is for the nations of world to agree and carry them out. There is no agreement, because powerful nations seek to dominate, and fail to follow the straight path.

As we know, the United Nations General Assembly has no power, except as a moral force. Post-World War II world have been run by the so-called Great Powers consisting of United States, Britain, France, Soviet Russia and Communist China. At this time, it is the interests of the two opposing blocs – the so-called Western democratic bloc verses the Eastern communist bloc. When the

161

Cold War ended, after the collapse of communism towards the end of the last century, capitalism reigns supreme, and the world is still run by the five veto-bearing so-called Five Permanent of the U.N. Security Council.

Calls by Third World nations for democratic reforms of the U.N. Security Council have been ignored. So has been the resolution of the 6th Special Session of the U.N. General Assembly in 1974 for a New International Economic Order. It is obvious that this universal chaos will continue until the U.N. Security Council itself agrees to make democratic reforms. This is a forlorn hope. To go by precedent, only a Third World War can break this impasse, and bring the Great Powers to their senses. Can we avoid this catastrophe? When an Afro-American Barack Obama was elected 44th President of the United States 0n 25th November, 2008, on the basis of his promise for change in American policy, he was acclaimed throughout the world. That hope has since evaporated. The multiple crises of the world, economic, financial, political, environmental remained unresolved The Sword of Damocles hangs over the world.

Yet mankind cannot and must not give up. The awakened humanity, awakening step by step, slowly at first and moving faster, as the crises multiply and get more complex, until the awakened mankind gets wiser to seek and find the straight path, that is now, that the old order is replaced by a new order, that is a new just world. A new just world is about to be born!

******

CHAPTER 22

Malays, Malaysians and the Promise of a New Malacca

- The historical background of Malaysia: Malay sovereignty
- The failure of Malay leadership
- The changes brought about by 2008 General Elections
- The general breakdown of world systems
- The way forward: a Malay-Malaysian Republic

1. The historical background of Malaysia: Malay sovereignty

It was the American philosopher George Santayana who said that those who forget their history are condemned to repeat it. Malaysia is a multi-racial country that traces its origin to the Malay kingdom of Malacca in the 15th Century, after which colonialism, mostly European, intervened for 446 years. When it gained its independence from the British on 31st August, 1957, it was called the Federation of Malaya (in Malay, "Persekutuan Tanah Melayu", literally "Federation of Malay Land" (Malaya, for short), On that day one million non-Malays, mainly Chinese and Indians, were given outright citizenship. Then on 16th September, 1963 the still British colonial territories of Singapore,[382] Sabah and Sarawak joined the Federation to become Malaysia. It was the

---

[382]In Internet Wikipedia, the writer noticed a distortion of history. Singapore was a part of the Malay Johor-Riau Empire before it was ceded to the British in 1819. It was not a nondescript island. This historical fact was glossed over by the editor – a grievous mistake!

demand of the Chinese Malaysians, through their political party the People's Action Party, headed by Lee Kuan Yew , of an equal Malaysia, expressed in the slogan "Malaysian Malaysia", that undid Malaysia, throwing out Singapore in 1965, and later led to the bloody racial riots, known as the May 13th incident, in 1969.

A so-called Social Contract came to be accepted, whereby the non-Malay, non-indigenous part of the population, were given citizenship rights in return for the so-called the "Malay special privileges". These consist of the position of the Malay language as the national as well as official language, Islam as the state religion, the rights of the Malay rulers, as well as Malay rights in the economy. This last came to be packaged in the New Economic Policy that was launched by the second Prime Minister, Abdul Razak Hussein, after the May 13 riots.

However, after 30 years, the time-span given for the policy to achieve its target, it failed to do so. To put it in one sentence, it was the failure of Malay leadership.

2. The failure of Malay leadership

A wise saying was quoted in *Sejarah Melayu* "the Malay Annals" regarding bribes, i.e. the power of money to buy favour. "Oh gold! God you certainly are not, but what the heart desires, you can bring about."[383] The occasion was when one faction of Malacca ruling class, bribed the Malacca Admiral, to inform the King that his Prime Minister, Tun Perak, was working to topple him! The information was a god-sent present to the King, who had long wanted to eliminate his powerful Prime Minister.

The story of the rise and fall of Malacca is no different from the stories of the rise and fall of other nations everywhere in the world. The base animalistic Hobbesian conception of society as

---

[383] Djambatan edition (1952); p. 284.

"war of one against all" is behind the power struggles. It is based on Adam Smithian theory of the scarcity of resources. The ruling faction of the ruling class therefore seeks by fair or foul means to control and limit the distribution of resources among themselves.

This has been the failure of Malay leadership in olden Malacca as well as in modern Malaysia. Can we accuse Malay leaders of this seemingly human weakness that occurs in other countries as well? We surely can, except that in the case of Malaysia, such a thing would lead to a Malay loss of power, which in turn would lead to Malaysia losing its historical Malay-based character. The kicking out of Singapore from Malaysia in 1963, although Singapore, being part of Johor, rightfully belongs to Malaysia, was a portend that led to the ugly May 13th incident we have already referred to above.

Is it a foregone conclusion that Malay leadership will fail in Malaysia? Can the conservative traditional Islamic ideology of PAS, (Malaysia's Islamic party) allied to Machiavellian PKR (Anwar Ibrahim-led People's Justice Party) and to Chinese-dominated DAP (Democratic Action Party) save Malay leadership? I do not think so. However, I am convinced that the true Islamic political philosophy, based on a scientifically-correct understanding of Quranic teachings, can overcome this problem.

Political leadership in Malaysia, guided by the teachings of the Quran, can raise itself above the Hobbesian animalism by raising its psychological-moral level from the animalistic to the humanistic level, and even above that.[384] The examples of the great prophets, especially Muhammad, whose leadership qualities history has thrown up for our study, can be emulated. This can resolve the question of power-struggles arising out of animalism.

---

[384] See Ch. 12, Note 239. See also Quran, 12:53; 75:2, and 89:27-30.

As for the Adam Smithian theory of scarcity of resources, human socio-economic history has not proved it. Modern science and technology are capable of economic production almost without limit. Once society feels itself morally bound to support its weaker members, unemployment and poverty will automatically disappear. An ethically-based society can easily re-order its distribution, giving enough to the lowest strata and not too much to the highest, so that the difference between the highest and the lowest income brackets is reduced to the minimum.

This is not to say that we do not believe in a non-racially based political system in Malaysia. We are only looking at realities, formed by historical circumstance, as we orderly move towards the objective of an equal Malaysia. Given good leadership and right policies, we shall achieve this objective in three generations.

3. The changes brought about by the 2008 general election

The UMNO-led (UMNO=United Malays National Organization) coalition, in its 52 years of government, has not experienced such a loss of power, as in this national election. It was unprecedented. Both coalitions did not fully expect the results. One can say, a wind of change has blown over the political landscape of Malaysia. Many Malaysians welcome it as the beginning of a two-party system. The euphoria it produced can be seen in the subsequent winnings of the by-elections by the Opposition. But can this development resolve our dilemma? Firstly, it is claimed that ethnically-based political parties are something of the past. It is true? Are our problems all traceable to "racialist" politics? Secondly, with this development, can we resolve the so-called "Malay problem", including the vexed question of Ketuanan Melayu or, to put it differently, a Malay-led nation-state of Malaysia?

Two facts are often forgotten or glossed over by our non-Malay Malaysian citizens. Firstly, Malaya, now, Malaysia, is part of a wider Malay world that includes Indonesia. Secondly, the Malay world is also part of the wider Islamic world. Therefore, any man coming from these parts, be he a Javanese, or a Pakistani, or an Arab, marrying into a Malay family, gets easily assimilated into Malay culture and regarded as a Malay.

Facts prove that we cannot resolve the "Malay problem" or the ethnic problem by forming so-called non-racial parties. When Onn Ja'afar, first president of UMNO, in 1956, wanted to open the UMNO door to non-Malays, his proposal was rejected by the Malays, and he was replaced by Tungku Abdul Rahman. The PAP (People's Action Party) of Lee Kuan Yew, now succeeded by the DAP of Lim Kit Siang and son Lim Guan Eng , had Malay and Indian members, but it cannot be said that it is free from the Chinese character of the majority of its members. We all agree that it is a Malaysian Malaysia that we aim for, but the basic character of this nation, whether it is Chinese, Indian or Malay must be defined. Until this national question is correctly understood and resolved, there would not and cannot be a Malaysian nation. The early progressive PUTERA-AMCJA coalition understood this national question, but they were suppressed and eliminated by the British colonialists.[385]

4. The general breakdown of worlds systems

It seems obvious that for the last five decades, the Western system of democratic government (Government/Opposition two-party or multi-party system) and the Eastern system of autocratic government cannot endure into the 21st Century. All systems have collapsed. I would say that a more just politico-economic world system is emerging. The monopoly of nuclear bombs by the West is not just or fair; yet non-proliferation of the technology is

---

[385] See Ahmad Boestamam, Carving the Path to the Summit, (1979: New York); pp. 97-111. This book is translated with an Introduction by William R. Roff from the Malay original, Merintis Jalan ke Punchak (Kuala Lumpur: 1972)

not the answer. Israel and Western security, it is claimed, are at stake. These reasonable concerns are surely not solved by the West lording over the world. A more logical and fair solution must be found. In fact, the current systemic financial-monetary breakdown is forcing the world community to seek a more equitable system.

5. A Malay-based Malaysian republic

It is equally obvious that any form of racialism or chauvinism is not the answer to the problems that Malaysia faces, be they economic, political, social, intellectual and cultural. Our multi-racial nation must be based on unity of purpose out of the diversity of languages, religions and cultures. It must be a government based on justice, conducted through a system of national consultation, led by a competent Malay-based national leadership for some time to come.

A Malaysian nation-state naturally must have its own national characteristics, yet these characteristics must not be a burden to the nation. The feudal system of the Malay rulers is a relic of the past, yet it defines a Malaysian characteristic. Can a non-Malay and a non-Muslim be the King or the President of a future Malaysian Republic? Can a non-Malay or a non-Muslim be the Prime Minister? Must there be a two-system of laws, the secular and the *Shari'ah* (Islamic law)? These are questions that must be resolved within the next few years, or a decade or two, at the most.

As I said above, Islam, as a natural religion, has a big, if indirect , role to play. It can not only unite through its universalism, but also promote a rationalist, scientific and revolutionary attitude in the Malaysian community. A study in depth of the teachings of the Quran would reveal that God's plan is for the universe to fully serve the purposes of man, hence humanism, and that Afterlife means life in this world, hence secularism is natural, and the Paradise and Hell are natural consequences of our own activity. It is up to our thinkers and leaders to reach this understanding and bring this way of life to our future society, consonant with the "Straight Path" recommended to us by God, the power that creates, fashions, guides and develops the universe.

*****

CHAPTER 23

A Life of Success and Happiness

- Definition of success and happiness,
- Following the Straight Path,
- The scientific methodology,
- Demythologization and secularism,
- Death and Life

1. Definition of success and happiness

One often hears that life is short; therefore, one should make the best of it. Definitely, in the sense of an individual's life, life is short. In the sense of species life, the life of the human family, it is very, very long, almost eternal. Therefore, whether for the individual or the species, it is very important for us to live life to the fullest and to know how to live a happy and successful life.

Success and happiness are defined differently by different types of people. According to the Quran, there are three types of people: the believers, the disbelievers, and the hypocrites. The believers are those who believe in the existence of the Truth and uphold it in their lives. The disbelievers are the opposite of the first: they openly oppose the Truth, and uphold and practice evil and falsehood. The third category is the people in between: they claim that they believe in the Truth, but in actual fact they do not. They practice evil and spread falsehood, as the disbelievers do.

To the first category, success and happiness are defined as essentially in non-materialistic, but moral and spiritual terms. Their values are moral and spiritual values, without denying the importance of material values. Thus, to them having more money, wealth and power is less important than having good moral and spiritual qualities of truth, justice and compassion. They do not reject money, wealth and power, but these are strictly only for the upholding of the cause of truth, justice and compassion. To the second and third categories, it is the opposite. They seek money, wealth and power in order to oppose the truth and spread evil in the world. As I have said earlier, the first category forms the humanist faction, and fights the oligarchical faction, made of the second and third categories, throughout human history, to establish their visions of human society.[386] The humanist faction fights to establish a society that is just, truthful and compassionate, while the oligarchical faction fights to establish an empire of slavery with them lording over it.

True success and happiness lie with the first category, the humanist faction. Their struggle and endeavour lead to the establishment of, in religious terminology, Paradise or, in secular terminology, a just World Society. The struggle of oligarchical faction only leads to chaos and destruction (poverty, starvation, diseases, so-called natural disasters, and wars), or, in religious terminology, Hell.

2. The straight path

Islam directs us to follow the straight path. The word 'Islam' here does not refer to the religious institution. It refers to the religion of God or the true religion, as taught in the Quran,[387] and that has been practiced by God's prophet-messengers or the humanist faction, throughout history. The 20th Century has exposed the

---

[386] See, Ch. 3, Note 81.
[387] See, Ch. 5, Note 69.

failures of the Capitalism, Communism and Theocracy. These have deviated from the straight path of Islam, or the Golden Mean of the Greek philosophers, and of Buddhism,[388] resulting in chaos and destruction in human society. It is our task now to seek this straight path.

A human being is made up of physical, emotional, mental and spiritual parts. In order to be happy, he or she must satisfy his or her needs in these departments. We know what the physical needs are. Emotionally he or she needs to be loved, respected and appreciated by the society. When the time comes, he or she needs to marry. As the Quran puts it, in his or her spouse, each finds tranquility, contentment and love.[389] Mentally, he needs to develop his mind through education, through reading, and through appreciation of beauty in its various forms. Spiritually, he needs to find peace and contentment with himself, his environment and his deepest soul needs. By this last, I mean a belief in some invisible power that is behind the universe – a religion, or a non-religion, as the case may be.

These four parts of a man are not separate. They are closely linked by his selfhood. The Quran defines a man as a self (Ar. *nafs*).

Thus, a human being can only achieve true happiness if he caters to all these needs. If he or she neglects any of these needs, he or she cannot achieve true happiness. Can an ascetic who neglects his physical needs achieve true happiness? No, he cannot. That is why the Quran is critical towards ascetism of mysticism.[390] Can an atheist who denies his spiritual need (by denying faith) achieve true happiness? No, he cannot. Again, that is why the Quran does

---

[388] See, Ch. 21.
[389] Quran, 30:21.
[390] See, Ch. 19, Note 356.

not support a life given to worldly concerns alone to the detriment of the greater spiritual needs.[391]

3. The development of civilization

However, all these needs have to be collectively sought. Man is said to be a gregarious animal. He lives in a society. These needs have not only to be sought; they have to be maintained and developed from generation to generation. Thus man creates civilization. This civilization has to develop and progress. There have been many civilizations in the past: Mesopotamian, Babylonian, Egyptian, Greco-Roman, Persian, Indian, Chinese, Arab, Southeast-Asian, Japanese, South American, African, Malay, European, Russian, and modern. We are now creating a global civilization. What lies in the future, we do not know.

This human development and progress is an ongoing process, and never ends. Death comes to an individual, or even to a civilization, but not to the human species. The human species will go on and on, for a very long time to come, almost for eternity, until the universe itself perished, and God Alone remains.[392]

4. Demythologization and secularism

As we have seen, myths were a part of human life. As we gather more scientific knowledge of ourselves and the world, these myths disappear, little by little, until they are no more myths. Is it a surprise that at the beginning of the 21st Century, when science and technology form a great part of our lives, we still hold to many long-held myths? To be more accurate, I should mention that a great part of humanity still lives in rural areas, where the science and technology has not yet penetrated. The European Enlightenment of the 17th and 18th centuries that gave priority to

---

[391] Quran, 28:77.
[392] See, Ch. 8, Note 189.

reason, however, went into excesses, and produced a counter-movement of Romanticism that down-played science and technology. This proved that the West proceeds by trial and error: it has possesses no basic guide.

From the beginning, the Muslim Community has its infallible Book of guidance, i.e. the Quran. However, they lost this Book of guidance about 300 years after Prophet Muhammad's death, as I have said.[393] So they lost out to Europe during the European Renaissance from the 14th to the 16th centuries. This produced what we call the modern Western civilization that has engulfed the whole world.

As I have mentioned, this world is the only world;[394] there is no mysterious world as the Hereafter. The Hereafter does exist, of course; it is the changed world that comes after, that we create and bequeath to later generations. It gets better and better, as we progress. Therefore, secularism, that has become a bane with religious-minded scholars, is wholly lawful, even in the eyes of God.[395] Why should God, Who created this world, hate it? One should distinguish between an obsession with the material side of life, which is bad, from a realistic recognition of it, which is right and lawful. A willful neglect of the lawful concerns of this world in favour of a so-called mysterious Hereafter would only condemn the human community to stagnation and even regression. An obsession with the material side of this world only brings chaos and destruction, as I have said.[396]

---

[393] See, Ch. 16.
[394] Quran, 7:25
[395] Quran, 2:201.
[396] See, Ch. 21.

5. Death and life

We should make the best of our short individual life, because it is our short individual lives that go to make our very, very long species life meaningful. We must make sure that our children and grand-children, in short, our posterity, inherit a progressively better world from us. It is also because, life being one[397], we are present in all the generations after we came into the world. Before we were born and came alive, we were potential in the earth. We were dead, so to speak. After having come into the world and live out our individual lives, we die again, and then we come alive again, to return finally to our Maker.[398]

Death and life is one. The first death is a state when we are not alive yet. We were potential in the earth. Then we came alive into this world and live out our short individual lives. Then we died. Then we come alive again, the second life, coming out of the grave, metaphorically-speaking.[399] This second life is a very long one, living either in Paradise, or in Hell.

Thus, we should not waste our life here, but the Hereafter, being the further development of life here (depending on the good works of earlier generations), is more important.[400] In this interpretation, the Hereafter already exists now. But the Hereafter that the Quran envisions includes outer space.[401] The Paradise that the human community is going to create in the future is far vaster and far better than the present world. This follows logically from the present rapid and incredulous development of science and

---

[397] Quran, 4:1.
[398] Quran, 2:28.
[399] Quran, 70:43.
[400] Quran, 28:77.
[401] Quran, 57:21.

technology. What lies in the future for humanity is incredibly beautiful, as the Quran informs us.[402]

*****

---

[402] Quran, 32:17.

CHAPTER 24

The Scientific Method

- What is the scientific method?
- The cultural mould,
- A life of total liberation from servitude,
- In this world, and no other,
- Realizing the manifestation of the God-Man.

1. What is the scientific method?

The Pakistani poet-philosopher, Muhammad Iqbal, made an insightful and true remark about Muhammad. In his *The Reconstruction of Religious Thought in Islam*, he said:

> "... the Prophet of Islam seems to stand between the ancient and the modern world. In so far as the source of his revelation is concerned, he belongs to the ancient world; in so far as the spirit of his revelation is concerned, he belongs to the modern world. In him life discovers other sources of knowledge suitable to its new direction. The birth of Islam ... is the birth of the inductive intellect. In Islam prophecy reaches its perfection in discovering the need of its own abolition. This involves the keen perception that life cannot forever be kept in leading strings; that in order to achieve full self-consciousness man must finally be thrown back on his own resources."[403]

---

[403] See p. 126. Please also See, Ch. 5, Note 117.

According to Paul Davies:

> "In primitive cultures, understanding of the world was limited to everyday affairs, such as the passage of the seasons, or the motion of a slingshot or an arrow. It was entirely pragmatic, and had no theoretical basis, except in magical terms. Today, in the age of science, our understanding has vastly expanded, so that we need to divide knowledge into distinct subjects – astronomy, physics, chemistry, geology, psychology, and so on. This dramatic progress has come about almost as a result of 'scientific method': experiment, observation, deduction, hypothesis, falsification. The details need not concern us here. What is important is the science demands rigorous standards of procedure and discussion that set reason over irrational belief."[404]

To fully understand the scientific method, its birth and its immense contribution to knowledge, we must quote the British philosopher, Robert Briffault, from his epoch-making book, *The Making of Humanity*, published in 1919:

> "It was under their successors at the Oxford school that Roger Bacon learned Arabic and Arabic science. Neither Roger Bacon nor his later namesake has any title to be credited with having introduced the experimental method. Roger Bacon was no more than one of the apostles of Muslim science and method to Christian Europe; and he never wearied of declaring that knowledge of Arabic and Arabic science was for his contemporaries the only way to true knowledge. Discussions as to who was the originator of the experimental method ... are part of the colossal misrepresentation of the origins of European civilization.

---

[404] *The Mind of God – the Scientific Basis for a Rational World* (1992); pp. 22-23.

The experimental method of the Arabs was by Bacon's time widespread and eagerly cultivated throughout Europe."[405]

He further says, "For although there is no a single aspect of European growth in which the decisive influence of Islamic culture is not traceable, nowhere is it so clear and momentous as in the genesis of that power which constitutes the permanent distinctive force of the modern world, and the supreme source of its victory – natural science and the scientific spirit."[406]

2. The cultural mould

The religion of Islam is also designated in the Quran as the true religion[407] or God's religion[408]. Yet, by the 13th Century, it had deviated so much from its original self that it was no longer fit to lead the world. As we all know, the torch of civilization was wrested by a re-awakened Europe. Why has this happened to Islam? To answer this question, we have to understand the nature of the old Arab society. It was a society full of superstitious beliefs.[409] On the other hand, as philosopher Iqbal, whom I quoted at the beginning of this chapter, rightly said, Muhammad stands mid-way between the old and the modern world. The old world was pre-scientific; the new scientific. This is symbolized by the first revelation that he received from God: the order "to read in the name of your Lord, who created."[410] The Quran appeals to

---

[405] See pp. 200-201.

[406] *Ibid.*, p. 109.

[407] Quran, 9:33; 48:28 and 61:9.

[408] Quran, 110:2.

[409] Read the lengthy reply made by the leader of the nascent Muslim community sent by Prophet Muhammad to Abyssinia, Ja'far bin Abu Talib, when questioned by the Christian King about their new religion. (See *The Life of Muhammad* – a translation of Ishaq's *Sirat Rasul Allah*, trans. by A. Guillaume); pp.150-51).

[410] Quran, 96:1-5.

reason.[411] This is the most difficult thing for the old culture to accept. While Muhammad was leading them, coupled with the fire that the Quran kindled in them, the reactionary features of the old culture were overcome, but not altogether eliminated. Rather, they remained in abeyance.

No sooner was Muhammad gone from their midst, deterioration began to set in. Civil wars broke out between the followers of Uthman ibni Affan, the third Caliph, and the followers of Ali. In 661 A.D., barely 30 years after the Prophet's death, autocratic feudal rule, in place of the republican democratic rule that Muhammad introduced, was instituted by Mu'awiyah!

3. Islam propagates total liberation from servitude

This is not what Islamic politics desired. Islam propagates governance based on justice through consultation and through the choice of qualified leaders, qualified meaning both professionally as well as morally. It rejects Machiavellianism in the social system. It rejects extremes, choosing what the Quran calls the "Straight Path"[412]

Islam does not also fully support the Western type of check-and-balance democracy, with two or more parties. In Britain and the United States the two major parties are not very much different in their treatment of countries under colonialism or imperialism. Philosophically, it is wrong to arbitrarily divide the country into two (the Government and the Opposition), just as it is illogical to deny the use of our two hands at any one time when we have two! Criticism and correction can come from within the party or coalition of parties in power, the government and society through freedom of expression as well as through consultation. It may be true to say that no Muslim country has yet been able to devise and

---

[411] Quran, 10:100.
[412] See, Ch. 21.

institute such a system. Yet, it cannot be said that the system is impractical, for in a family, that is what happens. The nation-state is just a big family.

Islam has come to bestow on the human being the role and mission of God's *khalifa* on Earth.[413] He is a new creation of God, separate from previous creation.[414] He is to re-make the world, indeed, the whole universe, in accordance with his desire, and, of course, in accordance with the Laws of God (Ar. *sunnatullah*). This is the awesome meaning of the symbolism of man's accepting God's tremendous offer of rulership over the universe, while no one else in the whole created order dares to do so. This symbolism is again shown in the divine order to the angles to prostrate before Adam.[415]

Human history has displayed acts so cruel, hideous and stupid, like the First and Second World Wars that could have wiped out civilization from the face of the earth. The fact that they have not does not guarantee that it will not happen in the future. However, the teachings of the Quran justify our optimism about the future of mankind, for the Quran visualized men living in outer space,[416] and ascending higher and higher in the ladder of evolution.

4. In this world, and in no other

As we have seen, myths and superstitions enter into religion, including the religion of Islam, the final scripture of which, the Noble Quran, is pro-reason and pro-science.[417] Since our understanding of the universe is still minimal, our understanding

---

[413] Quran, 2:30-34.

[414] Quran, 23:12-14.

[415] Quran, 2:34.

[416] Quran, 3:132; 57:21, where Paradise is referred to as extensive as the heavens, implying that men will colonize outer space in the future.

[417] Quran, 10:100. Again the symbolism about man's ability to know the world (2:31) indicates his future limitless scientific and technological advance.

of such Quranic concepts of Afterlife and Heaven and Hell is unclear and shrouded in mystery. Is it in this world or in some other world totally different from this world? Quranic language is replete with metaphors and allegories and our understanding of it is far from sufficient. However, a close study of these matters would lead us to the conclusion that Afterlife or the Hereafter is no more than a continuation of our life in this world. We must understand that this earth is part of the larger world that is the universe that must logically be a unity of multiple parts and a highly complex whole, since it is the creation of the One and Only True Power, that we call God. As believers, our mission is to create a Paradise on this earth that automatically includes other parts of the universe. Note that God describes Paradise to be as extensive as the entire universe.[418]

5. The manifestation of God-Man

Remember that the entire created order cringed from the divine offer to rule the world, with the exception of Man,[419] the *Homo sapiens*, that God distinguished as a new creation,[420] separate from the others, including the angels, whatever the word 'angel' means. Remember also that God taught Adam the knowledge of all things, and for this God ordered all the angels to prostrate to Adam. Thus knowledge would make Adam, that is, mankind, God-like. This is the profound meaning of the symbolism of the angelic prostration to Adam. Man can become God with the power of construction and destruction.

In a million years of man's history on the earth, we have seen this power displayed alternately. It is amazing that the destructive instincts of man have not wiped him out of existence. We refer especially to all the wars in the Twentieth Century which

---

[418] Quran, 3:132.
[419] See, Ch. 4, Note 93.
[420] Quran, 23:12-14.

historians describe as the bloodiest century. We may, therefore, infer that man is destined for greater glory.

We should not forget that in that metaphor, one of the angels refused to obey the divine order to prostrate to Adam, and automatically became the Devil. The disobedience is to symbolize the freedom in the world of men to disobey God, which is the source of evil. It is not God that is the source of evil in the world. It is men's disobedience to God that results in evil. The implication is that man can eliminate evil from his life if he completely obeys God. Does this mean that in the end there will be no Hell to burn the disbelievers? Yes, it does.[421] What then happens to freedom? If there is no freedom, you become robots. No, at that time, men freely choose to be good. Man has not only become God-like with power of construction and destruction; he has also become God-like in that he is goodness itself, as God is. Thus man is the crown of creation. The universe achieves its highest point when man becomes God, marking the point when men unite with God.

******

---

[421] Quran, 11:106-07. It is logical and rational to think of Hell as temporary.

CHAPTER 25

Demythologization and Secularism

- The role of myths in human life: from darkness to light
- Demythologization and secularization
- The role of science and truth.

1. The role of myths in human life: from darkness to light

The Quran informs us that God's religion, Islam, is to bring men out of darkness into light.[422] Thus, we were and are in darkness until His messengers came to us to bring us out of darkness into light.

Myths are a great part of the darkness. Myth has existed in every society. Indeed, it seems a basic constituent of human culture. For instance, the ancient Greeks had their myths of Olympian gods, with Zeus as their head. Also the myth of Prometheus, who stole fire from Zeus to give to men, and was chained as punishment. The Malays had their myths of their origins in Mt. Siguntang in Palembang in southern Sumatera; the Chinese their dragon myth, and the Indians their sacred cow myth. Sociologists and anthropologists who studied religions have related these myths in both non-literate and literate societies.[423] But, as light from God shines, these myths get cleared from our life. This process is called

---

[422] Quran, 14:1.
[423] See, for instance Sir James Frazer, *The Golden Bough* (1890), and Christopher Dewdney, *Acquainted with the Night* (2004).

the demythologization. It is accompanied by the process of secularization. It is a modern phenomenon. In particularly, it is associated with two Christian theologians, Rudolf Bultmann (1884-1976) and Karl Rahner (1904-1984). In the strict sense of the word, demythologization efforts have been limited to theological discussions in 20th century Christianity.

2. Demythologization and secularization

As we pointed out in a previous chapter, there is only one world, although of many levels.[424] There is no other world. The Quran uses the phrase "Lord of the Worlds, to refer to the whole unspeakably vast universe. It also refers to the many levels of this one unified world: the material, the emotional, the mental, the moral and the spiritual, as well as the various psychological states of man. Thus secularization of life takes place, as the myths gradually disappear (i.e. demythologization). Therefore demythologization and secularization go hand in hand and constitute an ongoing process.

However, there is not one type of secularization only. So far, the Western type, almost undistinguishable from modernization and Westernization, has been *amoral*, even *immoral*, inspired by Machiavelli's book, *The Prince* (1513). Secularization has been resisted by modern Muslim societies everywhere, except in Mustafa Kamal Atatürk's Turkey. In point of fact, Islam allows a certain type of secularization – the separation of rituals of religion from state policy, the former given autonomy to the particular religious group.[425]

---

[424] See, Ch. 2, pp. 1-2.

[425] See Kassim Ahmad's essay, "A Short Note on the Medina Charter" (2003), published at http://www.stormloader.com/qsmjam, the website of Quran Society of Malaysia. This separation is in line with verse 67 of Surah 22 of the Quran.

3. The role of science and truth

As science and truth advance, the processes of demythologization and secularization of life are going to move faster and faster, as they are necessary to the survival of the human species. Consequently, modernization of Muslim societies, which has been moving at a snail's pace, if not altogether resisted by their conservative clerical classes before now, will be quickened and completed in one or two generations.

I should speak about the advancement of truth, too, apart from that of science. In modern science, which began with the Arab-Islamic Renaissance (7th to 13th centuries) – a fact a large segment of Western scholarship seeks to erase from history[426] --, we can easily recognize the clear landmarks, Isaac Newton (1642-1727) with his introduction of scientific laws of mechanistic physics, Nicolaus Copernicus (1473-1543) with his revolutionary conception of the heliocentric universe, and Albert Einstein (1879-1955) with his General Theory of Relativity (1915), which revolutionized scientific thought by denying the existence of any absolute time. This is just to mention three names, among many, who contributed to the advancement of modern science.

As far as truth goes, it cannot be as easily shown. Truth is abstract. It is a conception of the mind. What is truth? We can say that truth is the congruence of thought or a statement to facts. Thus, we can say that "You are reading a book on Einstein." We can go on to say, "You can know the truth of the concept of relativity from reading that book." These two statements are *true* because they cohere with the facts.

Let us take some other statements that are more difficult to show or prove their truth:

---

[426] See Robert Briffault, *The Making of Humanity*, (1919); p. 189.

Do they not see that We bring them closer to the end with every passing day on earth.[427]

God has decreed that, "I shall win, I and My messengers."[428]

The difficulty lies in the fact there are two points of view, each with plausible arguments. The believers, the true upholders of the truth, take the side of God, and their arguments are the more convincing, because the course of history vindicates them. But, of course, the disbelievers, the true falsifiers, will not admit the weakness of their case, as they are not beholden to the truth.

Yet, sooner or later, truth will prevail, as the Quran states.[429] There will come a time when life will completely be divested of myths, and true knowledge, science and truth will prevail. Light will replace darkness, and God's purpose in creation will be realized.[430]

*****

---

[427] Quran, 13:41.
[428] Quran, 8:21.
[429] Quran, 17:81.
[430] Quran, 21:16-18.

CHAPTER 26

The "Second Coming"

- The myth of the Second Coming,
- Pauline Christianity,
- Living in comfort zone,
- The burden of freedom.

1. What is the "Second Coming"?

Most people need a crutch, being unable to stand on their own. So do nations. The belief that the dead Jesus Christ (c. 6 B.C.– c. 30 A.D.), a great prophet of God, (Peace be upon him) will come back again to save the world from the Anti-Christ and to rule the world in justice and peace is nothing more than a myth that mankind creates from time to time to console themselves! It was Paul (c. 4 A.D. – c.64 A.D.), originally a persecutor of the early Christians, who, after his conversion, became the major influence in promoting Christianity. It was also Paul (who incidentally never met Jesus) who was responsible for erecting Christian theology: the belief that Jesus was divine, that only through Christ can a man be saved, that he was resurrected bodily after death, to come down again at "the end of time" to establish God's Kingdom on earth. It is this belief in Jesus coming down again to establish God's Kingdom that is known as the Second Coming. The belief is so pervasive that even the famous Irish poet, William Butler Yeats (1865–1939), wrote an equally famous poem of that title.

2. Pauline Christianity

That Jesus is divine is Pauline Christianity. The Quran informs us that Jesus never said that he was divine. "God will say, 'O Jesus, son of Mary, did you say to the people, 'Make me and my mother idols besides God?' He will say, 'Be You glorified. I could not utter what was not right. Had I said it, You already would have known it. You know my thoughts, and I do not know your thoughts.... I told them only what you commanded me to say, that "You shall worship God, my Lord and your Lord." I was a witness among them for as long as I lived with them. When you terminated my life, You become the Watcher over them. ...'"[431] That was precisely what happened. The early Christians were monotheists. A Christian leader from Alexandria, Arius (250/256 A.D. – 336 A.D.) , led this monotheistic movement to spread the teachings of Jesus that was the legacy of Abraham. However, he was opposed by the Trinitarian Athanasius. At the time of the defining Council of Nicaea in 325 A.D, presided over by the Roman Emperor Constantine (who incidentally was still a pagan at that time), the doctrine of the Trinity was decided upon by the Church.[432] There were then around 300 versions of the Gospels, Only four were chosen as official: the Gospels of Mark, Matthew, Luke and John. The others were destroyed. However, the Gospel of Barnabas survived the destruction.[433]

---

[431] Quran, 5:116-117.

[432] In spite of this official, false and foreign doctrine of the Trinity, both the Old and the New Testaments contained clear statements on the necessity of belief in the One True God only, as in the Quran. See Deut., 6:4-5; Mark, 12:29-30.

[433] See Muhammad 'Ata ur-Rahman, *Jesus – the Prophet of Islam*, (Johor, Malaysia: 1978); Ch. 3. See also *The Gospel of Barnabas*, edited and translated from the Italian MS in the Imperial Library at Vienna by Lonsdale and Laura Ragg, (Oxford:1907); pp. x-xvii.

Christian apologists stretched logic to prove the divinity of Christ. The argument goes thus: even disbelievers in the divinity of Christ admit that he was a good man and not a liar; Jesus stated that he was divine; therefore he was divine! Any intelligent and fair person can see that the second proposition in the syllogism is questionable. None of the four canonical gospels were written by Christ. They were written many years after Jesus' death. It is mostly the work of Paul, who was desirous to present Christianity acceptable to the pagans in the Roman Empire. Remember that the Emperor Constantine who presided over the fatal Nicene Council in 325 A.D. was a still a pagan before he converted to Christianity.

3. Living in comfort zone

As I said earlier, this doctrine of the Second Coming is mankind's rationalization of its inability to establish a just society through perpetual struggle "to enjoin good and forbid evil", as the Quran pithily puts it. It is to avoid or postpone this struggle, and to wait rather for the coming of a special figure who would do it for them. At this time of the advent of Christ, there was a widespread expectation of the coming of such a messianic figure to establish a Just World. That this is a myth is proved by many facts, one of which is that past predictions of his coming have proved false. Likewise, predicting a date in the future from now (2010 A.D.) will be equally false.

Even Muslims, who should know better (because on the authority of the Quran, no man lives forever), believe in this doctrine. It is based on *hadiths* that predict the second coming of Jesus Christ. Obviously, such *hadiths* originate from this Pauline Christian teaching. Although the Quran is quite clear about the death of Jesus,[434] based on traditional methodology that the *Hadith* interprets the Quran, traditional theology makes the verse to

---

[434] Quran, 3:55; 5:117; 21:35.

mean God's taking Jesus up to Heaven to come down against at the Second Coming!

In Indonesian folklore, there is the figure of *Ratu Adil* or the Just King who will perform the role similar to that of Jesus at the Second Coming.

In troubled times, such myths thrive to satisfy man's psyche. Jesus' time was a troubled time. Ours too, after the two World Wars; hence the Yeats' poem, "The Second Coming" :

> *Things fall apart; the centre cannot hold;*
> *Mere anarchy is loosed upon the world*
> ....
> *Surely some revelation is at hand;*
> *Surely the Second Coming is at hand.*

I said that the doctrine belongs to Pauline Christianity. It does not belong to the true Christianity, as Jesus Christ, a great prophet of God, preached. This is not only clearly stated in the Quran. It is proved by the Gospel of Barnabas as well as by the teachings of the early Christian monotheist theologian Arius and the existence of other Unitarians at that time.

4. The burden of freedom

Man is made to be a vicegerent of God. That means he is a King who decides his own fate. He can remake the world, and in fact, the whole universe. Of course, he does this in consonance with God's will. He must struggle in God's cause, i.e. to establish good and destroy evil.[435]

There is a beautiful allegory in the Quran when God offered the whole creation the trust of responsibility to rule the universe. All the created orders, except man, refused to accept the trust, fearing

---

[435] Quran, 9:111.

that they may not be able to carry it out faithfully. Man's daring to accept the trust was mildly rebuked and mocked by God.[436] Sure enough man almost failed with the long trail of blood he leaves behind him, the two bloody World Wars being his worst failures. Of course, he could have avoided those misdeeds that he has committed, had he followed God's commandments fully, or even to a passable extent. Yet there is a bright side to man's dismal history. He has created a world civilization built upon a spiritual, yet humanistic and scientific world outlook, giving rise to a humanistic culture and modern science and technology. This combination will not only free man from old and new form of hegemony to build the Just Society, but will also take him live in outer space.

As another equally beautiful Quranic allegory has it, the angels vehemently objected when God told them that He wanted to create a *khalifa* to rule the world.[437] The objection of the angels is based on their knowledge of the behavior of beasts, from whom the humans emerge. God's answer implies His optimism about man.[438]

We can already see the outlines of the coming Just World, the result of centuries of struggles for freedom and justice by the humanist faction, symbolized by the myth of Jesus' Second Coming, in the awakened humanity everywhere today demanding justice and freedom for all mankind. The toppling of the cruel systems of Communism, free-market Capitalism, and religious Theocracy signaled the coming of that Just World that has been the dream of humanity since the dawn of history.

*****

---

[436] Quran, 33:72.
[437] Quran, 2:30.
[438] Quran, 2:30.

CHAPTER 27

Judeo-Christian Plot against Islam

- What is the Judeo-Christian plot against Islam?
- The root cause of the plot,
- The West's control of the United Nations,
- The setting up of the State of Israel in Palestine, and the ideological dead-end,
- The collapsing of Western-based ideological systems,
- The future lies in the world following the Straight Path.

1. What is the Judeo-Christian plot against Islam?

The Quran warns the Muslims of the Judeo-Christian plot against Islam early in its career under the last Prophet Muhammad. "Neither the Jews, nor the Christians, will accept you, unless you follow their religion. Say, 'God's guidance is the true guidance.' If you acquiesce to their wishes despite the knowledge you have received you will find no ally or supporter to help you against God."[439] At the same time, the Quran also states that those who call themselves Christians are nearest to the believers.[440] This is historically proved by the Christian King of Abyssinia, Negus, who treated Prophet Muhammad's fugitives with great honour

---

[439] Quran, 2:120.
[440] Quran, 5:82.

and respect.[441] In modern times, the Vatican has initiated inter-religious dialogues with Muslims and followers of other religions. The Second Vatican Council (1962-1965), in one of its documents, states "The Church has a high regard for Muslims ..." In another, it states, "The plan of salvation also includes those who acknowledge the Creator, among whom are in the first place, the Muslims. These profess to hold the faith of Abraham, and together with us they adore the one merciful God, judge of humankind on the Last Day."[442] Unfortunately these fine sentiments have not percolated down to Christian society at large, nor up to the U.N. Security Council.

The Jews, however, gave him great trouble. They not only refused to acknowledge his prophethood, in spite of prophesies of Muhammad's advent in the Old Testament.[443] They intrigued, conspired and fought against him. This is well documented in the Quran and in the early historical writings.[444] In the case of the Jewish tribe of Quraizah, their great crimes of reneging on their peace agreement with the Prophet and conspiring with the Quraysh enemy to exterminate the nascent Muslim community were punished with death (about 700), by the judgement one of their own leaders.[445] The term 'massacre' used by detractors of the Prophet, even by such a fair writer as Karen Armstrong, was hardly appropriate! It is like judging a punishment as unfair while completely ignoring the enormity of the crime![446]

---

[441] See, Ch. 24, Note 409.

[442] See *Recognize the Spiritual Bonds that Unite Us:16 Years of Christian-Muslim Dialogue* (1994: Vatican City); pp.5-7.

[443] See, Ch. 15, Note 279.

[444] Quran, Surah *Al-Azab* (33) and Surah *Al-Hashar* (59) and Martin Lings, *Muhammad: his life based on the earliest sources*, (1983); pp.220-233.

[445] Martin Lings, *Ibid*.

[446] Karen Armstrong, Muhammad: A Biography of the Prophet (1992); pp. 206-210.

The Quraizah case was an equivalent punishment for a clear act of aggression against the early Muslims. How does this so-called massacre compare with the unnecessary mass killings in the carpet bombing of Dresden by allied forces in February, 1945, the atomic bombing Hiroshima and Nagasaki by American President Truman in August, 1945, and the illegal invasion and occupation of Iraq by American and British forces in 2003? Is it not part of the Judeo-Christian West's continuing plot against Islam? Recall also that American President George W. Bush characterize the so-called War Against Terrorism as a crusade.

2. The root cause of Judeo-Christian West's hatred against Islam

History informs us that the Jews are a closely-knit group around their synagogue. They believe themselves to be the "Chosen People" of God. It is on this basis, jealousy, that they rejected Muhammad when he appeared. They could not accept the fact that the Arabs also could receive divine revelations. Although the Christians do not claim to be the "Chosen People" of God, they too rejected Muhammad for the same reason.

The Pauline Christians, especially post-Nicene, (note not the early Christians) turned Jesus into a deity and a member of a Trinity, "The begotten Son of God", through whom only can anyone obtain salvation. Thus both the Jews and the Christians doctrinally closed their door to Muhammad, who was the last prophet of God to the whole of mankind, and thereby closed their door to religious toleration and true humanist universalism.

Although the revolt against this perversion came in the European Religious Reformation of the 16th century, the Christian misrepresentation of Islam and Prophet Muhammad did not cease until the rationalist Enlightenment produced Orientalists of

195

increasing objectivity and scientific scholarship.[447] The Jews, however, after the destruction of their Temple in Jerusalem by the Roman Emperor Titus in 70 AD entered into their long period of Diaspora and settled in many European countries, becoming parts of the citizenry of those countries, although they were persecuted in those countries for their usurious financial activities as well as their part in the crucifixion of Jesus. It was not until 1974 that the Vatican formally cleared the Jewish people collectively of the murder of Jesus Christ. The ascendancy of Hitler in Europe in 1933 and the mass extermination of the Jews by him from 1941 to 1945, known as the Holocaust, changed Western relations with the Jews. They supported the Zionist movement and the eventual creation of the State of Israel in Palestine.

The Christian crusades against Islam, extending over a period of roughly two centuries (1095-1291), according to historians, consisted of eight major expeditions. The aim was to take possession of and maintain control over the holy city of Jerusalem and the places associated with the earthly life of Jesus Christ. However, the crusaders failed to achieve their purpose. In 1291 the Latin Christians were finally expelled from their bases in Syria.

3. The setting up of the State of Israel in Palestine: an ideological dead-end to Western-based systems

It would be easy to suppose that the State of Israel is an outpost for Western imperialism to control the strategic area of the Middle East. It was the British who in 1917 gave the Jews support for a "National Home in Palestine" in the famous Balfour Declaration. It was a Western-controlled United Nations that recognized the Israeli state in 1948. It is American imperialism, taking over from

---

[447] I mention a few: W.M. Watt, A. J. Arberry, A. Guillaume, Karen Armstrong and Maxim Rodinson.

the Britain and France after the Suez War in 1956 that arms Israel and guarantees its security.

However, Zionism was a nationalist political movement designed to set up a national home for the Jews in Palestine, as stated in the Balfour declaration, and answering to the needs of the Jews for a secure homeland against anti-Semitism in Europe. The Jews had their home in the ancient land of Canaan. During the Diaspora, after the destruction of the Temple by Titus in 70 A.D. until the mass killing of the Jews in Germany under Hitler, the Jews were persecuted in Christian Europe for their alleged killing of Christ as well as for their usurious financial activities. Thus their persecution in Europe and their historical ties to the ancient Land of Canaan gave birth to their nationalist political movement. In this respect, the Israelis shared a common purpose with the Arabs.

The truth is none of the European states wish to see an Israeli state in Palestine.* Unfortunately, the Arabs, influenced by a pan-Arab nationalism and backed by the Soviet Union in the Cold War conflict, chose to fight the Israeli state as soon as it was proclaimed in 1947 and recognized by the United Nations in 1948. Six wars ensued. Although the Arabs were defeated in all these wars, Israel's security is still not guaranteed and the problem of Palestine not resolved. Due to the enormity of the problem, involving as it does the Judeo-Christian *bloc's* traditional sentiment against Islam, it impinges on world peace. Note the impotence of the United Nations in this matter, due to the United States' support to it. It has also led to a Bush-proclaimed "Hundred-year War on International Terrorism" – another war against Islam --, forgetting that the Western-controlled United Nations, in terms of nuclear-weapons possession especially, constitutes "State Terrorism" against other states outside the "Nuclear Club". Overall, the General Assembly of the United Nations, despite being the highest policy-making body of the organization, cannot execute any decision unless it is approved by its Security Council, consisting of five veto-bearing so-called Permanent Members – a tiny minority and a truly democratic farce! It was in 1974 at a Special Session of the General Assembly that the historic resolution for a New International Economic Order was adopted. Up to now when the world is facing its greatest financial, monetary and economic crisis in modern history, it has not implemented this resolution. It has not done so, because it is not in the interests of the big powers to do so.

In the true sense of the word, the failure of the United Nations, representing humanity, in resolving the crucial issue of Palestine, is the failure of Western-based ideological systems – in short, the failure of Capitalism and Communism. It is a failure of a materialist, amoral and anti-spiritual worldview.

4. The "Straight Path"-- A Humanist, Moral and Spiritual Worldview.

The error of both Capitalism and Communism is that it totally rejects the spiritual dimension of human life. Man is both body and spirit, with the spirit controlling the body. It is truly said that man cannot live by bread alone. Bread satisfies his physical-biological needs. Faith in Truth, with a capital T and Truth standing for God, the Spirit that creates, sustains and guides the universe – only this can satisfy his intellectual-moral-spiritual needs. This faith is lacking in Western-dominated modern civilization, beginning with the strident spirit of rationalism and belief in scientific and technological progress. The First and the Second World Wars destroyed this shallow optimism. Read the pessimist literature of the period – Dostoyevsky, Albert Camus, Jean-Paul Sartre, W.B. Yeats and T. S Eliot. It is drenched with a desolate, lonely, if at times, brave pessimism. Listen to , the Irish poet, W. B. Yeats (1865-1939):

....

Thing fall apart; the centre cannot hold;
Mere anarchy is loosed upon the world,
The blood-dimmed tide is loosed, and everywhere
The ceremony of innocence is drowned;
The best lacked all conviction, while the worst
Are full of passionate intensity.
Surely some revelation is at hand;
Surely the Second Coming is at hand.
The Second Coming! ...[448]
Listen also to T. S. Eliot (1888-1965):-

....

I said to my soul, be still, and wait without hope
For hope would be hope for the wrong thing, wait without
love
For love would be love for the wrong thing,
There is yet faith
But the faith and the love and the hope are all in the
waiting.
.... [449]

This multifaceted crisis has been documented in many books. I shall mention only a few.[450]

The Quran describes the crisis simply, thus: "We have adorned everything on earth in order to test them, and thus distinguish those among them who work righteousness. Inevitable, We will wipe out everything on it, leaving it completely barren."[451] In another passage, referring to the same event, it says "We will

---

[448] From the poem "The Second Coming", 1921.

[449] "East Coker" in *Four Quartets*, 1974.

[450] Rene Guerion, *The Crisis of the Modern World* (Original French:1946; English translation:2001); P.A. Sorokin, *The Crisis of Our Age* (1941); Joseph Needham, *Within the Four Seas – the Dialogue of East and West* (1969); Thom Hartmann, *Threshold: The Crisis of Western Culture* (2009).

[451] Quran 18:7-8.

present Hell on that day to the disbelievers. They are the ones whose eyes were too veiled to see My message. Nor could they hear. Do those who disbelieve think that they can get away with setting up My servants as gods beside Me? We have prepared for the disbelievers Hell as an eternal abode. Say `Shall I tell you who the worst losers are? They are the ones whose works in this life are totally astray, but they think that they are doing good.'"[452]

The future lies in mankind seeking the "Straight Path" mentioned in the Quran. As we said earlier, the concept of the straight path is not new. It is as old as human community itself. Aristotle's "Golden Mean" and the Buddhist "Straight Path" refer to the same thing. The forms of this "Straight Path" must be worked out by us. As a system, it can take many forms, suited to the many human communities, each with its own history and national characteristics. Nevertheless it is not any path. It must exclude the deviating paths of "incurring God's wrath and going astray."[453]

*****

---

[452] Quran 18:100-104.
[453] Quran, 1:6-7.

CHAPTER 28

Peaceful Co-existence of Religions

- Let there be peace: avoid exclusivity and fanaticism,
- Inter-religious dialogue,
- Co-operation between different ways of life,
- The triumph of truth, freedom and justice.

1. Let there be peace: avoid exclusivity and fanaticism

There many religions living side by side in our modern world. In Malaysia, its Constitution stipulates Islam as the State religion, with other religions given freedom to be practiced by its adherents.

The Arabic word 'Islam' means 'submission (to God)'. It also means 'peace', as in the greetings *al-salamu 'alikum* or *salamun 'alaikum* (peace on you). Thus, Islam teaches peace. That means peace among nations and among religions is one of the Islam's requirements. In other words, we must tolerate and respect each other's religions, as the bottom line of living together. This is documented in the Quran.[454] Therefore, plurality of religions is a fact, and must be accepted. Religious exclusivity must be avoided.

---

[454] Quran, 109:6.

We must also avoid fanaticism, thinking that one's own religion is right and others are wrong. We have seen and experienced many tragedies because of exclusivity and fanaticism.[455]

Yet there is only one truth. There cannot be two truths. If there is more than one truth, chaos will reign in the Universe. Although, as I have said earlier, chaos has reined in the world, this is only a temporary state. Sooner or later, truth will prevail.[456] That is the time when the whole human community will accept the one truth and reject falsehood. Thus, respect and toleration that I have spoken of above is only necessary for the time being, as a necessary condition of our survival. A time will come when all of us will accept the one truth and reject falsehood; that is the time when true peace and justice will be freely upheld by the whole human community.

2. Inter-religious dialogue

Although inter-religious dialogue is a recent phenomenon (since 1960-es), it began with Scottish philosopher David Hume's book, *Dialogues Concerning Natural Religion*, posthumously published in 1779. Three fictional characters debate the existence of God. Then in 1960 Ninian Smart wrote *World Religions: A Dialogue* where six

---

[455] The author has much experience in witnessing these two diseases in Muslims themselves. Firstly, in our organization (*Forum Iqra' Bhd.*) calling Malaysians back to the Quran, groups of fanatics almost always harassed us at our functions. He was also involved at meetings with other Malaysian organizations to ask our Government set up a commission to conduct inter-religious dialogues to promote inter-racial and inter-religious understanding. Their proposal was rejected by the Government. Recently (in 2010) our Prime Minister set up a Committee to conduct inter-religious dialogues. The author has been reliably informed that this Committee could not take off due to harassment by Muslim fanatics!

[456] Quran, 17:81. See also Hans Kung and others, *Christianity and the World Religions – Paths to Dialogues with Islam, Hinduism and Buddhism* (1985); p. xv.

characters, a Christian, a Jew, a Muslim, a Hindu, and two Buddhists took part. In these two books, the purpose is to understand religion or to understand the different religions.

It is only later, after the Second Vatican Council (1962-1965) issued documents aimed at fostering inter-religious understanding and cooperation to promote world peace that a new type of religious dialogues takes place. Again this dialogue is accelerated after the publication of Huntington's controversial book on the clash of civilizations,[457] more so after the suicide attacks on the United States on 11th September, 2001. According to Christian theologian Huns Kung, an actual dialogue took place in 1982 at the University of Tubingen in Germany.[458]

What is the purpose of these dialogues? Apart from promoting understanding and cooperation among different religions, in the end the question of truth cannot be avoided. Is there a true religion? How can the truth of the true religion be established? As I said earlier, the real elephant exists, although different descriptions of the elephant are given by the proverbial blind men. In the same way, the truth, the one truth, exists. This truth can be established through civil and reasoned debate.[459]

3. Cooperation between different ways of life

In the meanwhile, the multi-national and multi-religious human community must learn to live together side by side and cooperate in the works of civilization. As the United Nations Organization has proved, it is eminently possible to do so. In fact, we have the standing example of the early Arab-Muslim nation-state formed by its leader, Prophet Muhammad. This first Arab nation-state

---

[457] See Samuel P. Huntington, *Clash of Civilizations and the Remaking of Word Order* (1966).
[458] See Note 456 above.
[459] Quran, 16:125.

consisted of Muslims, Jews and pagans and was ruled in accordance of the first written constitution in the world, known as the Medina Charter, promulgated by Prophet Muhammad himself.[460] The cul-de-sac that we have now reached is due to exclusivity and fanaticism; in other words, Big-Power chauvinism. The only way to break through this Big-Power chauvinism is to intensify and enlarge the movement of awakened humanity to demand for universal freedom and justice. The time is not far off for this victory to be realized.

4. The final triumph of truth, freedom and justice

As it is, this movement, which has as its aims, in the apt phrase of the Quran, "to enjoin good and forbid evil", has attained many successes: almost universal independence for the nation-states, the fall of theological state-system in the West and the East, the fall of Marxist communism, and the current fall of free-market capitalism. I am convinced that the humanist faction's (the oppressed peoples') long and persistent fight for true freedom and justice throughout the world will soon be crowned with complete victory.

This complete victory has not come easily. It has taken many centuries and many great sacrifices: from the burning at stakes of Prophet Abraham (although God protected him from the fire) in ancient Iraq and the crucifixion of Spartacus in ancient Rome, or even earlier, through the struggles and fights of prophets Moses, Jesus, Muhammad and countless others, bringing us into the modern and globalized world that is now.

It is surely a justified and worthwhile fight, and that is to put it mildly. Praise then be to God, the Lord of the Worlds!

---

[460] See Kassim Ahmad, "A Short Note on the Medina Charter" in http://www.stromloader.com/qsmjam (political section).

CHAPTER 29

The Great Deterioration and the Necessity for Perpetual Renewal

- The pull of the earth, and the desire for the easy road,
- Living in comfort zone,
- Can we overcome the deterioration?
- Apply the scientific method.

1. The pull of the earth: the desire to take the easy road

As I said before, most human beings succumb to the pull of the earth, preferring to take the easy road, rather than to strive, and take the hard road.[461] This is the instinct of animalism, as opposed to carrying out his God-given mission of ruling over himself and the Universe.[462] At every step of the way, he must exert himself so that he can ascend the ladder of evolution to higher and higher states of existence. If he fails to do that, he will regress, and what I have called the great deterioration will take place.

The example of Prophet Muhammad's followers is a standing example of this deterioration. I have already described their unexampled rise from a little-known people to the summit of

---

[461] Quran, 90: 10-17.
[462] Quran, 2: 30-34. The Arabic word *khalifa* means ruler. Man is God's vicegerent. His mission is to change the world to his liking.

power and civilization in a very short time.[463] Then as rapidly they fell, to be replaced by other peoples. The democratic republic he set up gave way to dynastic rule after just after 30 years of his death, set up by long-time enemy, the Muawiyah family, who only accepted Islam after its final victory in Mecca. Political factions, soon to be followed by theological factions, broke out. Baghdad in the East and Cordova in the West fell. The stars of Islam were dimmed forever. The stars of Europe and the West shone in their state.

2. Living in comfort zone

In earlier times, it was Prophet Abraham's people. He fought against paganism to establish monotheism and freedom for his people. He took his people to the summit of the then civilization. Then human society regressed, until Muhammad came on the scene to pick up the pieces and reconstruct human life again.

In later times, the Pilgrims Fathers brought into a tired and decrepit dying old world of Europe a new rising, creative and dynamic world, a beacon of liberty and a new hope for mankind, the United State of America![464] One of the Founding Fathers, Benjamin Franklin, said, answering a question at the Constitutional Convention: "I give you a republic, if you can keep it!" Sure enough, even Great America could not retain its humanist republic for long. Soon it was enlisted by the cunning English to become, like itself, imperialistic. From the time of the 26th President, Theodore Roosevelt (pr. 1901-09) a so-called special relationship with the erstwhile colonialist Britain was formed. America fought on the side of the British in the Second World War to save the British Empire a little while more.

---

[463] See Ch. 3, Note 86.
[464] See Rose Wilder Lane, *Islam and the Discovery of Freedom* (1997); pp. vi-vii.

The Second World War was followed by the Cold War in quick order, and now we are at the beginning of another Hundred Years' War against Terrorism. These endless wars – whose work are they, if not the Devil? Mao Zedong spoke the truth when he described our age as "Great Disorder under Heaven".

So, can we say that deterioration is normal? They say: "To err is human." So we get used to the idea. Robert Briffault called it "custom thought".[465] Yet, as I have pointed out, the human being is free and destined for higher and higher achievements. His capacity for achievements is almost limitless. Deterioration, therefore, is not normal; nor is it human. Deterioration means extinction, like the dinosaurs, while the human being embraces life ever-ascending and life-eternal.

Deterioration is, in fact, a deviation from the norm, the norm being a process of evolution. The human being is destined to ascend from the animal nature from which he springs. The norm is for him or her to ascend the psychological ladder until he achieves unity with God, i.e. the Abode of Heavenly Bliss.[466] When he or she regresses and deteriorates, it is therefore deviation. This is because, as I have pointed above, the pull of his lower nature, metaphorically, the earth. This lower nature likes to wallow in the mud. It is a comfort zone, with the myths and superstitions of the former society, from which he rose to heights unheard of due to a change in himself. In this societal dross, it stops him or her from developing, leading him or her to extinction. When a species cannot cope with the environment, it becomes extinct. This is natural law, and no creature can evade it. In human society, when that society regresses and deteriorates, it too becomes extinct and replaced by other fitter societies.

---

[465] See his excellent *The Making of Humanity* (1919); pp. 69 ff.

[466] "As for you, O content soul. Return to your Lord, pleased and pleasing. Welcome into My servants. Welcome into My Paradise." (Quran, 89: 27-30)

3. Can we overcome the deterioration?

Can human society avoid this deterioration? It is reasonable to suppose that a human being progresses through trial and error. So does a society. But all societies, past and present, had received their books of guidance from God. As we know, God's Final Scripture to mankind is the Quran. We also know that human societies, having progressed, have also regressed. This is due to their having deviated from the right path of God. To overcome this regression and deterioration, therefore, human society must keep as closely as possible to the said righteous path. Again take the case of Muhammad's followers: why did they deviate and regress? The answer is that Muhammad's later followers did not understand fully the right path, and condoned and accepted as correct the deviations that crept in, in the second, third and fourth centuries of Islam. To put it concisely, the leadership of the society could not maintain for long the path that Mohammad showed them, either because the leadership was weak in understanding its Islamic role, or that the leadership has been usurped by alien elements altogether.

4. Apply the scientific method

Therefore, a scientific understanding of leadership role in accordance with Islamic teachings is extremely important. Muhammad understood his role almost instinctively. Caliphs Abu Bakr and Omar, who succeeded him, also understood their leadership role well. When subsequently alien elements (those who were opposed to Islam) rose to constitute powerful forces in the nascent Muslim society, the true teachings of Islam became diluted and later replaced by alien teachings coming from Judeo-Christians, as well as pagans. By the time of Imam Ghazali (1058-1111), the deviations had been complete. False teachings, i.e. those that clearly contradict the teachings of the Quran, (in the form of *Hadith/Sunnah*, the *Ijma* or the consensus of scholars, and

208

mysticism) had crept into Islam and had corrupted it beyond recognition.

What should have happened is that each succeeding generation should re-evaluate its heritage. This would have eliminated the errors and proceed with a perpetual renewal. There is no holiday or rest for mankind's upward journey. However, idol-worshipping the so-called Great Masters stood in the way of such a step.

Thus, a long time elapsed before a reform movement started. It started with the theologian Ibni Taymiyah (1263-1328), and came to full fruition with the political activist Jamaluddin al-Afghani (1839-97) and the modern scholar-theologian Muhammad Abduh (1849-1905). However this reformation movement's achievements were limited to some legal and theological reforms only. The fundamental cause of the deviations, however, was the setting up of the *Hadith/Sunnah* as an equal or secondary source of theology and law with the Quran, as well as the setting up of an *ulama* class -- a veritable priesthood not sanctioned in Islam -- with sole authority to interpret Islam to the masses.

These two deviations amount to idol-worship which is strictly forbidden in Islam.[467] I have written about the self-made prison that the Muslims have set up.[468] There is a way for Muslims to totally liberate themselves, that is to totally subject their theology-ridden religion to the test of the Quran and only follow that which passes the test.[469] However, I must admit that this possibility is quite remote, since Muslim deviations have been locked into their religious system. The likelihood is that their liberation can only

---

[467] The setting up of leaders (prophets, religious and political) as idols constitutes idol-worship. Quran, 33: 67.

[468] See www.kassimahmad.blogspot.com

[469] The Quran must of course be interpreted correctly. See Kassim Ahmad, *Hadith: A Re-evaluation* (1997); pp. 126 ff.

come when the now-formed Global Community intervenes to make the breakthrough to a new just world that I believe is now in the making. I shall deal with this topic in another chapter.

*****

CHAPTER 30

The Fall of Empires, of Muslims and the Divine Law of Replacement

- Why the fall?
- The historical law cannot be violated,
- The corruption of Islam,
- Divine law of replacement.

1. Why the fall?

The story of the rise and fall of nations, civilizations and empires is a fascinating one. Fascinating, because it fallows the laws of history, or the historical process. Thus, history is not whimsical. It unfolds according to a certain logic or law that can be studied. Because of this we can avoid its pitfalls if obey the law and do not deviate from it. The Quran informs us about this historical law:

> *Have they not roamed the earth and noted the consequences for those who preceded them? They used to be more powerful, more prosperous, and more productive on earth. Their messengers went to them with clear signs. Consequently, God was not the One who wronged them; they are the ones who wrong themselves.*[470]

> *Such is God's system throughout history, and you will find that God's system is unchangeable.*[471]

---

[470] Quran, 30:9.
[471] Quran, 48:23

In this chapter, I am only taking about the fall, because it does seem that no nations in the past or the present can avoid from falling after a certain period. The Quran informs us:

> Each community has a predetermined life span. Once their interim comes to an end, they cannot delay it by an hour, nor advance it.[472]

> There is not a community that We will not annihilate before the Day of Resurrection, or inflict severe retribution upon them. This is already written down in the book.[473]

2. The historical law cannot be violated

There had been many nations, civilizations and empires in the past, and all of them had fallen. It looks as if the fall had been pre-determined, and could not have been avoided. The most famous if these nations, perhaps, were the Romans (510 B.C. – 23 B.C.). They rose and became a very powerful nation, inheriting from the older Greeks as well as from the Mesopotamians and the Egyptians, and perhaps from the Indians and the Chinese as well. After 500 years they fell as a consequence of their violating the law, to be replaced by the Arabian Muslims (622 A.D. – 1258 A.D.)[474] The Arabian Muslims, in spite of their having a divinely-protected scripture (Quran) for their guide, in time fell too, also as a consequence of their violating the law, to be replaced by the Judeo-Christian Europeans and Americans. This brings us to what has come to be known as the modern period of world history, from the beginning of the European Renaissance in the 14th Century.[475]

---

[472] Quran, 10:49

[473] Quran, 17:58

[474] This refers to the fall in the east. In the west, it is the fall f Granada in 1492.

[475] Actually, the world entered the modern period with the advent of Prophet Muhammad with his famous exhortation to mankind: "Read, in the name of your Lord Who created!" (Quran, 96:1). See, Ch. 5, Note 117.

Why the fall?

Actually the fall is only confined to the physical entity. The Roman nation or empire, the structural edifice, fell, but not its good civilizational or moral values. As the Romans took over from the Greeks and others, so the Romans bequeathed to succeeding nations those values that are useful to the further development of the Human Community. Thus the Human Community is a progressively developing community, forever carrying forward the torch of civilization and progress. What dies is not the Human Community, but the individual nation making up the Human Community that has failed in its mission to carry forward its onward march. The Quran elucidates:

> He sends down water from the sky, causing the valleys to overflow, then the rapids produce abundant foam. Similarly, when they use fire to refine metals for their jewelry or equipment, foam is produced. God thus cites analogies for the truth and falsehood. As for the foam, it goes to waste, while that which benefits the people stays close to the ground. God thus cites the analogies.[476]

The fall was not pre-determined, as also was its rise. As we have seen, the human being is free to determine its fate. So is a human society. Its fall is due to its own freely-made choice. The Quran states the law:

> God does not change a blessing He has bestowed upon any people until they themselves decide to change.[477]

> Thus, God does not change the condition of any people unless they themselves make the decision to change.[478]

---

[476] Quran, 13:17
[477] Quran, 8:53
[478] Quran, 13:11

Therefore, it can avoid this fall if it adheres strictly to the laws of the historical process that I mention above. These historical laws are the same throughout history. They are summarized in the Great Prayer that I discussed in Chapter 2. "Guide us in the right path, the path of those You have blessed, not of those who have deserved wrath, nor of those who have strayed."[479] God blesses those who uphold truth, justice and compassion. He is angry with those who rebel against Him, i.e. those who act against truth, justice and compassion. Those who stray are those who purport to obey Him, but who exceed certain limits of devotion to Him by practicing what He does not preach. The second category would include those who, even unwittingly, idolize their prophets.[480]

Following the right path means being righteous. Righteousness is defined in the Quran, thus:

> "Righteousness is not turning your faces towards the east or the west. Righteous are those who believe in God, the Last Day, the angels, the scripture, and the prophets, and they give the money cheerfully to the relatives, the orphans, the needy, the traveling alien, the beggars, and to free the slaves; and they observed the Contact Prayers (salat) and the obligatory charity (zakat); and they keep their word whenever they make a promise; and they steadfastly persevere in the face of persecution, hardship and war. These are the truthful; these are the righteous."[481]

3. The corruption of Islam

Let us apply these criteria to the early Arabian Muslims, who, after all, claimed to be strict monotheists. We have seen that their rise was extremely rapid.[482] So was their fall. Hardly thirty years

---

[479] Quran, 1:6-7
[480] One form of idol worship is to idolize prophets and leaders. (Quran, 33:67)
[481] Quran, 2:177
[482] See, Ch. 3, Note 86.

after Prophet Muhammad's death, directly against the Prophet's teachings, they broke into political and theological factions, giving rise to civil wars and later to the formation of two permanent sects, the majority Sunni sect and the minority Shiah sect. New teachings, not sanctioned, by the Quran arose, and by 1258, the capital of Muslim east, Baghdad, fell to the Mongol hordes, and in 1492 the capital of Muslim west, Granada, fell to the Christians. The liquidation of the Ottoman Empire by the Turkish nationalist Kamal Atatürk in 1924 completed the fall of corrupted Islam.

With the expansion of the Arab-Muslim empire came great wealth, leading to extravagant and ostentatious living by the elites. What with the usurpation of power by former enemies of the Prophet, the Muawiyah clan![483] Increases in taxes to pay for soldiers and corruption among the elites leads to alienation of the lower classes and the provinces. The introduction of *Hadith/Sunna* (the so-called Prophetic traditions) as a principal source law and theology on par with the Quran, the fabrication of *Hadith*, the introduction of a new religious elite, the so-called *ulama*, to dictate on religion, the break-up of knowledge into religious and secular knowledge, the introduction of mysticism that is alien to Islam – all these deviations go to make the new corrupted Islam that came to be the religion of the Muslim masses!

Thus over-materialism leading to a hedonistic mode of life, corruption of the elites, oppression of the masses, and mysticism led to Islam's downfall.

As with the Arabian Muslims, so with all nations, empires and civilizations… Their decline and downfall were brought about by their own actions of in violation of the laws of the historical process. They became unjust; they did not uphold the truth; they were not compassionate to the poor and the disabled. Because of

---

[483] See Martin Lings, *Muhammad* (1983); p. 308; Philip K. Hitti, *History of the Arabs* (10th Edition: 1970); p. 189.

these, they fell. They did not fall from external causes alone. The external causes, like foreign attacks, were subsidiary to the internal causes.

4. Divine law of replacement

But historical process goes on, and must go on. It is an immutable law. So the failed nation is replaced by one or ones better. This nation or group of nations carry on the work of progress and civilization until the mission of the Human Community is completely realized. We can call this the law of replacement, stated thus in the Quran:

> *If you turn away, He will substitute other people in your place, and they will not be like you.*[484]

It can also be called the law of revival. A nation that dies for violating the laws of history, can also be revived, if it takes steps to correct and overcome its past mistakes that caused its decline and downfall. That being the case, the door is not closed for any nation or human community to rise again. We have seen this happen. Old medieval Europe died, but it is replaced by a new renaissance Europe. So was ancient Egypt. So were ancient India, China and Japan. But, of course, this revival can be complete or partial, depending on the course each of these human communities takes. If it takes complete measures to recover, and continue to do so at each generation, its recovery and revival will be complete and continuous.

Let us now pose this question for the Muslim Community. After its decline and fall with the fall of the Ottoman Empire in 1924, Muslim communities revived with the achievement of national independence everywhere, with the exception of Palestine. Obviously, this revival is only partial, even after considering the

---

[484] Quran, 47:38.

reformist movement initiated by Jamaluddin al-Afghani and Muhammad Abduh at the end of the 19th and the beginning of the 20th centuries. That is why we see problems in all the Muslim countries: problems of modernization, of corruption, of misgovernment, and of poverty and diseases. Can they achieve complete revival and lead civilization and the Human Community again, as they did in the early days? Of course they can. They only have to correct their mistakes and follow the right path that the Quran recommends them to. This is easier said than done. But, as the saying goes, where there is a will, there is a way.

As concrete practical measures, the Muslims must first put the Quran as the sole principal source of law and theology above everything else. Other sources are secondary, and these must not run counter to the principal source. The secondary sources include everything else from governmental decisions to teachings of political and religious leaders and as well as philosophers. Secondly, they must free themselves from the dictatorship the so-called *ulama* class and listen to all view in all matters, including the interpretation of the Quran.[485] Thirdly, the arbitrary division of knowledge into so-called religious and secular must be discarded, as all branches of knowledge are interrelated and equally important.

*****

---

[485] I have worked out a scientific methodology of *tafsir*. See Kassim Ahmad, *Hadith – A Re-evaluation* (trans.) (Arizona: 1997); pp. 126 ff.

CHAPTER 31

A New Just World – Paradise on Earth

- The fruits of a long persistent struggle
- The Devil fails and Divine optimism justified
- The U.N. General Assembly's resolution on New Economic Order
- The U.N. and the work of its various agencies,
- There is no other place for Paradise to be in

1. The fruit of a long persistent struggle

If we were to take a referendum today on the possibility of establishing a new just world, the probability is that we would get at most 30% of the world's adult population saying 'Yes'.[486] We have been taught to accept geopolitics as natural to man that the just world of man's age-old dream can only be realized in the next world, or, in religious terminology, the Hereafter. No one really knows where the Hereafter is, or what it is like.

The Quran, however, informs us: "That is the day when everyone will be completely exposed; none of them will hide anything from God. To whom belongs all sovereignty on the day? To God, the One, the Supreme. On that day every self will be requited for

---

[486] This 30% includes Malaysia's own NGO, the International Movement for a Just World, currently chaired by social activist D. Chandra Muzaffar. I also want to mention an early document on the topic (1980) by Rajni Kothari of Centre for Study of Developing Societies in Delhi, India.

whatever it had earned. There will be no injustice on that day. God is most efficient in reckoning."[487] Note the sentence: *There will be no injustice on that day.* Can it not mean a coming Age when where there will be complete justice in the world?

On the surface, the 'day' refers to the Day of Judgement when God dispenses justice to all men in accordance with their works on earth. But any serious student of the Quran can see that it is a metaphor standing for man's accountability. Man will judge his own self, as indeed the Quran elsewhere states.[488] This judgement will take place on this earth, and not in any other world.[489] Such an interpretation is certainly more logical and more beautiful, reflecting God's power, wisdom and beauty as Creator and Fashioner of the universe.

This new just world will come about as the supreme result of the continuous struggles of oppressed peoples everywhere under the leadership of their humanist factions for millennia, from Spartacus (d. c.71 B.C.), or even earlier, through divine prophet-messengers Abraham, Moses, Jesus and Muhammad, right through to recent times, to even now and into the future. In religious terminology, it is God's Kingdom; it is Paradise.

It is to be expected that such a major change in human history, surpassing all previous revolutions, cannot take place without great struggles and sacrifices. It is no less than the replacement of the old global unjust imperialistic order by a new just humanistic order. No wonder this earth-shaking event is described in such catastrophic terms in the Quran:

> Your Lord's requital is unavoidable. No force in the universe can stop it. The day will come when the sky will violently thunder.

---

[487] Quran, 40:16-17
[488] Quran, 17:13-14. See, Chapter 2, Note 61.
[489] Quran, 7:25

The mountains will be wiped out. Woe on that day to the disbelievers...[490]

When the horn is blown once. The earth and the mountains will be carried off and crushed, utterly crushed. This the day when the inevitable event will come to pass. The heaven will crack and fall apart. The angels will be all around, and your Lord's dominion will then encompass eight (universes). On that day you will be exposed; nothing of you can be hidden.[491]

However, these terrifying images of the Day of Resurrection are changed into more naturalistic descriptions in the following verses:-

God is the One who sends the winds to stir up clouds, the We drive them towards barren land, and revive such lands after they were dead. Thus is the resurrection.[492]

He is the One who designs the night to be a cover, and for you to sleep and rest. And He made the day a resurrection.[493]

2. The Devil has failed, and Divine optimism justified

Thus the Day of Judgement or the Resurrection refers to a major change in the evolution of the universe and in human society. Recall that the Quran informs us that the creation of human being, the coming into being of the *Homo sapiens*, represent a new stage in God's creation. He is God's vicegerent, a ruler who is given knowledge and power to chart his own fate and, therefore, to change the world and the universe. While the angels objected to the creation of this unique being because of his inner tendency to cause chaos and the shedding of blood, God entrusted him with

---

[490] Quran, 52:7-11.
[491] Quran, 69:13-18.
[492] Quran, 35:9.
[493] Quran, 25:47.

the rulership of the universe! In that profound metaphor, God foresees that man, in spite of his tendencies to evil, represented by the Devil (who rebelled against the Lord), will ascend the ladder of creation to become master of the universe. It is this humanity that will create the new just world that is God's kingdom, and that is Paradise.

3. The significance of the United Nations

In the last chapter, I refer to the ever-ascending historical process that cumulates humanity's civilizational values and carry humanity forward.[494] The historic formation of the United Nations Organization at the end of the Second World War, in spite of its many weaknesses that I have referred to,[495] represents a big achievement in humankind's forward march to higher states of being. In its 65 years it has achieved many great things. Among them, we can mention the U.N Charted itself, the Universal Declaration of Human Rights, and the notable resolution on the formation of a New International Economic Order passed by its special session in 1974. This resolution reflected a practical need of the Human Community for a fair international economic system. Although it remains unimplemented, it nevertheless points to what mankind must work for to create a better world. It is a landmark event in our march towards this new just world.

It is to be remembered that the United Nations replaces a failed earlier attempt – the League of Nations – by the Human Community to achieve true internationalism. Even now, we are still far from achieving this true internationalism. We are still not over the hill in terms of the threat of nuclear war. We have not resolved the problem of Palestine. We have not resolved the problem of starvation and poverty and diseases in many parts of the world, in spite of the rapid development of science and

---

[494] See, Note 7.
[495] See, Ch. 27; pp. 3-4.

technology. Yet, in spite of these, we have seen the rapid development of world consciousness to resolve these questions. All these are signs that we are rapidly moving toward a new just world.

*****

CHAPTER 32

Science, Philosophy and Religion

- Three methods of cognition,
- The Christian origin of the animosity between science and religion,
- Their coming meeting point,
- The coming birth of the unified world,
- At the threshold of a major event in human history.
- God's optimism is justified.

1. Three methods of cognition

A unified integrated epistemology should consist of the three methods of knowing. Against, the Quran reveals this to us in the most casual manner that hardly any translator notices its significance. There are (a) through sensory evidence,[496] (b) through logical or rational evidence,[497] and (c) through direct or supra-sensory or supra-rational evidence.[498]

Take a simple case. You can see a pen in front of you. That is the first step: you testify to the existence of a thing through sensory evidence. Then you ask how the pen comes to be there. The answer is that it has been made by a craftsman from materials

---

[496] "Then you will see it with the eye of certainty." (Quran, 102:7) The Arabic phrase is 'ain'ul-yakin.

[497] "If only you could find out for certain." (Quran, 102:5) The Arabic phrase is 'ilm'ul-yakin.

[498] "This is the absolute truth." (Quran, 56:95) The Arabic phrase is haqq'ul-yakin.

from the earth. This is the second step: you testify to the existence of a thing logically through logical evidence. The final question to ask is regarding both the craftsman and the earthy materials: where do they come from? Here the Western materialist empirical answer is the same as in the second step, denying that both of them come from a Creator-God Who exists by Himself, i.e. a Necessary Being. Thus this mechanistic empirical epistemology, by denying a spiritual dimension to the world, meets a dead-end, in a cul-de-sac that is Logical Positivism that we have referred to in an earlier chapter.*

However, there is also a Western scientific-philosophical stream that embodies the unified, integrated three-dimensional epistemology. One historical philosopher, P. A. Sorokin propounded this view in his book, *A Modern Historical and Social Philosophies*.[499]

Richard Carrington also said the same thing: "If the reader agrees that enlightened people must now give up all magical explanations of man' place in nature, he has a right to ask what alternative approach can be made to the problem. To me there is no doubt whatever that our basic attitude must be scientific, but there again, there is a danger of semantic confusion. The word science, like the word God, has been narrowed down to a special meaning, which in many people's minds is entirely separate from religious and artistic experience, and is indeed hostile to these other means of knowing. If I say that the basic approach to the problems of the universe and of man should be scientific, I do not mean that the religious and artistic experience must be rejected as invalid. They should indeed be extensions of the scientific method, which enable the scientific picture to be enormously

---

[499] See pp. 247-48.

expanded and enriched. Their different approaches are not in the slightest degree contradictory, and each can gain enormously by an understanding of the methods of others. The ability to harmonize the findings of these three techniques of knowing is in fact an apt and concise definition of wisdom – a state of mind which is generally regarded as the most desirable which man can attain."[500]

According to a Malaysian researcher, Islamic epistemology is a new field and still undeveloped.[501] We can begin from the pointer from the Quran that we have mentioned above and learn much from the creative developing stream in Western science and philosophy.

2. The animosity between science and religion

In the West, the Church had a long history of animosity to science. This was due to certain contents of the Bible that contradict scientific facts as well as to literal interpretation of the sacred book. Author A. D. White published a two-volume account of this under a toned-down title *A History of the Warfare of Science with Theology in Christendom* in 1895 (more than a century ago). It is an excellent account of this subject from the early times till recently. Nevertheless, the matter is the conflict between science and false religion,[502] not just a wrong interpretation of religion by a priestly

---

[500] See *A Million Years of Man*, pp. 188-89.

[501] See Syed Muhammad Dawilah al-'Edrus, *Islamic Epistemology* (1992); p. xi.

[502] As we said below, Prophet Jesus's teachings were a continuation of the religion of Islam begun by earlier prophets. However, at the Council of Nicaea in 325, the false doctrine of the Trinity and the divinity of Jesus Christ was first promulgated. See K.N. Cameron, *Humanity and Society – A World History*; 275-76. The Quran was revealed to confirm, rectify and supersede previous scriptures. It therefore condemns this doctrine: "O people of the scripture, do not transgress the limits of your religion, and do not say about God except the truth. The Messiah, Jesus, the son of Mary, was a messenger of God and His word that He had sent to Mary, and a revelation from Him.

class. That is why this conflict essentially originates from the West, and has continued to the present-day.

It was the philosophers of Islam, notably Ibn Rushd (known to the West as Averroes) who promulgated the congruence of religion and philosophy and by implication science. Several scholars have written on the topic of the congruence of the contents of the Quran with the discoveries of modern science. However, later the triumph of traditional Asha'arite theology over the rationalism of the Mu'tazilites made consequent Muslim theology dogmatic, and this is strengthened by the rise, in imitation of Christianity, of a priestly class among the Muslims during their Middle Ages (16th – 20th centuries), and led creeping anti-scientific views into Muslim societies.

To arrest this decadence, a modern reform movement was initiated by thinker and political activist Jamaluddin al-Afghani (1839-1897) and scholar and theologian Sheikh Muhammad Abduh (1849-1905) at the end of 19th and the beginning of the 20th centuries. Since the movement failed to address a basic fallacy in traditional Muslim theology and law – the elevation of the Prophetic Tradition to a position equal to the Quran – it could not achieve a complete liberation of the Muslim mind.

The Christian Church persecutions of early Renaissance scientists in the 15th and 16th centuries are well-known. In 1543 the Church condemned Copernicus book *On the Revolution of Heavenly Bodies* as deviationist. On 16th February, 1600 Giordano Bruno (1547-1600) was burnt to death in Rome for his apostasy in teaching the infinity and multiplicity of the worlds. Before this, he was jailed

---

Therefore, you shall believe in God and His messengers. You shall not say, 'Trinity'. You shall refrain from this fro your own good. God is only one god. Be He glorified; He is much too glorious to have a son. To Him belongs everything in the heavens and everything on earth. God suffices as Lord and Master." (4:171)

for seven years in the cells of the Inquisition. He was charged in court for apostasy in 1591. In 1632 Galileo was ordered by the Church to repent and recant his own teachings that the earth orbited the sun. He was also jailed for several years. In 1616 the Papacy silenced Galileo and pronounced by the mouth of Cardinal Bellarmine that the Copernican theory was "false and altogether opposed to Holy Scripture." Copernicus' book was suspended, but the suspensory edict was never ratified by the Pope. It was virtually repealed in 1757, and "in 1822 the sun received the formal sanction of the Papacy to become the centre of the planetary system."[503]

However, these religious persecutions were not new. They had their precursors in the ancient world. Anaxagoras of Clazomenae, an Ionian philosopher, was indicted for rationalism by Athena in c. 432 B.C. Sarton remarks, "Whatever were the real causes of Anaxagoras' accusation – his friendship with Pericles or perhaps his Persian leanings – the pretext was religious … He was certainly not the first victim in the incessant war between bigotry and science, but his is the first Athenian known one. We may not call him a martyr of science … but he was the first man in history who was punished for thinking freely, for following the dictates of reason and his conscience rather than the opinions of the community."[504]

William of Occam (d. 1347), a native of Surrey, was tried for heresy and imprisoned at Avignon. He denied that any theological doctrines were demonstrable by doctrine and showed the irrational nature of many church doctrines. He attacked the theory of papal supremacy and headed a Franciscan revolt against

---

[503] W. C. Dampier, *A History of Science*, p. 113.
[504] *A History of Science*, Vol. 1; p. 244.

the control of Pope John XXII. His work marked the end of mediaeval scholastic dominance.[505]

Socrates (470-399 B.C.) was sentenced to death by poison by the Athenian state on the following charge: "Socrates is guilty of rejecting the gods acknowledged by the state and of bringing in strange deities; he is also guilty of corrupting the youth. He was found guilty by a majority of 281 out of 501 judges. The Athenian democracy was devout to the point of superstition, and Socrates' rationalism though tempered as it was by mysticism, was shocking to them."[506]

It is obvious that science and rationalism pose a danger to most people in all societies and climes. This is because they fear what may happen to them if their actions incur the wrath of God or of the gods that they believe in. It is this fear that gives rise to religious dogmatism that is really opposed to true religion. True religion cannot be opposed to truth, which, with science and philosophy, it shares as the three approaches to knowledge and reality.

3. The coming meeting point – the false dichotomy between the religious and the secular

In spite of the opposition of traditional Asha'arite theology, we make bold to say that it is Islam that will bring about the meeting point between religion, philosophy and science. As we stated earlier, the saving grace of the Muslims, in spite of their deviation from the religion of divine unity, like the rest of the religious communities, is the incomparable Quran that they still possess. Of course, the Quran belongs to the whole world, not to the Muslims alone. What is unique about the Quran is that its basic and

---

[505] See W. C. Dampier, *A History of Science*; p. 94.
[506] See G. Sarton, *A History of Science,* Vol. I ; p. 265.

universal teachings cohere with the truth. This means that it is congruent with reason and science.

The Quran is being studied and scrutinized by the whole world, most seriously so in the face of the current collapse of all the reigning ideological systems of the world. The straight path that it advocates, neither Eastern, nor Western[507] is what mankind needs now. It also answers the basic aspirations for peace, justice and love for all mankind of all religious groups, namely Hindus, Buddhists, Taoists, Confucius, Jews, Christians and Muslims.

To conclude this chapter, I shall quote from professor of philosophy, Errol E. Harris, on the coming meeting point of religion, philosophy and science:

> *Consequently, the existence of God is the absolute and most indispensable presupposition of science, and so far from there being an alienation of science from religion in the modern era, there is an can only be the closest **rapprochement** between them if both scientific and religious concepts are rightly interpreted. Such alienation as there has been was due to the influence of empiricism, which created for itself a nature vacuously actual and banished from its purview the mind as a ghost in which only the superstitious could believe. God had then to be imagined as the Supreme Ghost and all things religious as ghostly – and therefore non-existent. But empiricism, though it persists is a relic of the past without scientific basis, and has proved itself to be in this age of evolution, relativity and quanta, an outworn and outmoded superstition.*[508]

*****

---

[507] A phrase from the Quran. (Quran, 24:35)
[508] *Nature, Mind and Modern Science* (1954); p. 452.

CHAPTER 33

God's Grand Plan:
the Triumph of the Religion of Truth

- What is God's grand plan?
- The role of Man, vicegerent of God
- The role of the Devil, the enemy of God
- The eventual triumph of the religion of truth.

1. What is God's grand plan?

Renown British physicist, Stephen Hawking, at the end of his book, *A Brief History of Time*, says, "… If we find the answer to that (i.e. a complete theory of everything that can tell us why we and the universe exist), it would be the ultimate triumph of human reason – for then we would know the mind of God."[509]

Apart from the strange phenomenon of witnessing a self-confessed atheist taking about the mind of God (proving that true atheism is non-existent, since it is in the nature of man to believe in something), we can actually know the mind of God, because He has revealed it to us. I have already talked about Quranic epistemology as consisting of a combination of evidence from the senses (sensory evidence), from logic (logical evidence), and from intuition or inspiration (direct evidence from his soul (Ar. *ruh*), i.e.

---

[509] *A Brief History of Time* (New York: 1988); p. 185.

from God).[510] The Quran is God's final scriptures to mankind given to Prophet Muhammad. Let us take a peep at the mind of God about the creation of the universe and the creation of man from it.

> We did not create the heavens and the earth, and everything between them just for amusement. If We needed amusement, We could have initiated it without any of this, if that is what We wanted to do. Instead, it is Our plan to support the truth against falsehood, in order to defeat it. ...[511]

> I did not create the jinns and the humans except to worship Me alone.[512]

> He is the One who helps you, together with His angels, to lead you out of darkness into light. He is Most Merciful towards the believers.[513]

> He is the One who created the heavens and the earth in six days – and His domain was completely covered with water – in order to test you, to distinguish those among you who work righteousness. Yet when you say, "You will be resurrected after death," those who disbelieve would say, "This is clearly witchcraft."[514]

> Everything We created is precisely measured.[515]

> Do you not see that God has committed in your service everything in the heavens and the earth, and has bestowed you with His blessings – obvious and hidden? Yet, some people argue

---

[510] See, Chapter 14; p. 3.
[511] Quran, 21:16-18.
[512] Quran, 51:56.
[513] Quran, 33:43.
[514] Quran, 11:7.
[515] Quran, 54:49.

about God without knowledge, without guidance, and without the enlightening scripture.[516]

Everything perishes, except His presence …[517]

2. The role of Man, vicegerent of God

The above verses give us eight characteristics or, one might also say, purposes of existence.

First, existence, or the universe, has a serious purpose. It is no less than to prove that truth prevails over falsehood. Order, harmony, beauty and goodness prevail over chaos, disorder, disharmony, ugliness and evil.

Second, man should serve God alone (although He does not need it), because in the service of God alone man can accomplish he mission on Earth. Serving other than God means throwing himself forever into servitude; thus disabling himself from carrying out his mission.

Third, it is God's wish to bring man out of darkness into light. He is born into a world which bequeaths him a mixture of enlightenment and ignorance. It is only with enlightenment that he (and his society) can make progress.

Fourth, humankind must be able to distinguish between good and evil, so that evil can be overcome by good, thus quickening the achievement of the just world of man's dream.

Fifth, everything in the universe is created by God to serve mankind, positively or negatively. We know that man can only gain knowledge through trial and error. Both pen and cane are necessary to teach him.

---

[516] Quran, 31:20.
[517] Quran, 28:88.

Sixth, the universe is lawfully run on the basis of truth and logic. It is not capricious. This would facilitate man's understanding of it, enabling him to control it and therefore freely chart his own destiny, as God desires. That is the meaning man being God's vicegerent (Ar. *khalifa*).

Seventh, the universes as well as man, the Homo sapiens, who emerged from it about a million years ago, are not eternal. All things that have a beginning must come to an end, when they attain the purpose of their existence.

Lastly, only God is eternal. At a point in time, many millions of years from now, the universe will collapse and return to where it came from -- God. Only God has no beginning and has no end. He is the Ever-living on Whom all depend. He is the Absolute Being, Who gives rise to all other beings.

The above verses surely elucidate matters that Hawking and other disbelievers are asking about. However, let me pose some questions, however silly they may sound.

First question: Why must God create man to prove that truth triumphs over falsehood?

Answer: If He did not create man and the universe (since man grew out of the universe), there would be nothing. We would not be able to have this dialogue!

Second question: Why is it so important that truth triumphs over falsehood?

Answer: Because truth is one of the highest values. Because all the good people want it so. Because you and I want it so. Because good values will bring about the new just world that we have fought so hard and sacrificed so much to establish.

3. The role of the Devil, enemy of God

Third question: Why cannot God do this Himself without relying on such a wayward creature as man to do it?

Answer: Of course, God, being All-Powerful, can do this Himself. Has He not created this mighty structure, the universe, without anybody's aid? But if He were to do it Himself, and not his free agent, Man (in spite of his waywardness), where lies the proof of God's power, wisdom and knowledge? It also proves that the Devil, arrogating to himself the task of seducing man away from God, has failed in his mission to frustrate God's plan and purpose. The Devil is, therefore, weak. This is Proof Extraordinary that God alone deserves to be worshipped.

Lastly, the silliest of all questions: "I did not ask to be born into this world. So why did God create me?" Implicit in this statement is that man is not to be held responsible for all the evils in this world.

Answer: Since you are free to say that, I shall hold you responsible for what you say freely. Why then do you procreate? You love this life, don't you? Then you must bear the consequences of your actions.

In the above imaginary questions and answers, I have dealt with the role Man, as God's vicegerent, and role of the Devil, the enemy of God and of man. I have dealt with these matters in detail in previous chapters.

4. The eventual triumph of the religion of truth

Thus, God's Grand Plan of creation – making truth prevail over falsehood – will be realized. It is in this sense that Islam, the religion of truth, God's religion, will triumph over all other religions. It is not the corrupted Islam that came to be practiced by the Muslim masses about three hundred years after Prophet Muhammad's death until now. It is the Islam that has been forever preserved in the Quran. It is the Truth Convergent, the Truth-in-Chief, that is preserved in all nations, as Verse 17 of *Surah Al-Ra'ad* (13) informs us. It is this invincible truth that will give birth to the new just world that I discussed in chapter 31 above. This is predicted in the Quran thus:-

When triumph comes from God, and victory, you will see the people embracing God's religion in throngs. You shall glorify and praise your Lord, and implore Him forgiveness. He is the Redeemer.[518]

*****

---

[518] Quran, 110:1-3.

CHAPTER 34

Conclusion

At last we have come to the end of the book. In this concluding chapter, I shall gather all the trends of thought in the book and summarized them.

First, the universe is not eternal. It was created by a Power we call God. In the beginning there was nothing except this Power which is Spirit Extraordinary. When the time comes, which is hundreds of millions of years from now, the universe itself with all that it holds will collapse from lack of energy, and only this Power remains.

The atheist denies the existence of this Creator-God simply because he does not see Him. This is unreasonable, as no one also sees the roots of a tree, yet the tree is there. Moreover , without its roots the tree cannot exist at all. He also denies His existence due to his dislike of regression. "Who creates this God?" , he proudly and triumphantly asks, blithely forgetting that he himself (i.e. man) comes from the creative act of this supreme Power.

Second, this Power, being Goodness Itself, subjects the whole universe, not just this earth that we are inhabiting at the present moment, to serve mankind, His crowning achievement. It is to Man alone He allots freedom of choice that He gives to none other created order. Due to this Goodness also, God always sends messages to mankind to guide them on their journey from non-knowledge to ever-increasing knowledge and from a low to ever higher psychological states, the many worlds of God's creation.

However, mankind, pulled by animalism, very often regresses. He therefore quite often has to begin again. But the divinely-controlled historical process helps him to accumulate the good values that go to improve his civilization. A point is reached when the Divine message could be protected from human corruption by an internal mechanism. This is reached with God's Final Scripture to him that is the Quran.

Third, the Muslim portion of mankind who was given the Quran, also regressed and deviated, reducing them to the same position as the other corrupted religious communities about 300 years after Prophet Muhammad's death. Fortunately, mankind has the Quran intact. Apart from that, a portion of all human communities have within them the good values that God has taught them. It is these good values that converge to form the Global Community in which we are living now. At the same time, this Global Community is interacting with God's Final Scripture, the Quran. It is this combination that will finally save mankind from total destruction, and carry them on their onward journey to complete freedom and happiness.

Fourth, the atheist or more correctly the disbeliever wants to be smart. He wants freedom, but does not want to bear the consequences of his actions. He commits all sorts of evils, and blames God for all the evils in the world!

On the other hand, he cleverly argues that since God is All-Knowing, my so-called free actions have already been determined by God. So how can I get punished for what God has already pre-determined?

He yet gets cleverer still. I did not ask to be born into this world, he claims. So why should God bother what I do? So he goes on a rampage to create chaos, precisely as the angles predicted he would do.

But fortunately, God's Law favours the triumph of truth over falsehood. This is highly significant. This is the **fifth and last** point. Even though the disbelievers in God are numerous at any one time in any community, their struggles and plots are in vain. Their big numbers do not count. Truth counts, because God, this Supreme Power, is the Truth. This is the meaning of human existence. This is what makes life meaningful, contrary to the opinions of disbelievers.

*****

APPENDIX I

Rejoinder to Dr. Robert D. Crane's Essay

"The Nature and Role of Hadith: An Analysis of A Re-Evaluation"

By: Kassim Ahmad
10 March, 2011
darul_hilmah33@yahoo.com.my

I was pleasantly surprised to suddenly come across the above essay while surfing the Internet about a year ago. When I added an addendum to my book, translated English version, Hadith – A Re-evaluation (1997:U.S.A) , titled "A scientific Methodology for Understanding the Quran", I anxiously waited for reviews or comments from Muslim scholars in Malaysia or elsewhere. Without desiring to boast, I believe this was the first attempt at such a colossal task. I waited in vain, until I accidently found Dr. Crane's quite lengthy essay. Regardless of some of his negative remarks, I am therefore extremely appreciative of his comments.

That said, what irked me was the author's unfounded barbs against me regarding the late Dr. Rashad Khalifa and the American thinker, Lynden H. LarRouche, Jr. The slanders that he flung at these fine individuals do not bear repeating and do his reputation no good. Needless to say, I am no slavish follower of any leader or thinker.

I shall not waste words. This erudite scholar, nevertheless, made many pitfalls. He claimed that the translated English version was different from the original Malay one. The translator, Syed Akbar Ali, as I stated in my preface to the translation, submitted the translation to me in late 1987. I left it in my computer until I found a way how to get it published in 1995. (Remember the Malay original is banned by Malaysian authorities.) I then went over the translation and made "what additions and changes" I thought necessary. I further stated in the preface that "this is not an exact translation of the Malay original, although the format and arguments remain the same."

He claimed that the Code 19, discovered by Rashad Khalifa is "a deliberate fake", without disclosing that it is based on Surah Al-Muddathir (74), verse 30 of the Quran and the numerous proofs of the Code's existence in the Quran. Obviously, he was unreasonably swayed by the slander against the Code!

He claimed that the sixth pillar of Muslim faith, belief in predetermination, is "old hat for advanced students of the Quran and Hadith". If that was so, why did Muslim leaders allow the error (because it contradicts the Quran) to continue for centuries?

He criticized me for regarding Jesus's "Second Coming" as spurious. The Quran categorically rejects such nonsense. Man must work for his own salvation. There is no short-cut to it. For this reason, he took me to task for discussing the Anti-Christ and Gog and Magog. The fact of the matter is that enemies of Jesus's true teachings did exist and continue to exist, symbolized in the person of the Anti-Christ; so do the enemies of God and mankind, symbolized in the figures of Gog and Magog, mentioned in both the Bible and the Quran.

He was flatly wrong in criticizing Rashad Khalifa for his claims to be a prophet, for the simple reason that Rashad made no such claim! What Rashad claimed (and I disagree with him) was that he was the Messenger of the Covenant. Cannot he differentiate between these two simple terms: a prophet and a messenger?

A grave error, repeated by most Muslims and shared by Dr Crane, is the so-called *salawat* to Prophet Muhammad, taken out of context by Surah *Al-Ahzab* (33), verse 56. It is tantamount to idol-worship, not forgiven by God, unless the believer repents in good time. I shall not go over this matter here, as I have fully explained it in my book.

I was greatly disappointed that such a scholar as Dr. Crane fails to appreciate that discrepancy between rise of the official compilation of the Hadith (250 -300 years after the Prophet's death) and the fabricated hadith that the Prophet left two books, the Quran and the Hadith. Truth is bitter, but it wills out.

To his credit, Dr. Crane reproduced in full my nine principles of a scientific methodology of *Tafsir* with favorable comments.

I am a little disappointed that this well-read scholar did not appreciate my work as it is. Again without wanting to sound boastful, it is the first comprehensive, logical and methodological refutation of the Hadith, as partial criticisms have appeared before. I made this clear in my book.

However, Dr. Crane's concluding remarks are nice. I shall quote them in full: " In summary, we might say that this monograph by Kassim Ahmad carries a lot of baggage, but that its overall message and most of the analysis is needed today more than ever to help Muslims understand their own religion better so that they can explain it to well-meaning non-Muslims who are willing to learn.

Note: Dr. Crane's essay follows.

The Nature and Role of Hadith: An Analysis of a Re-evaluation

by Dr. Robert D. Crane

A highly controversial document is circulating among Muslim intellectuals calling into question the validity of hadith as a source of guidance.

This document, an 80-page monograph, entitled Hadith: A Re-Evaluation was written about 1990 by Kassim Ahmad and was somewhat sanitized in 1997 by Syed Akbar Ali to remove some of its politically and ideologically sensitive baggage.

The present analysis of Kassim Ahmad's production is divided into four sections: 1) background intelligence analysis, so we know where the author is coming from; 2) purpose and objectives of the author in writing this particular piece, so we know where he is going; 3) major contribution of this piece to the thinking and literature on the subject; and 4) weakness of the author's arguments.

Background Intelligence

One approach to any potentially enlightening study is to determine initially where the author is coming from by glancing through the bibliography, footnotes, index, and table of contents, in that order, and only then to consider the text.

My first conclusion from this background check is that this translation has left out some of the original, and that the apparent omissions suggest that the original was prepared before Rashad Khalifa destroyed his credibility in the late 1980s. What is left of the original indicates that Kassim Ahmad was not only familiar with Rashad Khalifa, but used Rashad's translation of the Quran as his favorite (p.77). He also bought into Rashad's Number 19 theory (p. 68), which has been exposed by computerized analysis as a deliberate fake designed to corrupt the words of the Quran in order to fit his theory.

As old-timers will remember, Rashad was the most powerful force during the mid- and late 1980s in bringing Euro-American women to Islam, especially the most able, creative, and dynamic of them, such as Karima Omar, who had a fantastic humor column every month in Islamic Horizons. He then built on his asserted discovery of what Kassim Ahmad on page 68 refers to as The Miracle of Code 19 to assert further that this revelation to him from Allah proved that he was a prophet. He developed this to assert that he was the fifth most important prophet, right after Abraham, Moses, Jesus, and Muhammad. He then proceeded to introduce new customs, like encouraging women to lead the prayers of both men and women together. As a result he was assassinated. His most promising students hung together for awhile, but some of them then left Islam and most simply disappeared, which was a major tragedy in the history of Islam in America.

In his introduction on page one, Kassim Ahmad writes that his book builds on Ibn Khaldun's formula of hadith interpretation. This, he says, requires all acceptable traditions to be validated by the Quran and rational criteria. This position, however, though a scientific one, was still not clear enough until in 1985 the works of an outstanding Egyptian Muslim scholar, Dr. Rashad Khalifa, particularly his The Computer Speaks: God's Message to the World, Quran, Hadith, and Islam, and his superb translation of the Quran opened for me a way to solve the problem of the hadith: how they came about; the social factors that brought them into existence; a review of the classical criticism; the actual place of the hadith in relation to the Quran; their negative effects on the Muslim community; their connections to the decline and fall of the

243

Muslims; and the way out of this impasse. This seven-fold task is exceptionally well accomplished.

Nevertheless, this monograph has unnecessary baggage. The most recent of Kassim Ahmad's forty-four bibliographic entries are in the 1980s, except for two, Mahmud Saedon A. Othman's Al Sunnah in 1990 and the quite anomalous listing of Lyndon La Rouche' s The Science of Christian Economy, published by his Executive Intelligence Review in 1991. The text that had once referred to Lyndon La Rouche was deleted from the translation, no doubt because LaRouche, although brilliant and exceedingly well informed, was and is a demagogue and a kook. The fact that Kassim Ahmad was taken in by these two brilliant imposters, Rashad Khalifa and Lyndon La Rouche, shows a lack of discriminating judgement. Fortunately, the most compromising parts of the original appear to have been deleted ex post facto in 1997 in the translation, though the above mentioned traces remain.

Purpose and Objectives

The objectives of this monograph are the seven he enumerates on page one, as listed above. These are to solve the problem of the hadith [by showing] how they came about; the social factors that brought them into existence; a review of the classical criticism; the actual place of the hadith in relation to the Quran; their negative effects on the Muslim community; their connections to the decline and fall of the Muslims; and the way out of this impasse.

The author's underlying or overarching purpose is developed in beautiful prose throughout the monograph, as in a work of literature. He proceeds from appropriate verses of the Quran, since his entire theme is that the only authentic source of divine guidance is the Quran, and not the hadith, and that failure to appreciate this is the cause of civilizational decline.

His first two chapters are introduced by such verses. The introductory chapter one, entitled "Why We Raise this Problem", is introduced in a heading quoting Surah *al-Zumar*, 39:17-18< "Therefore, congratulate My servants who listen to all views, then follow the best. These are the ones guided by God; these are the intelligent ones." This sets the tone for the entire monograph.

Kassim Ahmad lists his favorite English translations of the Quran and praises the magnificent one by Muhammad Asad. Asad's comment on the above ayah from *Al-Zumar* reads: "According to Razi, this describes people who examine every religious proposition (in the widest sense of this term) in the light of their own reason, accepting that which their mind finds to be valid or possible, and rejecting all that does not measure up to the test of reason. In Razi's words, the above verse expresses a praise and commendation of following the evidence supplied by one's reason (*hujjat al-aql*), and of reaching one's conclusions in accordance with [the results of] critical examination (*nazar*) and logical inference (*istidlal*).

Chapter Two, entitled "Refutation of the Traditionalists Theory", is introduced by a heading quoting Surah *al-Isra* (17):36, "Do not accept anything that you yourself cannot ascertain. You are given the hearing, the sight, and the mind in order to examine and verify." Although some commentators restrict the target of this ayah to slander and detraction (*humaza* and *lumaza*), Kassim Ahmad prefers to extend its meaning to the entire realm of cognitive psychology, perhaps because of the immediately following ayah: "And walk not on the earth with haughty self-conceit." Of course, this interpretation can turn into a double-edged sword, as shown by some later conclusions that could be understood to support the fatal hallucinations of the author's apparent mentor, Rashad Khalifa.

The author's overall purpose in writing this monograph, as stated on page 4, is to encourage the Muslim community and their intelligentsia to critically re-evaluate the whole heritage of traditional Islamic thought, including theology and jurisprudence, [in order] to seek the true causes of Muslim decline and thereby to lay the ground for a new Muslim Renaissance. As stated this might appear to be self-serving narcissism by a Muslim seeking to transform his glorious past into a utopian future at the expense of everyone else or at least with indifference toward the other. In fact, the purpose is much broader, namely to correct the errors of both Muslim and European post-Christian thought so that all civilizations can build a better global future through interfaith reliance on the transcendent.

He opposes both modernist and traditionalist theses on how to build a better world, because they both fail to appreciate the wisdom of what he calls the first scientific-spiritual culture in history, namely, classical Islamic thought. He writes on page 5, The modernist thesis, in brief, states that the Muslims declined because they remained traditional and have not modernized themselves according to Western secular values. The traditionalist thesis, on the other hand, blames the secularization of Muslim societies and the neglect of orthodox Muslim teachings as the major cause of Muslim decline. Both of these extremes he refers to as false ideologies. These spread only because the Muslims failed to follow the powerful and dynamic Islamic ideology as preached in the Quran, which subjected all knowledge, both local and foreign, to its own discriminative teachings and methodologies in order to gain insights into the justice and mercy inherent in the Will of God.

The thesis of this book, he writes on page 8, is that mankind, including the Muslims, have deserted the true teachings of God. Modern secular rebellious Europe not only turned against its own religious priesthood, in which action it was right, but also against religion altogether, in which action it was wrong. This is the cause of the present Western impasse. A similar fate befell the Muslims, who abandoned the Quran by elevating the *ahadith* and sunna to a divine source of truth in competition with it in order to support competing political powers and supportive religious movements. So it came about, he writes on page 9, that while Europe embraced either liberalism or Marxism, the Muslim world embraced the hadith, with the philosophies of secular humanism infecting the elites of Muslim societies.

Since this monograph is not a political tract, at least not in its edited version, it is not clear whether Kassim Ahmad here is referring to the Muslim Brotherhood, which under Syed Qutb metamorphosed into a modern political movement patterned after Western secularism, or whether he is referring to the still more radical Wahhabis and Deobandis who carried the logic still further and eventually produced the likes of the pseudo-religious Osama bin Laden who want to save the world by destroying it.

The purpose of this monograph is perhaps best developed on page 64, where Kassim Ahmad gives his prognosis for the future of the world. He forecasts: Despite the heresy of certain concepts like taqlid or blind imitation that have been dominant since the 12th century, there has always been a strong anti-*taqlid* movement that has manifested itself through the likes of Ibn Rushd (d. 1198), Ibn Khaldun (d. 1406), and Shah Wali Allah (d. 1762). The anti-*taqlid* movement obtained its strongest impetus from the reform movement of Muhammad Abduh toward the end of the nineteenth century. It is most likely that within a short period of a few decades, the anti-*taqlid* movement in Islam and the theistic spirit that is growing in Europe will unite and return to the Quran in its entirety.

He cautions that, a return to the Quran does not mean that we destroy all the books of hadith and all the books of the religious scholars, nor do we mean that we no longer need the religious scholars. It only means that we must refer to the Quran alone as infallible guidance.

He concludes: Muslims have three major tasks. Firstly, they must evaluate critically everything that has been inherited from their Islamic tradition, in strict accordance with the bidding of the Quran. Secondly, Muslims have to learn to accept things that are from outside their fold but which by themselves are inherently good and therefore originate from God. The third and final task is to build the second Islamic civilization that will doubtless be far superior to the first because it will be the combined efforts of all united humanity. All these three tasks are interrelated. Our Muslim thinkers must also seek to reach out to those intellectuals and thinkers in other faiths and cultures, for they also seek to do good in the world. They must cooperate with the followers of other religions, those who believe in God and the Last Day and do good.

In our effort to elicit the full purpose of this monograph, as written before the death of Rashad Khalifa, we should note portions of the monograph that might be regarded as *mutashabihat*, from the root *shub-bi-ha* (make similar; compare; be doubtful), referring to portions of the Quran and of any writings that can have more than one meaning and therefore are doubtful except through interpretation by experts. On page 71, Kassim Ahmad states his preference for the school of thought that such portions of the Quran can be known and that a class of people, the experts, can have such knowledge by God's leave. He cites in proof thereof Surah al *Baqara* 2:30-34 where God tells us that He has endowed man with the ability to know all of His creations, above the knowledge even of His angels.

Ironically, on page 19, perhaps the key sentence in the entire monograph is Kassim Ahmad's assertion that, this means, on the

248

one hand, that the Quran explains itself, and, on the other, that God will, at the proper time, give man the necessary knowledge to understand it.

Major Contribution to Thought and Literature

Perhaps the single most controversial sentence in this monograph is Kassim Ahmad's assertion on page 47 that, the majority of the hadith in the six [classical] collections cannot be accepted any more.

The bulk of the monograph is designed to substantiate this conclusion. The evidence has been marshaled many times before, among others by Fazlur Rahman, who thereby became one of America's most controversial scholars.

Ahmad goes through the standard critiques. The role of the hadith as a source of law was not adopted until Imam Shafi'i did so 200 years after the death of the Prophet and decades after the death of even the last of the *taba tabi'in*. And the Six Authentic Books of Hadith of the Sunni majority (Bukhari, d. 256; Muslim, d. 261; Abu Daud, d. 275; Tirmidhi, d. 279; Ibn Maja, d. 273; and Al-Nasa'i, died 303) were not compiled until after that, mainly from the years 220 to 270; and the four Shi'a collections (Al-Kulaini, d. 328; Ibn Babuwayh, d. 381; Jaafar Muhammad al Tusi, d. 411, and Al-Murtada, d. 436) until a century after that, when it was simply impossible reliably to ascertain the *isnad* of any hadiths.

Ahmad then does a creditable job in trying to show, as he put it on page 27, that, the so-called Prophetic traditions did not originate from the Prophet. They grew from the politico-religious conflicts that arose in the Muslim society then, during the first and second centuries. It constituted a new teaching altogether, seriously deviating from the Quran that the Prophet Muhammad brought to them. It was done against his will, but skillfully attributed to him. He goes into some detail to show that the Prophet

Muhammad and the first four caliphs forbid the collection of any hadiths, and that the justification for doing so came from spurious hadiths invented for this purpose.

Ahmad concludes on page 29-30 that many hadith began to emerge and multiply at the same time as the emergence of divisions in the early Muslim community in three civil wars, beginning under Ali's rule right up to the end of Mu'awiya's rule. Power struggles giving rise to divisions led to the fabrication of hadith to support each contending group, and the fabrications of hadith further deepened divisions.

He notes the odd phenomenon of the hadith being elevated to an idol in the form of a source of guidance in competition with the Quran (p. 26) and even to a form of spirituality for Muslim fundamentalism. (p. 62), while the Quran itself is undermined by using the hadith to declare the doctrine of abrogation, so that whatever parts of the Quran might conflict with one's favorite hadith are declared to be abrogated by a part or parts that agree with this hadith.   Perhaps in observance of the political correctness that governed prior to 9/11, Ahmad does not point out that the Wahhabi practice in the modern world has been taken to the extreme of abrogating several hundred Quranic verses, so that this divine revelation is gutted of all meaning or perverted into a travesty of truth.

The specific conflicts between *ahadith* and the Quran are well documented, such as the lashing of adulterers prescribed in the Quran and the stoning invented later in the hadith (p. 48); the Quranic provision for freedom of religion and the bizarre hadith in Bukhari and Abu Dawud, if anyone leaves his religion, then kill him (p. 50); and the five pillars of the *aqida* in the Quran (Anyone who disbelieves in God, His angels, His scriptures, His messengers, and the Last Day has indeed strayed far away, which does not include the so-called sixth pillar, *Qadr*. Ahmad laments that this sixth pillar, which appears in the hadith, has been used for centuries not to recognize that the ultimate planner is Allah but to instill a fatalism that more than anything else has caused the absurd situation today where the followers of the Quran are the most despised and oppressed people on earth.

All this is old hat for advanced students of the Quran and hadith. Although such critical analysis must always be maintained, this bulk of Ahmad's monograph, Hadith: A Re-Evaluation, is not really a contribution to the thinking and literature on the subject.

The major contribution of this particular analysis of the nature and role of the hadith is Kassim Ahmad's emphasis on principles in an iterative process of inductive-deductive-inductive reasoning. This was emphasized by the Prophet Muhammad, *salla Allahu 'alayhi wa sallam*, and by all the classical scholars, who developed the *maqasid al shari'ah* over the course of many centuries. This great intellectual paradigm of thought culminated in the hierarchy of human responsibilities and rights propounded by *Al Shatibi* and never again even approached in any other civilization, but now essentially dead.

A corollary of this emphasis on principles is the focus on distinguishing between principles and historically determined forms. Ahmad states on page 23 that, whenever God pleases, He provides us with both the principles and the methods, but the punishments of hand-cutting for theft and a hundred lashes for adultery mentioned in the Quran are forms, not principles, of punishment. Furthermore, these forms are connected to specific historical circumstances. The Quranic principles for punishment are two: firstly, that every crime must be punished in accordance with the severity of the crime, i.e. the principle of equivalence; and secondly, the principle of mercy.

Similarly, the principles of governance, which come under the *shari'ah* purpose (*maqsud* or universal principle) known as *haqq al hurriya*, according to Kassim Ahmad, are sovereignty of the people under God's sovereignty, government based on just laws, complete freedom of religious worship, obedience to God and due obedience to leaders, leadership to be exercised by those who are competent and morally upright, and government through consultation. But methods and institutions vary according to time and circumstances. The [specific] methods and institutions used by the Prophet are not universally and eternally binding.

Ahmad explains the difference on page 75 in his conclusion that, a careful study of the Quran would reveal that its contents consist of two types of statements: the universal and the particular. The universal statements refer to absolute truths, while the particular statements refer to relative truths that are limited to certain concrete situations. He uses the famous command from which the second surah of the Quran, Surah al *Baqara*, gets it name, when the Jews of the time were asked to sacrifice a cow, and they got hung up deliberately on the form of the cow, asking repeatedly about its size, age, and color, in order to avoid the principle.

The most useful contribution of the entire monograph is the set of rules for Quranic interpretation, based on the principle that the Quran is not only the best but the only reliable source for its own interpretation. He distinguishes nine principles of Quranic interpretation that come from the Quran itself. These are:

8. Two types of verses must be distinguished, which establish the principle of distinction between straightforward and metaphorical language (Quran 3:7);

9. The principle of unity of the Quran's contents, meaning that its verses are not contradictory, but in perfect harmony (4:82);

10. The congruence of Quranic teachings with truth and logic, establishing the principle of truth, and its congruence with science and right reason (41:41-42, 42:24, 23:70-71, 8:7-8, 17:81, and 10:100);

11. The principle of self-explanation, i.e., that Quranic verses explain one another (55:1-2 and 75:18-19);

12. The principle of good intention, i.e. that the Qur?an cannot be comprehended by anyone who approaches it with bad intention (41:44, 56:77-79, and 17:45-46);

13. The principle of topical context, i.e., that the meaning of any verse or verses must be understood in the context of the topic under discussion (17:58, 53:3-4, and 59:7);

14. The principle of historical context, i.e., that verses relating to a particular historical condition must be interpreted in the light of that condition (4:25 and 92:4-3);

15. The principle of easy practicability, i.e., that the teachings of the Quran are meant to facilitate and not to render things difficult for mankind (22:78, 20:2, 5:6 and 101-2, and 4:28); and

16. The principle of distinction between principle and methodology and putting principle above methodology (22:67 and 2:67-71).

Much of this erudite monograph is devoted to examples of how to apply these principles in practice. Ahmad laments that he needs many years before he can apply such guidelines in detailed evaluation of all the hadith in the major collections, but implies that he is now doing precisely that.

Weakness of the Author's Arguments

Compared with what Kassim Ahmad offers to the student of Islam, emphasizing his methodological and substantive weaknesses would appear to be merely nit-picking.

The only major fault that I find with his whole approach, and one of which most authors are guilty, is suggested in his statement on page 63: In the realms of philosophy, religion, the social sciences, and the arts there can only be one optimum form which will maximize the efficiency of all social behavior in human societies. The weakness of this approach is its failure to distinguish between human-made systems or realms, in which there can be no optimum form, and divine revelation, in which by definition there is an optimum, even though exactly what this is will always remain beyond human certainty.

Secondly, in his statement lumping philosophy and the social sciences and the arts together with religion, Ahmad fails to distinguish between essence and form. In philosophy, there clearly is a distinction between the essence of positivist relativism, which denies the existence or even possibility of truth, and the essence of what America's founders called traditionalism, which denies the truth of such relativism. In religion, on the other hand the essence of all religions, regardless of the diversity in outward expression, is awareness of an ultimate reality beyond all forms, which Muslims and Arabic-speaking Christians call Allah and some Christians call Being (which is beyond existence) or even Beyond Being (beyond the trinity). The essence of religion, furthermore, involves recognition that from the Oneness of the ultimate comes ineluctably the coherence of existence, which Muslims call *tawhid*.

Thirdly, Ahmad's statement about optimum form seems to contradict his apparent preference for tolerance, diversity, and pluralism, which are three ascending levels of the same thing, namely, a respect for what Allah has created and planned, whether it is in the color of one's skin or in one's choice of religion.

The struggle to overcome this mindset of optimum form is beautifully explored in William R. Hutchison's new book, Religious Pluralism in America: the Contentious History of a Founding Ideal, which will be reviewed, *insha Allah*, on behalf of the Islamic Foundation in Leicester, England, in the next issue of this online journal, http://www.theamericanmuslim.org Hutchison, who teaches the history of religion at Harvard's Divinity School, is considered to be the leading authority in the world on the history of religion. His thesis is that America, despite its nominal claims, has not advanced very far up the ladder of progress from tolerance to diversity to pluralism.

Tolerance, by my own definition, is what the Soviet Communists used to call peaceful coexistence, which is a codeword and in Soviet jurisprudential literature a well-defined legal term meaning a tactical truce in a strategic war finally to liquidate the enemy. This contrasts with recognition of diversity as a simple fact of life. This, in turn, contrasts with pluralism, which recognizes the pluralism in the universe, ranging from atoms to trees to clusters of galaxies and on to religious traditions as part of the divine plan as an essential means to recognize the Oneness of God.

Rashad Khalifa may claim secret knowledge of the ultimate form, but the Quran warns us not even to discuss anything about which in this life we can have no knowledge.

Another perhaps related weakness is Kassim Ahmad's penchant for categorical statements about the realm of the *ghaib*. He appears to contradict his own maxims when he makes the categorical statement on page 65 that, there will be no Second Coming of Christ and neither will there be any superhuman savior to save the world. Our salvation lies in our own hands and through applying the teachings of the Quran creatively and scientifically. He adds on page 37, encouraging the Muslims to hang their hopes on something called the Mahdi is actually a subtle attempt to make defeatists and pessimists of them. The suffocating belief in fate: to make the Muslims submissive to other than God and to wait for someone to come along to save them. The truth is that no one will help us unless we help ourselves first.

Yet, on page 69 he accepts the coming of Gog and Magog and the Anti-Christ toward the Last Days, and states, we are required to believe in them, but we are to leave them to be interpreted by God and those who are experts in this field. The details of both the Mahdi and the Anti-Christ come from the hadith. His rejection of the Mahdi because he does not like the possible effect of a messiah on Muslim dynamism, and his acceptance of the Anti-Christ apparently because he sees no harmful effect of such a belief, seem to exemplify subjective selection of what Muslims should and should not believe.

His failure to consider alternative interpretations of the Quran is exemplified by his categorical statement on page 71 that the word *mutawaffika* (from the root *WaFaYa*, to complete, perfect, fulfill) cannot mean other than what it says, that is, that Jesus died, though not on the Cross. He dismisses Marmaduke Pickthall's translation of this passage, "And remember when Allah said, 'O Jesus! Lo! I am gathering thee and causing thee to ascend to me, and cleansing thee of those who disbelieve.'" and counters it with Rashad Khalifa's translation, "Thus God said, 'O Jesus, I am terminating your life on earth, raising you up to me, and ridding you of disbelievers.'"

There has always been a minority position among the *shuyukh* of Azhar that the Quranic statement that Jesus did not die on the cross, although he appeared to do so, means that spiritually he did not die. Denial of Jesus's death undermines the entire basis of Pauline Christianity, which is based on the belief that original sin requires the ultimate sacrifice of Jesus's death on the cross for any person to go to heaven. This indeed is one of the passages of the

Quran that appear to be *muhkamat* or clear and decisive, based on the root *HaKaMa* for exact and firm, but, in fact, may be among the *mutashabihat* or unclear passages and therefore not subject to categorical statements.

Entire sections of this monograph are simply weak in their arguments. The most egregious would seem to be his contention on page 19-20 that, we do not learn to pray from the hadith; that, the *salat* prayers today were not originally given to Muhammad during the Night Journey; and that neither the Quran nor the hadith are needed to teach us how to pray, because the Quran clearly states that the obligatory prayers and all other religious observances of Islam were originally taught to Abraham.

From this he concludes on page 54 that the forms of prayer do not have to come from the hadith but have been inherited one generation after another from Abraham. This may be Rashad Khalifa's basis for innovating in the form of prayer by encouraging women to be imams. This free-wheeling approach to the forms of prayer seems to conflict with his statement on page 76 that the ordinary forms of prayer are required in principle, but that only under normal circumstances are we required to perform these prayers in the usual way. This leaves the way open to define subjectively what is normal and abnormal.

The reader will find many such surprising views, but the most surprising and suspect is his contention on page 72 that, God puts the believers and the Prophet on the same level. This is meant to counter the idolization of Muhammad, but it can be interpreted to permit reverence for someone living today as a prophet.

In summary, we might say that this monograph by Kassim Ahmad carries a lot of baggage, but that its overall message and most of the analysis is needed today more than ever to help

257

Muslims understand their own religion better so that they can explain it to well-meaning non-Muslims who are willing to learn.

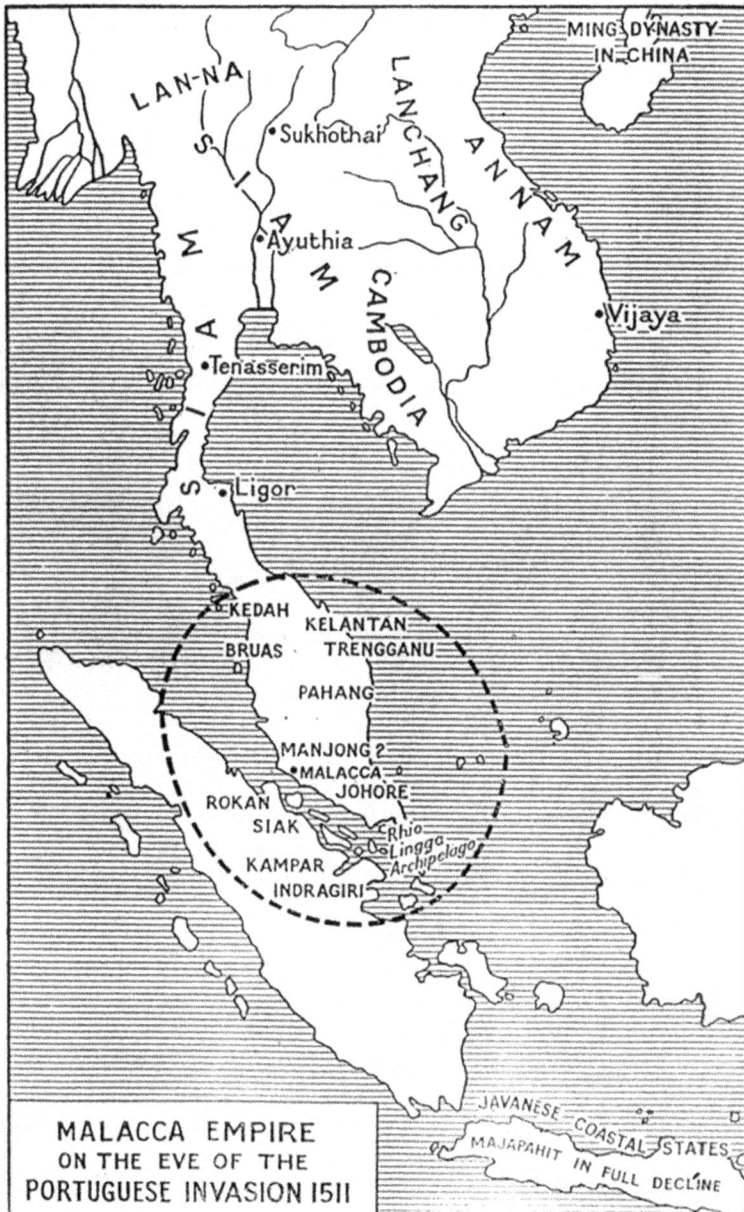

MING DYNASTY IN CHINA

LAN-NA

LANCHANG

ANNAM

SIAM

•Sukhothai

•Ayuthia

CAMBODIA

•Vijaya

•Tenasserim

•Ligor

KEDAH

KELANTAN

BRUAS   TRENGGANU

PAHANG

MANJONG?
•MALACCA
JOHORE

ROKAN
SIAK

Rhio
Lingga
Archipelago

KAMPAR
INDRAGIRI

MALACCA EMPIRE
ON THE EVE OF THE
PORTUGUESE INVASION 1511

JAVANESE COASTAL STATES
MAJAPAHIT IN FULL DECLINE

THE SPREAD OF ISLAM
in the Indonesian Archipelago

وَاللّٰهُ اَنْبَتَكُمْ مِّنَ الْاَرْضِ نَبَاتًاۙ

THE DIVINE PLAN HAS RAISED YOU UP FROM THE EARTH IN THE FORM OF A (GENEALOGICAL) TREE: (AL-QURAN 71 : 17)

أَمْثَالَكُمْ أَمْثَالُ

خَلَقَاَخَرَ
MAN

أُمَمٌ

GORILLA   CHIMPANZEE

مِنْ يَّمْشِىْ عَلٰى رِجْلَيْنِ

CETACEA
THE MOST SPECIALISED
AQUATIC MAMMALS
WHALES & PORPOISES;

ORANGUTAN   GIBBON

— **SIRENIA**
SEA-COWS (MANATEE & DUGONG)

CAMELS
ELEPHANTS   **HORSES**

ANTHROPOIDS

HOMINIDS

NEW
WORLD
MONKEYS

FISSIPEDIA
CARNIVORA WITH
SEPARATED TOES
(CATS, DOGS, BEARS)

AARDVARK
PRIMITIVE
AFRICAN
MAMMALS,

RUMINANTIA
CUD-CHEWING
DIVISION
OF UNGULATA.

مِنْ يَّمْشِىْ عَلٰى اَرْبَعٍ

HOMINOIDS

OLD
WORLD
MONKEYS

PINNIPEDIA
SEALS AND
WALRUSES WHICH
HAVE SPECIALISED
TEETH AND LIMBS
CONVERTED INTO
FLIPPERS.

UNGULATA

—**HOOFED ANIMALS WITH**
MODIFIED LIMB-BONES,
TYPICALLY ONLY ONE OR
TWO TOES, GRINDING TEETH

MARMO-
SET

EDENTATE
PRIMITIVE ANIMALS
LIKE INSECTIVORES
BUT WITH FEWER
TEETH OR NONE
AT ALL.

CARNIVORA

— **RODENTIA**
RATS, MICE, SQUIRRELS
WITH GNAWING TEETH.

TARSIERS

LEMURS

AYE-AYE

— **LAGOMORPHA**
RABBITS, HARES,
WITH GNAWING TEETH.

TREE-SHREW

PRIMATES

—**CHIROPTERA**
FLYING MAMMALS (BATS)

INSECTIVORA
PRIMITIVE MAMMALS HAVING
CHARACTERISTICS MUCH LIKE
THOSE OF FOSSIL MAMMALS
(SHREWS, MOLES, HEDGEHOGS)

— **MARSUPIALIA**
POUCH BEARERS
(LIKE KANGAROO, WOMBAT)

طَيْرٍ يَّطِيْرُ بِجَنَاحَيْهِ

BIRDS

— **MONOTREMATA**
EGG LAYING MAMMALS
(PLATYPUS, ECHIDNA)

مِنْ يَّمْشِىْ عَلٰى بَطْنِهٖ

REPTILES
(SOME OF THEM CREEP)

MAMMAL-LIKE
REPTILES

—**BONY FISH**

AMPHIBIA

REPTILES

— **SHARK-LIKE FISH**

A BRANCH OF
GENEALOGICAL TREE
REPRESENTING
SUB-PHYLUM VERTEBRATA

JAWLESS FISH

وَاللّٰهُ خَلَقَ كُلَّ دَاۤبَّةٍ مِّنْ مَّاۤءٍ

261

A CHRONOLOGY OF BIBLE EVENTS AND WORLD EVENTS

Creation undated

Noah builds the ark undated

2500 B.C. Egyptians discover papyrus and ink for writing and build libraries in the ancient Near East

2400 Egyptians import gold from Africa

2300 Horses domesticated in Egypt, chickens domesticated in Babylon, coal in wars

2371 Sargon, in Babylon, christian, bows & arrows used in wars, Sargon conquers Syria to become king "world conqueror"

2100 Glass made by the Mesopotamians

Abraham born 2166

Abraham enters Canaan 2091

Isaac born 2066

Jacob & Esau born 2006

Jacob flees to Haran 1929

Joseph born 1915

Joseph sold into slavery 1898

Joseph rules Egypt 1884

Joseph dies 1805

2000 Native Americans emigrate to North America from northern Asia

1900 Egyptians use irrigation systems to control Nile floods, invented the square wheel used in China, Stonehenge, England, a center for ancient Near East worship, horses and higher animals used in religious ceremonies

1750 Babylonian mathematicians document already understand cube and square root, Hammurabi of Babylon provides first of all legal codes

1700 Egyptian mathematics document describe medical and surgical practice

1530 Sandals used in Egypt, Mexican Sun-Pyramid built

Moses born 1526

Have you ever opened your Bible and asked the following:

• What does this passage really mean?
• How does it apply to my life?
• Why does some of the Bible seem irrelevant?
• What do these ancient cultures have to do with today?
• I love God, why can't I understand what he is saying to me through his Word?
• What's going on in the lives of these Bible people?

Many Christians do not read the Bible regularly. Why? Because in the pressures of daily living they cannot find a connection between the timeless principles of Scripture and the ever-present problems of day-by-day living.

God urges us to apply his Word (Isaiah 42:23; 1 Corinthians 10:11; 2 Thessalonians 3-4), but too often we stop at accumulating Bible knowledge. This is why the Life Application Bible was developed—to show how to put into practice what we have learned.

Applying God's Word is a vital part of one's relationship with God, it is the evidence that we are obeying him. The difficulty in applying the Bible is not with the Bible itself, but with the reader's inability to bridge the gap between the past and present, the conceptual and practical. When we don't or can't do this, spiritual dryness, shallowness, and indifference are the results.

The words of Scripture itself cry out to us, "Do not merely listen to the word, and so deceive yourselves. Do what it says" (James 1:22). The *Life Application Bible* does just that. Developed by an interdenominational team of pastors, scholars, family counselors, and a national organization dedicated to promoting God's Word and spreading the gospel, the *Life Application Bible* took many years to complete, and all the work was reviewed by several renowned theologians under the directorship of Dr. Kenneth Kantzer.

The *Life Application Bible* does what a good resource Bible should—it helps you understand the context of a passage, gives important background and historical information, explains difficult words and phrases, and helps you see the interrelationships within Scripture. But it does more, much more. The *Life Application Bible* goes deeper into God's Word, helping you discover the timeless truth being communicated, see the relevance for your life, and make a personal application. While some study Bibles attempt application, over 75% of this Bible is application-oriented. The notes answer the questions, "So what?" and "What does this passage mean to me, my family, my friends, my job, my neighborhood, my church, my country?"

Imagine reading a familiar passage of Scripture and gaining fresh insight, as if it were the first time you had ever read it. How much richer your life would be if you left each Bible reading with a new perspective and a small change for the better. A small change every day adds up to a changed life—and that is the very purpose of Scripture.

The best way to define application is to first determine what it is *not*. Application is *not* just accumulating knowledge. This helps us discover and understand facts and concepts, but it stops there. History is filled with philosophers who knew what the Bible said, but failed to apply it to their lives, keeping them from believing and changing. Many think that understanding is the end goal of Bible study, but it is really only the beginning.

Application is *not* just illustration. Illustration only tells us how someone else handled a similar situation. While we may empathize with that person, we still have little direction for our personal situation.

Application is *not* just making a passage "relevant." Making the Bible relevant only helps us to see that the same lessons that were true in Bible times are true today; it does not show us how to apply them to the problems and pressures of our individual lives.

What, then, is application? Application begins by knowing and understanding God's Word and its timeless truths. *But you cannot stop there. If you do, God's Word may not change your life, and it may become dull, difficult, tedious, and tiring.* A good application focuses the truth of God's Word, shows the reader what to do about what is being read, and motivates the reader to respond to what God is teaching. All three are essential to application.

Timeline dates and events:

- The exodus from Egypt 1446
- Ten Commandments given 1445
- Hebrews enter Canaan 1406
- 1400 First period of Chinese literature; intricate vases used in Egypt
- 1380 Palace of Knossos on island of Crete destroyed by a raging earthquake
- 1358 Egyptian king Tutankhamun (King Tut) begins to rule
- 1375 Judges begin to rule
- 1250 Silk fabric manufactured in China
- 1209 Deborah becomes Israel's judge
- 1200 Labor strike in Thebes; first Chinese dictionary
- 1183 Destruction of Troy (Trojan War)
- 1162 Gideon becomes Israel's judge
- 1105 Samuel born
- 1075 Samson becomes Israel's judge
- 1050 Saul becomes Israel's first king
- 1010 David becomes king
- 1000 City of Peking built
- 970 Solomon becomes Israel's king
- 959 Temple in Jerusalem completed
- 930 Kingdom divided
- 875 Elijah prophesies in Israel
- 874 Ahab becomes Israel's king
- 860 Celts invade Great Britain; iron development popular in Northern Europe
- 850 Evidence of highly developed medical and stone sculptures for soldiers in Africa
- 848 Elisha prophesies in Israel
- 835 Joash becomes Judah's king
- 830 Development of caste system in India; Chinese astronomers understand planetary movements; writing enters south of Europe
- 814 Founding of Carthage, a Phoenician trading post
- 800 California Indians build wood-reed houses to cross rivers
- 793 Jonah becomes a prophet
- 776 First known date of Olympic games

Application is putting into practice what we already know (see Mark 4:24 and Hebrews 5:14) and answering the question, "So what?" by confronting us with the right questions and motivating us to take action (see 1 John 2:5, 6 and James 2:17). Application is deeply personal—unique for each individual. It is making a relevant truth a personal truth, and involves developing a strategy and action plan to live your life in harmony with the Bible. It is the Biblical "how to" of life.

You may ask, "How can your application notes be relevant to my life?" Each application note has three parts: (1) an explanation that ties the note directly to the Scripture passage and sets up the truth that is being taught, (2) the bridge that explains the timeless truth and makes it relevant for today, (3) the application that shows you how to take the timeless truth and apply it to your personal situation. No note, by itself, can apply Scripture directly to your life. It can only teach, direct, lead, guide, inspire, recommend, and urge. It can give you the resources and direction you need to apply the Bible; but only you can take these resources and put them into practice.

A good note, therefore, should not only give you knowledge and understanding, but point you to application. Before you buy any kind of resource Bible, you should evaluate the notes and ask the following questions: (1) Does the note contain enough information to help me understand the point of the Scripture passage? (2) Does the note assume I know too much? (3) Does the note avoid denominational bias? (4) Do the notes touch most of life's experiences? (5) Does the note help me apply God's Word?

NOTES

In addition to providing the reader with many application notes, the *Life Application Bible* offers several explanatory notes, which are notes that help the reader understand culture, history, context, difficult-to-understand passages, background, places, theological concepts, and the relationship of various passages in Scripture to other passages. Maps, charts, and diagrams are also found on the same page as the passages to which they relate. For an example of an application note, see Mark 15:47. For an example of an explanatory note, see Mark 11:1, 2.

BOOK INTRODUCTIONS

The Book Introductions are divided into several easy-to-find parts:

Timeline. This puts the Bible book into its historical setting. It lists the key events of each book and the date when they occurred.

Vital Statistics. This is a list of straight facts about the book—those pieces of information you need to know at a glance.

Overview. This is a summary of the book with general lessons and application that can be learned from the book as a whole.

Blueprint. This is the outline of the book. It is printed in easy-to-understand language and is designed for easy memorization. To the right of each main heading is a key lesson that is taught in that particular section.

Megathemes. This section gives the main themes of the Bible book, explains their significance, and then tells why they are still important for us today.

Map. This shows the key places found in that book and retells the story of the book from a geographical point of view.

OUTLINE.
The Life Application Bible has a new, custom-made outline that was designed specifically from an application point of view. Several unique features should be noted:

1. To avoid confusion and to aid memory work, each book outline has only three levels for headings. Main outline heads are marked with a capital letter. Subheads are marked by a number. Minor explanatory heads have no letter or number.

2. Each main outline head marked by a letter also has a brief paragraph below it summarizing the Bible text and offering a general application.

3. Parallel passages are listed where they apply in the Gospels.

HARMONY OF THE GOSPELS
A harmony of the Gospels was developed specifically for this Bible. It is the first harmony of the Gospels that has ever been incorporated into the Bible text. Through a unique and simple numbering system, you can read any Gospel account and see just where you are in relation to the entire life of Christ. The harmony is located after the Gospel of John and explained in detail there.

PROFILE NOTES
Another unique feature of this Bible is the profiles of many Bible people, including their strengths and weaknesses, greatest accomplishments and mistakes, and key lessons from their lives. The profiles of these people are found in the Bible books where their stories occur.

MAPS
The Life Application Bible has more maps than any other Bible. A thorough and comprehensive Bible atlas is built right into each Bible book. There are two kinds of maps: (1) A book introduction map, telling the story of that Bible book. (2) Thumbnail maps in the notes, plotting most geographic movements in the Bible.

CHARTS AND DIAGRAMS
Hundreds of charts and diagrams are included to help the reader better visualize difficult concepts or relationships. Most charts not only present the needed information but show the significance of the information as well.

CROSS-REFERENCES

A carefully organized cross-reference system in the margins of the Bible text helps the reader find related passages quickly. See page iii for more information on the NIV Cross-Reference system.

TEXTUAL NOTES AND SECTIONAL HEADINGS

Directly related to the New International Version text, the textual notes examine such things as alternate translations, meaning of Hebrew and Greek terms, Old Testament quotations, and variant readings in ancient Biblical manuscripts. The NIV text also contains sectional headings in order to help you more easily understand the subject and context of each section. NOTE: The standard New International Version sectional headings have been altered for this particular edition, particularly in the Gospels where they have been eliminated in favor of the "Harmony of the Gospels" feature.

INDEX

This book contains a complete index to all the notes, charts, maps, and personality profiles. With its emphasis on application, it is helpful for group Bible study, sermon preparation, teaching, or personal study.

266

SELECT BIBLIOGRAPHY

Translations of the Quran. There is no perfect translation. Rashad Khalifa's translation is the best in modern English. The author uses this, but consults others when necessary.

Abdullah Yusuf Ali, The Holy Quran, New Revised Ed., Amana Corporation, Maryland, U.S.A., 1989.

Arthur J. Arberry, The Koran Interpreted, Vols. I-II, George Allen & Unwin, London, 1955.

Maulahum Muhammad Ali, Te Holy Quran, New 2002Ed., Ahmadiyya Anjuman Isha'at Islam Lahore Inc., Ohio, U.S.A.

Mohammed Marmaduke Pickthall, The Meanig of the Glorious Quran, Islamic Book Trust, Kuala Lumpur, 2001.

Muhammad Asad, The Message of the Quran, Dar'ul- Andalus, Gibralta, 1980.

Rashad Khalifa, Quran: The Final Testament, Revised Ed.II, Universal Unity, Tucson, Arizona, U.S.A., 2002.

Sheikh Abdullah basmeih, Tafsir Pimpinan Ar-Rahman, Bahagian Agama, Jabatan Perdana Menteri, Kuala Lumpur, 1980.

The Holy Quran, Vols. 1-5, Islam International Publications, United Kingdom, 1988.

Yuksel Edip, Layth Saleh al-Shaiban & Martha Schulte-Nafeh, Quran – A Reformist Translation, Brainbow Press, U.S.A., 2007, 2011.

Other References:

Life Application Bible, Tyndale House Publishers, Illionis, U.S.A., 1991.

New Encyclopedia Britannica, 15th Edition, 1991.

Mohammad Iqbal, The Reconstruction of Religious Thought in Islam, Sh. Muhammad Ashraf, Lahore, n.d.

Rashad Khalifa, The Computer Speaks: God's Message to the World, Renaissance Productions International, Tucson, U.S.A., 1981.

Kassim Ahmad, Hadis – Satu Penilian Semula, Media Intelek, Kuala Lumpur, 1986. Translated into English as Hadith – A Re-evaaluation by Syed Akbar Ali, Monotheist Productions International, Tucson, U.S.A., 1997.

---------------- Hadis – Jawapan Kepada Pengkritik, Media Intelek, Kuala Lumpur, 1992.

---------------- Delima Umat Islam – Antara Hadis dan Quran, Forum Iqra', Malaysia, 2002.

---------------- Kontroversi Hukum Hudud, Forum Iqra', Malaysia, 2002.

---------------- "A Short Note on the Medina Charter", www.stormloader.com/qsmjam

Bertrand Russel, History of Western Philosophy, Allen & Unwin, London, 1961.

----------------------, Mysticim and Logic, Allen & Unwin, London, 1910.

Abul Kalam Azad, The Opening Chapter of the Quran, Islamic Book Trust, Kuala Lumpur, 1962.

Pitrim A. Sorokin, Modern Historical and Social Philosophies, Dover Publications, New York, 1963.

----------------------, The Crisis of Our Age, One World Publications, New York, 1992.

Frank J. Tipler, The Physics of Immortality, Pan Books, London, 1996.

Lyndon H. LaRouche, The Secrets Known Only to the Inner Elites, Campaigner Special Report, No. 11, New York, 1978.

----------------------, The Science of Christian Economy, Schiller Institute, Washington, D.C., 1991.

-----------------, The Economics of the Noonsphere, EIR News Service, Washington, D.C., 2001.

Philip K. Hitti, History of the Arabs, 10th Ed., MacMillan Press, 1970.

William Blum, Rouge State: A Guide to the World's Only Superpower, Common Courage Press, Monroe, U.S.A., 2000.

Internet, Wikipedia.

Robert Briffault, The Making of Humanity, Islamic Book Foundation, England, 1919.

Barbara Marx Hubbart, Conscious Evolution, New World Library, Novato, California, U.S.A., 1998.

Tom Hartmann, Threshold: The Crisis of Western Culture, 2009.

Jamila Khatoon, The Place of God, Man and the Universe in the Philosophic System of Iqbal, Pakistan Iqbal Academy, Karachi, 1963.

Syed Muhammad Naguib, The Mysticism of Hamzah Fansury, University of Malaya Press, Kuala Lumpur, 1970.

James A. Haught, 2000 Years of Disbelief: Famous People with the Courage to Doubt, Prometheus Books, 1996.

Arthur J. Arberry, Avicenna on Theology, J. Murry, London, 1951.

Kenneth W. Morgon (Ed.), Islam – The Straight Path, Ronald Press, New York, 1958.

J. Halipota, The Philosophy of Shah Waliullah, Sind Sagar Academy, Lahore, n.d.

Micahel H. Hart, The 100 – A Ranking of the Most Influential Persons in History, Golden Books Centre, Kuala Lumpur, 1989.

W.C. Dampier, A History of Science, 1968.

Maxime Rodinson, Mohamed (tr. Anne Carter), Penguin Books, Great Britain, 1971.

Syed Muhammad Dawilah al-Edrus, Islamic Epitemology: An Introduction to the Theory of Knowledge in the Quran, The Islamic Academy, Cambridge, Universiti Sains Malaysia, 1992.

A Concise History of Islam, Djambatan/Armsterdam, 1957.

George Sarton, Introduction to the History of Science, Vol. I, Baltimore, 1927.

Ahmad von Denffer, Ulum A-Quran, The Islamic Foundation, United Kingdom, 1988.

Fazlul Karim (compiler), Al-Hadis (an English translation of Mishkat-Ul-Masabih), Vols. I-IV, The Book House, Lahore, 1988.

Guillaume (tr.), The Life of Muhammad – A Translation of Ishaq's Sirat Rasul Allah, Oxford University Press, London, 1974.

M. Hamidullah, The First Written Constitution in the World, Sh. Muhammad Ashraf, Lahore, 1975.

Abdullahi Ahmad An-Na'im, Towards an Islamic Reformation, Syracuse University Press, 1992.

M.M. Azmi, Studies in Early Hadith Literature, Beirut, 1986.

Ahmad Amin, Fajar Islam, Dewan Bahasa & Pustaka, Kuala Lumpur, 1980.

Majid Khadduri (tr.), Islamic Jurisprudence, Shafi'e Risala, John Hopkins Press, Baltimore, U.S.A., 1961.

N. J. Coulson, A History of Islamic Law, Edinburgh University Press, 1964.

Ahmad Ibrahim, Islamic Law in Malaysia, Malaysian Sociological Research Institute, Singapore, 1965.

Ibn Al' Arabi, The Bezels of Wisdom, (tr. R. W. J. Austin), Paulist Press, New Jersey, U.S.A., 1980.

Fazlur Rahman, Islam (2nd ed.), University of Chicago Press, U.S.A., 1979.

Seyyed Hossein Nasr, The Three Muslim Sages, Harvard University Press, U.S.A., 1964.

----------------------------, Living Sufism, Unwin Paperbacks, London, 1980.

Hilaire Belloc, The Great Heresies, World Library Classics, Great Britain, 2009.

Bansi pandit, The Hindu Mind, New Age Books, New Delhi, 2001.

D. White, A History of Warfare of Science with Theology in Christendom, Vols. I-II, Dover Publications, New York, 1960.

Rene Guedon, The Crisis of the Modern World, Sophia Perennis, New York, 2001.

Ahmad Boestamam, Carving the Path to the Summit, (tr. William R. Roff), Ohio University Press, 1979.

Paul Davies, The Mind of God – the Scientific Basis for a Rational World, Simon & Schuster, New York, 1992.

Muhammad 'Ata ur-Rahman, Jesus – the Prophet of Islam, Omar Brothers Publications, Malaysia, 1978.

The Gospel of Barnabas, Oxford Clarendon Press, 1907.

Martin Lings, Muhammad: his life based on the earliest sources, Foundation for Traditional Studies, Malaysia, 1983.

Karen Armstrong, Muhammad: A Biography of the Prophet, HarperSanFrancisco, U.S.A., 1992.

Hans Kung et all, Christianity and the World Religions, 1986.

Sameul P. Huntington, Clash of Civilizations and the Remaking of World Order, Simm & Schuster, New York, 1996.

Rose Wilder, Islam dan the Discovery of Freedom, Amana Publications, 1997.

Stephen Hawking, A Brief History of Time, Banthma Books, U.S.A., 1988.

Hodgson, Marshall G. S., The Venture of Islam: Concience and History in World Civilization, Vols. I-III, University of Chicago Press, Chicago/London, 1970.

W. Montgomery Watt, Muhammad at Mecca, Oxford University Press, 1953.

-----------------------------, Muhammad at Medina, " "" , 1956.

-----------------------------, *Islamic Political Thought*, Edinburgh University Press, 1986.

INDEX

www.ingramcontent.com/pod-product-compliance
Lightning Source LLC
LaVergne TN
LVHW011345080426
835511LV00005B/129